Irish Musical Studies

1: MUSICOLOGY IN IRELAND

Edited by

Gerard Gillen & Harry White

IRISH ACADEMIC PRESS

The typesetting for this book
was produced by Gilbert Gough Typesetting
for Irish Academic Press
Kill Lane, Blackrock, Co. Dublin

BRITISH LIBRARY CATALOGUING IN PUBLICATION DATA
Musicology in Ireland. – (Irish musical studies; 1).
1. Ireland. Musicology
I. Gillen, Gerard   II. White, Harry   III. Series
780.720415

ISBN 0-7165-2456-2

Printed by
Betaprint Ltd, Dublin

Contents

Contributors

MARTIN ADAMS is Lecturer in Music at Trinity College, Dublin. His book-length study of Henry Purcell's compositional development is nearing completion.

BARRA BOYDELL lectures at the Dublin College of Music, where he directs the Graduate Diploma course in performance. His *The Crumhorn and Other Renaissance Windcap Instruments* was published in 1982.

BRIAN BOYDELL is a Fellow of Trinity College, Dublin, where he was Professor of Music from 1962 to 1982. His *A Dublin Musical Calendar, 1700-1760* was published by Irish Academic Press in 1988.

ANN BUCKLEY is a Fellow of Darwin College, Cambridge and a specialist in ethnomusicology and historical musicology. She has contributed the chapter on 'Music in ancient and medieval Ireland' to volume 1 of the Royal Irish Academy's *A New History of Ireland*, due to be published shortly. Her current research projects include the preparation of the volume on Ireland for the German series *Handbuch der europäischen volksmusikinstrumente*, and an edition and study of the lyric lai in Old French and Latin to *c.* 1300.

MÁIRE EGAN-BUFFET is College Lecturer in Music at University College, Dublin. She has co-edited a volume of the complete works edition of the music of Claude Goudimel. Her edition of the 14th-century Dublin play with music, *Visitatio Sepulchri*, prepared in collaboration with Alan Fletcher, will be published by the Royal Irish Academy.

PATRICK F. DEVINE is Lecturer in Music at St Patrick's College, Maynooth. In 1987 he completed a doctoral thesis on the early music of Anton Bruckner. His current research interests include the music of Gabriel Fauré.

PETER DOWNEY lectures in Music at St Mary's College of Education, Belfast. He holds a doctorate in musicology from Queen's University, and is a past contributor on organological topics to *Early Music* and other journals. His historical reconstruction of a 'Festal Mass at Vienna, 1649' has been released by Novello Records.

PAUL EVERETT is Lecturer in Music at University College, Cork. His many publications include articles on early 18th-century Italian manuscripts and *The Manchester Concerto Partbooks*, his doctoral thesis in press with Garland (New York). He is currently preparing a book on the chronology of the music of Vivaldi.

HORMOZ FARHAT is Professor of Music at Trinity College, Dublin. He is a composer and a musicologist and a widely-acknowledged authority on the music of the Middle East. His study of the *dastgáh* concept in Persian music is shortly to be published by Cambridge University Press.

GERARD GILLEN is Professor of Music at St Patrick's College, Maynooth. His research interests include the history of the organ, performance-practice and 17th-century keyboard music. His study of Irish organs in the classical tradition (written with John Brennan) will be published by Positif Press, Oxford.

DAVID GREER was formerly Hamilton Harty Professor of Music at Queen's University, Belfast. He is currently Professor of Music at the University of Durham. A specialist in early English music, he was editor of the *Proceedings* and subsequently the *Journal* of the Royal Musical Association from 1977 until 1990.

DESMOND HUNTER lectures in Music at the University of Ulster at Jordanstown. In 1989 he completed a doctoral dissertation on ornamentation in English keyboard music, 1530-1650, and he has papers on this and other related topics forthcoming from various English presses.

MÍCHEÁL Ó SÚILLEABHÁIN teaches Ethnomusicology at University College, Cork and is a specialist in Irish music. His publications include an edition of Bunting's *Ancient Music of Ireland* (with Donal O'Sullivan) published by Cork University Press in 1983. He is also active as a performing musician and his most recent recording (with the Irish Chamber Orchestra) was released in 1989 entitled *Oileán/Island.*

MICHAEL RUSS is Lecturer in Music at the University of Ulster at Jordanstown and holds a doctorate in post-tonal analysis from C.N.A.A. supervised by Arnold Whittall. He has recently published on Webern; he has a paper on Musorgsky in press and is currently writing a book on Musorgsky's *Pictures at an Exhibition* for publication by Cambridge University Press in 1991.

NICK SANDON is Professor of Music at University College, Cork. A specialist in late medieval and early renaissance music and liturgy, he has published numerous papers and articles on a wide variety of topics. He has also published several editions of medieval and renaissance music, and he is co-author of *The Oxford Anthology of Medieval Music.* BBC Radio Three has broadcast many of his liturgical reconstructions, including the series *The Octave of the Nativity* and *Trinity Sunday at Worcester Cathedral.* He is General Editor of the early music publishing house Antico Edition.

HUGH SHIELDS is Senior Lecturer in French at Trinity College, Dublin. He is editor of *Irish Folk Music Studies* and is currently writing a book on narrative song in Ireland. He has contributed on aspects of Irish music to various Irish and foreign journals.

HARRY WHITE is College Lecturer in Music at University College, Dublin. He has published papers on sacred-dramatic music and counterpoint in the early 18th-century and on aspects of music in Ireland in various Irish and international journals. He is currently editing a volume of Johann Joseph Fux studies, to be published by Scolar Press (London) in 1991.

The editors wish to acknowledge most gratefully
grants in aid of publication from

The Senate of the National University of Ireland

The Faculty of Arts Publications Committee
of University College, Dublin

The Maynooth Scholastic Trust

The Publications Committee of St Patrick's College, Maynooth

The School of Music of Trinity College, Dublin

Preface

Irish Musical Studies is the first volume of an occasional series, designed to offer a conspectus of musicology in Ireland. While it is not representative of every aspect of such research,[1] the purpose of this volume is to register, for the first time, the existence of a discipline of scholarly musical thought which has taken firm root in Ireland within the past twenty years. Prior to this period, there were important individual contributions made to musicology in Ireland, notably within the field of Irish music itself, but it is only in the recent past that the discipline has enjoyed widespread attention and cultivation, most especially within Irish university departments of music.

Most of the contributors to *Irish Musical Studies* teach or have taught for a considerable length of time in such departments, and their work both within this volume and beyond it is illustrative of the range of interests which occupy musicologists in Ireland at large. As this collection of essays indicates, such interests include medieval and baroque organology, source studies, notation, music theory and analysis, and a host of historical topics. The publication here of essays on Purcell, Goudimel, Fauré, Vivaldi, Hamilton Harty and Bartók, for example, is intended to convey the international scope of musicology, as it is practised in Ireland. Other essays, notably on music in eighteenth-century Dublin, on theoretical aspects of Irish Folk music and on the history of that music, equally affirm the vital pursuit of these and many other Irish topics by scholars who live and work in this country.

The volume as a whole does not, however, purport to be exhaustive in the range of research interests which it embraces. Its purpose, rather, is to give some material notion of that range, and also to stimulate further discussion on the future and scope of musicological studies in Ireland. Recent publications such as Richard Kearney's *The Irish Mind* (Dublin, 1985) show that scholars in the humanities have been particularly concerned to query the achievement of literary, philosophical, critical and other aspects of Irish culture. Music, however, has been conspicuous by its general absence from these debates. To propose a journal of musicology in Ireland would not be justified by the size and present scope of the field (in any event, most musicologists in Ireland rightly prefer to publish as a rule in international journals), but an occasional series of *Irish Musical Studies* would help to determine the progress of musical studies in Ireland and to display the work of Irish musicologists for the sake of interdisciplinary information and assimilation.

With these objectives in mind, it is reasonable to hope that subsequent volumes of *Irish Musical Studies* might be devoted to topics which only very recently have enjoyed the scrutiny of musicologists. Such topics include the sociology of music in Ireland, aspects of contemporary Irish composition and the history of Irish music in the second half of the nineteenth century.

One final point needs to be borne in mind with regard to the present volume. The emphatically positivist approach which underlies most of the essays in *Irish Musical Studies* reflects the growth of musicology in its first maturity in Ireland, as it has done formerly elsewhere. While many would justifiably argue that this first phase of factual accumulation and presentation ought to give way to a second phase of critical evaluation and cultural interpretation (an essential progression in terms of the general history of Irish ideas), the present volume would appear to represent the status quo of musicology in Ireland. This status is vulnerable to exciting and promising change, as recent research indicates, but in the meantime, *Irish Musical Studies* testifies to the indispensable prior commitment to the history and theory of music, without which critical and cultural assessment cannot succeed. If the logical progression from this commitment appears to be the recognition of musicology as a discipline in its own right, as a specialization to take its place alongside composition, performance and (music) education in Irish institutes of higher learning, it will survive to this second phase, as it has done in Britain, Europe and the United States.

The editors wish to express their gratitude to Sarah M. Burn, who prepared the music copy for the book. They also thank most sincerely Michael Adams and Gerard O'Connor of Irish Academic Press for their firm support and wise counsel in the preparation and publication of this volume.

The editors wish to make a further acknowledgement, to the memory of the late John Blacking, who died after a long illness in January 1990. It was this illness which prevented Professor Blacking from contributing to *Irish Musical Studies*. Both the world of musicology at large and this volume in particular are the poorer for his passing. His was a distinguished voice (along with that of the late Frank Llewelyn Harrison) which greatly enriched the practice of musicology in Ireland.

---

1.   See Harry White, 'Musicology in Ireland', *Acta Musicologica*, LX (1988), Fasc. III, 290-305 for an overall survey of the discipline in Ireland to date.

Musical Instruments in Ireland from the Ninth to the Fourteenth Centuries

A REVIEW OF THE ORGANOLOGICAL EVIDENCE

ANN BUCKLEY

The sources for the history of any aspect of music in medieval Ireland are complex, of variable reliability and largely random in nature. Excepting the notated liturgical books from the twelfth century onwards, information about music is incidental and not of a primary purpose. There are no manuscripts containing notation of secular repertories, no theoretical writers addressing specifically Irish musical practices, and because of the feudal and non-centralised structure of Irish courts, no account books or rolls which might have preserved information on the engagement of musicians for regular or extraordinary occasions of state. The only such documents are the annals, the oldest MSS of which date to the sixteenth century but which incorporate information from layers of older sources. In these are recorded the obits of a number of musicians associated with the most important chieftains' families; occasionally other references to musicians may be gleaned from accounts of the activities of their patrons. The annals provide the only information on actual historical figures.

In spite of this unpromising state of affairs, however, the sources abound in allusions to music, music-making, musicians, instruments, with an intensely detailed vocabulary to describe all manner of sounds. This last is surely no surprise in a culture which manifested such sensitive awareness in matters of rhyme, alliteration and assonance – as witness medieval Irish and Hiberno-Latin poetry. The Irish soundscape is well documented in the native literature; the range of linguistic terminology for musical (and non-musical) timbres, forms and instruments is extremely rich. The problem for historical enquiry is its unspecific nature. References are descriptive – and usually subjective, emotive, metaphorical, everything but technical or systematic.

There are three categories of evidence: literary, iconographic and material. The first, already alluded to, has by far the richest legacy in quantitative terms. It derives from manuscripts ranging in date from the eleventh to the sixteenth centuries, but often based on older sources. These layers are identifiable on a linguistic basis though they remain unspecific for purposes of organological investigation, hence the problems of terminology are infinite. No clearcut definitions exist, for they were not part of the purpose. The texts are mainly oral-tradition poetry and literature composed for court entertainment, not for posterity, and certainly not as communication and explication for the benefit of outsiders. They presume knowledge and common understanding on the part of all. The same words for musical instruments are maintained over several centuries and must be assumed to have undergone shifts in meaning: etymology can be a helpful guide to genre classification (chordophones, aerophones etc.) but not to any approximation of typology. Thus it is quite clear that *cruit* and *timpán* were stringed instruments, but when does the first cease to refer to a lyre and become a harp? when does the second refer to a plucked, a beaten, or a bowed instrument? The confusion is further compounded by the multiplicity of uses of the terminology even by individual scribes: for example, the word *céis* is glossed in one instance as having at least five possible meanings.[1] The problems for aerophones are similar: were instruments called *cuisle ciúil*, *fedán*, *píb*, organologically distinguishable? Do these terms signify a typological classification between wind instruments with single and double reeds, and those with a fipple, or are they simply a reflection of the variety of linguistic borrowings? There is so little consistency here too that such an enquiry cannot be taken very far. Undoubtedly the musicians themselves would have been aware of these factors – and indeed most likely had a distinguishing terminology; but they were not of importance to men occupied with the affairs of state, the preservers of the legal code and the guardians of genealogy and history. Hence the wind-instrumentalists grouped together with the lowly jugglers and entertainers according to the laws of status in the Brehon Laws are referred to as *fedánaig* (from Latin, *fistula*, 'pipe') in one collection called *Uraiccecht Bec* (Ancient Laws V, 108-9)[2] and as *cuislennaig* (from Old Irish *cuisle*, a pipe, tube, vein) in another, the *Críth Gablach* (Ancient Laws IV, 338-9),[3] as though each referred to wind instruments in general. On the other hand, the extent and contexts of these literary references provide unparalleled insight into the social history of music-making, the use of instruments, the status and rights of musicians, as well as their obligations.

The second evidential category, iconography, presents similar problems insofar as musical instruments are usually depicted as one element of a scene in religious carvings: not for the purpose of conveying information of a musicological nature but to preach the Christian message, portraying scenes of adoration and ritual of which music was a component. As in the case of literary references the purpose was not to convey accurate depictions of instruments; many illustrations are stylised, unrealistic copies of foreign works of art (e.g. manuscript illuminations, carvings) whose details may well have been ill-understood by native craftsmen, and even at times by the makers of the originals. Musical instruments are particularly vulnerable to inaccurate artistic representation.

Most Irish iconography is to be found on high crosses of the early and late ninth century, with a few scattered examples on stone and metalwork from the twelfth to fourteenth centuries. (Irish manuscripts rarely contain illustrations of musical instruments.) The scenes include players of undefined quadrangular chordophones and various forms of assymetrical and round-topped lyres, sometimes in the company of a wind instrument player and in a few cases paired with a player of triple pipes as though to emphasise the opposition of good and evil, sacred and secular. There are carvings of bells, an important symbol of ecclesiastical office, and it is these which are most frequently represented among material survivals.

With the exception of bells, whose preservation was guaranteed by virtue of their spiritual importance, the third category, that of material evidence, is represented by objects which in their time or soon after were apparently discarded or abandoned, thus not consciously preserved or found in a context of direct use. But their variety, particularly in the excavated sites of medieval Dublin, is most suggestive and represents the only hard evidence at our disposal. With the emergence of artefacts from all of the categories one might expect to find represented, we can begin the scientific, systematic task of reconstructing a history of musical instruments in Ireland.

In the ensuing discussion I propose to deal with iconographic and material evidence according to typology, unifying the information from an organological point of view as far as possible, endeavouring thereby to avoid unnecessary repetition of basic information. I shall attempt to explore the specific implications of these sources by examining them within the broader perspective of contemporaneous north-west Europe. To limit the enquiry to a positivistic account of what survives would hardly do justice to the enormous riches which clearly existed. A more open-ended approach will undoubtedly raise more questions than it answers but it may hopefully succeed in placing Irish materials clearly in their wider geographical and cultural contexts. The focus will be on organology and typological identification, and will be directed to chordophones and aerophones, which are the most frequently occuring both in iconography and among surviving artefacts. Investigation of the evidence for idiophones and membranophones must be deferred for lack of space[4] – as also an account of medieval Irish literary references to music.[5]

CHORDOPHONES

The structural distinctions between harps and lyres is a focal point in this discussion. A harp has a broadly triangular shape comprising horizontal stringholder and diagonal soundbox with the strings attached to both. European harps have their stringholder (or neck) at the top, and a forepillar at the hypoteneuse which joins the ends of neck and soundbox. The strings are thus perpendicular to the latter.[6] Lyres are quadrangular in profile in which strings are fixed with tuning pins to a yoke or arm at the top of the instrument, stretched over a soundbox (i.e. parallel to it) and attached to a tailpiece fixed at the end. They include instruments with bridges and without. The soundbox in a lyre does not extend through its complete length but a hole in the upper half of the instrument allows access to the strings from both sides.

Irish iconographic representations are found for the most part carved on panels of the granite high crosses and may be divided into two types: 1) large and small instruments of doubtful identity, round-topped, broadly quadrangular in outline, in some respects resembling harps and having parallel strings, in others the left arm is thicker, suggesting a soundbox. In no case is this feature visible at the bottom of the instrument, clearly distinguishing these images from 2), which represents lyre-type instruments with a round-topped quadrangular or an oblique profile (and one example which appears to combine both), in which the strings fan upwards to the stringholder and are stretched down over a bridge which sits on the soundbox. In some, but by no means all, illustrations the bridge and the tailpiece are visible.

The oldest chordophone depictions are found on eighth/ninth-century carvings on the Barrow Valley group of high crosses (Castledermot, Graiguenamagh, Ullard, cf. plates I-IV) and the north pillar beside the cross at Carndonagh, Co. Donegal (plate V) which carry representations of quad-rangular instruments of various sizes. The larger and slightly later 'scriptural' crosses of the Monasterboice school, which may date from the end of the ninth century[7] (the Monasterboice Cross of Muireadeach, the Clonmacnois Cross of the Scriptures and the Cross of St Colm Cille at Durrow, cf. plates VI-VIII), contain only lyre-type instruments. This is not the only distinction between the two groups. The figures on the older crosses are isolated in separate panels on the west face, the side on which Crucifixon scenes are also disposed; they are not in company although the right hand is always raised in a playing position. The musicians on the scriptural crosses are invariably on the east face, always reserved for scenes of glory and redemption, the Risen Christ, Christ in Judgement. They are always in company, usually including that of other musicians. As though to reinforce a distinction (between the instruments, or the contexts of their use) one of the older crosses (Kells Cross of Patrick and Columba, cf. plate IX) depicts a lyre player in attendance at the Miracle of the Loaves and Fishes. Although not a Biblical 'quotation' as such, it may suggest the appropriateness of music to accompany feasting in a medieval Irish context. On the scriptural crosses the relevant scenes concern the Last Judgement. The faithful on Christ's right (i.e., the left arm as one looks at the cross) appear to sing his praises to the accompaniment of musical instruments. On the crosses at Monasterboice and Durrow a lyre player is seated on the side of the Just on the left arm. On the former a player of a wind instrument is seated behind and a third figure holds a book, pointing to the text with his right-hand finger (perhaps singing from the psalter); behind him another figure looks at the book over the shoulder of the leader. On the Durrow carving wind and strings are also combined, though the former is placed closer to the central scene. On Clonmacnois a wind instrument is shown both right and left of Christ in Judgement (cf. plate X) and a clearly-defined lyre is played by a figure on the south shaft (plate VII). The Monasterboice carving represents the richest scene: as well as the detail of instruments and (singing?) monk with a host of others behind on the side of the Just, there is another group to Christ's left, turned away from Him and being ushered off the scene (along the right arm), except for a player of triple pipes on Christ's immediate left – perhaps an instrument associated with the devil, *musica profana*, and worldly pleasures. Another set of triple pipes is featured on the centre panel of the south shaft of Clonmacnois (plate XI) exactly opposite to the lyre player on the north, which seems to reinforce this symbolism in the structural disposition of the images. The implication on the later crosses seems to be that music is suitable only for occasions of joy and celebration. I shall return to the question of aerophones later in the discussion.

The main problem of identification concerns the earlier Irish crosses of the Barrow valley (Castledermot, Ullard, Graiguenamanagh), which represent the least reliable organological evidence. First of all, it is not clear what kind of evidence it is. There are no indications from archaeological sources that such instruments existed historically. They are certainly inaccurate from an organological point of view. Because of their quadrangular profile and perpendicular playing position they could have been intended as psalteries or lyres. They may have been copied from Carolingian or Byzantine manuscript paintings or carvings and their hybrid nature suggests that they were not known locally; Carolingian ivories were influential in Irish art of this period, serving as models for many of the earliest carvings.[8] Lack of precision is by no means exclusive to Irish illustrators. A twelfth-century example of a similar hybrid is seen on the ivory cover of the Psalter of Mélisande (London British Library MS Egerton 1139) made in Jerusalem before 1144 for the daughter of its French king, Baudoin II, and wife of his successor, Foulques d'Anjou (1131-1144; cf. Steger 1961b, 54-5, 216-7, *Dkm*. 40; Bachmann 1969, pl. 55; Gaborit-Chopin 1978, 127, pl. 189.) Another example is the painting on the first folio of a psalter from St Rémy de Reims now in the Library of St John's College, Cambridge (MS B.18), also twelfth century. Here David plays a quadrangular chordophone with one straight and one curved arm, the former nearest the player, i.e. facing in the opposite direction to the Durrow Cross carving. It has six parallel strings although eight tuning pegs – a further indication of its doubtful authenticity (cf. Steger 1961b, *Dkm.* 38; Seebass 1973, pl. 111).[9]

In addition to harps and lyres, ninth and tenth century European manuscript iconography contains illustrations of many types of quadrangular and triangular chordophones held in a vertical position which are neither harp-types nor lyre-types, but psalteries. By definition such instruments have parallel strings running over a soundbox and fixed with pins at both ends.[10] It is not always possible to distinguish between psalteries and triangular harps, which in the case of the former depends on a visible soundbox underneath the strings, and in the latter the presence of a forepillar and clear delineation of a soundbox fixed diagonally to the neck or stringholder. The literary and iconographic tradition of psalteries derives from the *De universo* of Hrabanus Maurus (*c.*780-856), in which he describes *psalterium* both as '*quadratus*' and '*in modum deltae literae*' (McKinnon and Remnant 1980, 383b). Their pre-twelfth-century history is not at all clear and it is not certain that they existed in practice, whether triangular (delta-shaped) or quadrangular.[11] Some triangular chordophone depictions may in fact be inaccurately drawn harps which lack the thicker side representing the soundbox, or which give the impression of a soundbox behind the strings because the player's hand or sleeve cannot be seen on the other side, or indeed where a forepillar is absent. Soundholes provide more reliable evidence for a flat soundbox, but these do not appear with any regularity until the twelfth century by which time trapezoidal psalteries were used in Western Europe as a result of Arabic influence, as also the 'pig's head' formation which was only found in Europe (cf. McKinnon and Remnant 1980, 385a).

It is worth examining the older Irish carvings for these features. Ullard and Graiguenamanagh show one thick side on the left of the frame, suggesting a harp soundbox, but with the strings running parallel rather than being attached to it. The Castledermot crosses show a frame of more or less equal thickness on both sides, and again with strings parallel to the arms; no soundbox is apparent on either arms or base.[12] In no case could it be discerned behind the strings in these much weathered stone carvings, nor are tuning pegs, string-holders, or bridges to be seen. On no account can these carvings be interpreted as harps: the (non-)relationship of strings to soundbox rules out such an hypothesis. Similarly, they are doubtful as lyres owing to the absence of a soundbox in the lower section. That they could be related to psalteries is unlikely given the obvious frame surrounding the strings. They must therefore be regarded as hybrids, inaccurate copies, or uninformed impressions, whether of actual musical instruments witnessed by the stonemasons or (what is more likely, in view of their vagueness) derived from iconography from another region. The carving on the Carndonagh pillar resembles a psaltery on which six parallel strings are attached to the same number of pins visible at both ends. It appears to have a thin frame and therefore also resembles a harp-lyre hybrid but without any indication of a soundbox, whether lateral or basal. If a psaltery was intended, the thin lateral frame could conceivably be interpreted as the perimeter of a soundbox underneath the strings.

If one applies the lyre theory to the Barrow Valley crosses, then the frame is explicable: all of the carvings show round-topped instruments but they lack any sign of a soundbox or tailpiece by which one could more easily identify them. The variability in thickness between the left and right arms on Ullard and Graiguenamanagh is another unrealistic aspect. Noteworthy, however, is that all of them appear to have six strings (it is not possible to be certain about this from the present state of the carvings) which is a strong argument in favour of the influence of lyre-type instruments on the stonemasons' consciousness, since the six-stringed lyre was the most common chordophone throughout north-west Europe in this period. The theory is reinforced by an illustration in an Irish psalter, British Library MS Cotton Vitellius F.XI, f 2^r, which is more or less contemporary with the scriptural crosses (Henry 1960, pls. IV, VI; also V for illustration of the Clonmacnois carving; Rensch 1969, pl. 6b): another David figure, seated and holding an instrument which can best be described as a stylised lyre, rectangular in profile with a round left arm, a highly improbable zoomorphic straight right arm, and up to twelve parallel strings. The soundbox occupies the lower section of the instrument and is clearly visible behind the strings which are attached between peg-arm and tailpiece, stretched over it in the manner of a lyre; the tailpiece protrudes below the soundbox. In the upper half the strings are accessible from both sides, the player's left hand being clearly visible at the back.

In most respects this is a lyre-type instrument such as is depicted on Clonmacnois and Kells West Cross (cf. plate XII) and comes closer to realistic representation than the quadrangular instruments on the older crosses. It could nonetheless have been the type of picture which served as a model for craftsmen, its quadrangular profile and parallel strings being common to both. The cross depictions, however, lack a stringholder and obvious soundbox at the base, which is why they appear closer to the harp type. However, we are not in a position to make a final assessment or to reach a conclusion on their reliability as organological data, and possibly we never shall be. Opinions among scholars vary and may be summed up by the observation that those who deny that these are realistic instruments base the argument on the incompatiblity of their structural features and on the lack of verifiable evidence such as might be recovered in archaeological excavation (Lawson 1981, 237 and n. 4; Homo-Lechner, personal communication), with which I am in agreement. Those who argue in favour suggest that the iconographic representations have some kind of literal authority *per se* (e.g. Porter 1983, 260), the weakest possible argument in a medium fraught with every kind of difficulty, one which needs to be treated with the utmost caution in view of the eclectic nature of its transmission and the complex messages (sometimes deliberately so) which they were intended to convey; details such as forms and structures of individual objects seem so often to be purely impressionistic. This is not to say that such impressions are mere intellectualisations which lack hard information for scholarly interpretation, but I emphasise the need to enquire beneath the surface structure rather than to regard it as profound reality.[13]

Plucked lyres are common on the ninth-tenth century crosses; an earlier one is found on the head of the Cross of Patrick and Columba, Kells, Co. Meath (as mentioned above). Representations include both assymetrical and round-topped forms, the former on the Cross of Patrick and Columba at Kells and the Cross of Muireadach, Monasterboice, the latter on the Kells West Cross, the Cross of the Scriptures, Clonmacnois, and the crosses at Killamery and Kinitty (cf. plate XIII); the example on the Durrow cross has one straight and one curved arm.[14] The two crosses which portray both tailpiece and bridge, Clonmacnois and Durrow, have strings in obvious fan formation. The latest lyre depiction is very clearly shown on the cover of the Shrine of the Stowe Missal (also known as St Maelruain's Gospel) dating from 1381 (cf. plate XIV). This instrument also has one curved and one straight arm and appears very similar to the Durrow exemplar apart from having only three strings to Durrow's six.

How might this evidence be interpreted in terms of likely practice? How does it relate to what is known of instruments in other parts of north-west Europe?[15] The earliest evidence for stringed instruments in that greater region is provided by excavated fragments of lyres from Scandinavia, Germany and England suggesting that these were the most common stringed instrument up to *c.*1000 AD. Fragments of eighteen six-stringed lyres have so far been identified, the earliest of which is of mid fifth-century date, with the majority from the seventh and eighth centuries. Lyre bridges with notches for six strings have been found in several sites including eighth and ninth century Sweden and West Germany, and tenth century Viking York and the Netherlands (Bruce-Mitford 1980, Hall 1984, 115-6, Lund 1981, 1984, Rimmer 1981), as also at a thirteenth-century level in the Louvre excavation in Paris (Homo-Lechner 1988, 64-65).

Both lyres and harps were known in the Mediterranean region up to the time of the Late Roman Empire and it is undoubtedly possible that either or both types (if not identical forms) were used further north during that period and earlier. Depictions on Gallo-Roman coins appear bound by forms from ancient Greece and seem therefore of little value for European practice (Harrison 1986, 254) but studies of iconographic representations from the east Hallstatt zone (early Iron Age eastern Europe) are currently assisting greatly in developing experimental hypotheses for prehistoric European lyres (cf. Megaw 1988, 349). Literary references attest to the use of stringed instruments among the Gauls, but whether harps as well as lyres there is no way of knowing from terminology and the lack of descriptive detail.

From the fifth to the tenth century the use of lyres was widespread in north-west Europe: they were the court instruments used in the accompaniment of epic recitation, praise poetry, and general entertainment of the nobility. As with Irish *cruit* players, their counterparts in England, Germany and Scandinavia were also holders of important appointments in the service of the king. Lyres appear to have predominated until *c.*1000 when triangular harps were in the ascendant. Prior to this date little is known about the history of triangular harps but they are found in manuscript iconography from *c.*800 and this evident change of emphasis suggests that they may have superseded lyres by the tenth or eleventh centuries. The latter did not become extinct in these islands, however, but continued in use at least up to the fourteenth or fifteenth century in England, possibly the sixteenth in Ireland, and late as the nineteenth century in Wales and Scandinavia. Triangular harps did not dominate for perhaps quite so long but they were the aristocratic instruments *par excellence* of the central middle ages.[16] During this period also, bowed instruments rapidly gained currency in north and central Europe (particularly in those regions dominated by Norman culture) but they did not supplant harp-playing until much later. Bowed instruments did not achieve the same status as harps in those areas peripheral to centralising Norman administration such as Ireland, Scotland and Wales where harpers continued to enjoy privilege in public and private music-making for as long as the local aristocratic culture survived. The shift from plucked lyre to plucked harp was clearly a technological improvement, offering greater musical possibilities and therefore flexibility of expression to performers; but a shift from plucked harp to bowed fiddle was a change of medium of expression and probably not suited to all repertories and styles. Bowing did, however, make its presence felt in the development of bowed lyres; but these instruments always remained secondary, never achieving the eminence of their plucked antecedents or seriously challenging the triangular harp.

The earliest Irish depiction of a triangular harp[17] is found on an eleventh-century book shrine with ornamental metalwork known as *Breac Maedóic* (cf. plate XVI). It is a large instrument and although it appears to have about eight strings, at least twelve tuning pins can be discerned. We are without further iconographic evidence until the Shrine of St Patrick's Tooth (*Fiacail Phádraig c.*1376; cf. plate XVII). The details of literary references such as those of Gerald of Wales, however, indicate the likelihood of its long-established use by the twelfth century. The shift probably took place some time between the ninth and tenth centuries as elsewhere in these islands. In a poem written by Patrick, second Bishop of Dublin (late eleventh century) he appears to have attempted to distinguish between two types of *cithara*, that which he described as '*cithara chordis que sex resonare solebat . . .*' which he was taught to play by a certain woman, and a description later in the poem of a great city with its assemblies, feasts and music played on various instruments including '*cytarasque novas*' (cf. Rimmer 1985, 25).

It is not clear when the practice of bowing reached Ireland but European evidence points to its use in Catalonia from the early eleventh century with the impact of Arab influence, from whence it spread to the rest of the continent (cf. Bachmann 1969, 61-2, 136ff.). Whether fiddles as such (or bowed lyres) were yet in common use in the north-western corner of the region is far from clear but there are two pieces of evidence from Ireland attesting at least to their existence there. A fragment of a bow was recovered from a mid-eleventh-century level during excavation of Christchurch Place, Dublin. It shows evidence of Scandinavian influence, having an animal-head carved terminal in Ringerike style (cf. plates XVIIIa-b). By this time Irish art represented a fusion of local and Scandinavian styles and thus it is impossible to determine whether the object in question was an import or the product of local manufacture. From about a century later survives the stone carving of a musician playing a bowed lyre among the church ruins on St Finan's Island, Lough Currane, Waterville, Co. Kerry (cf. plate XV). The instrument appears to have six strings, in which respect it precisely conforms with the older plucked lyres, and with the Welsh *crwth* which survived into modern times (but for which no medieval predecessor has been identified with that number of strings). It is badly weathered now; the details are more clearly visible on the photograph made by Lynch in or before 1908.[18]

Although no medieval chordophone bodies or bridges, or fragments thereof, have yet been discovered in Irish excacavations[19] further evidence of their use is attested in a number of pegs (broken and entire) which have emerged in recent years, two from thirteenth century levels in Cork and four from the Dublin sites of which three date to the mid or late eleventh century (Christchurch Place) and one to the thirteenth (High St). They are all made of yew; a third, longer, example (9.5 cm.) from Cork is of bone. This may have belonged to a sturdier instrument such as a harp (Hurley 1982, 305-9) as also one from Dublin's High St (8 cm.). The others are on average 5 cm. in length and probably came from lyres or fiddles. They include pegs with recesses at the top to facilitate tuning by gripping with thumb and index finger, and others with a top of square cross section which would have required the use of a tuning key (cf. Buckley 1988, 155ff.). A noteworthy feature of all of the Irish finds is the absence of a hole bored either at the lower end (indicating use in lyres, harps, fiddles) or near the top (for use in psalteries) in order to hold the string firmly when under tension. Such evidence is usually present in complete pegs which have been discovered in Britain (cf. Durham 1977, Lawson 1978a) though some have a groove cut in the base (Lawson 1986, 126, figs. 2b, c; 127, fig. 3a).[20] Pegs not provided with some form of grip are usually unfinished objects which were discarded for a variety of technical reasons (a fault in the material, an error in manufacture).

One of the Dublin pegs was split lengthwise and only half of it remains (cf. Buckley 1988, fig. 12, item 12071) suggesting, perhaps, that it broke in two while a groove was being cut. In the case of complete pegs without bored hole the possibility remains that the string was secured by being lapped, a technique which survived as late as some seventeenth- and eighteenth-century harpsi-chords in which the wrest-pins do not have a drilled hole. We remain deprived of basic information, however, in the case of the Irish pegs: had these objects actually been used in an instrument? Without microscopic examination of the evidence for markings (e.g. from the winding of a string, or from insertion in the socket of a pegbox) this is impossible to ascertain; similarly, if there is no sign of use, microwear analysis could help explain why.[21] Analysis of the bone pegs found at St Aldate's Oxford have led to the most interesting discovery of all – the site of a psaltery builder's workshop. There the incomplete pegs had been discarded because of a flaw in the bone, or breakage during manufacture. This site also yielded a spool of fine bronze wire apparently used for stringing the instruments (Durham 1977, 163-6, 194).

AEROPHONES

The oldest references to aerophones also occur in the Laws, as was indicated at the beginning of this discussion. Players of certain of these instruments were clearly frequenters of the court but unlike their string playing colleagues they were low class entertainers only fit for the company of buffoons, jesters and various kinds of tricksters. In *Críth Gablach* they are the *cornairí* and *buinnirí*, players of horn and *buinne*, of which the latter could refer to any kind of narrow pipe, including a reed or a stalk, and also a *tibia* (including in its biological sense of shinbone).[22] Animal tibiae are among the most common organological relics in music archaeology all over Europe. They were used as rim-blown or fipple flutes and as reed-blown instruments. In the first instance the instrument is held in a perpendicular position and the player blows across the top of the tube (as in panpipes) causing the column of air to vibrate. In fipple flutes a window is cut in the surface at the proximal end in order to provide an edge activating the column of air and a 'block' (fipple) is inserted into the mouthpiece, the air-column being forced between the fipple and the side of the instrument, hence 'block-and-duct' flutes. The blocks have not survived in excavated objects, as they would have been made from perishable material such as wood or cork. In reed-blown instruments a single or double reed (probably made from cane of some kind) are used to produce air vibrations in the tube. The reeds could be inserted into the mouth, or covered with a case or a horn terminal (as in the Welsh *pibcorn*), or fitted with a stock to which a bag was attached (i.e. bagpipes). Although the term *buinne/tibia* suggests bone, there is no reason to assume it was confined to instruments made exclusively of that material, anymore than applies in the case of horns. Again there is widespread evidence for wooden aerophones of the same type as just described, though not in the same quantity because of their more perishable constitution. It might reasonably be assumed that the Irish word applied to both. Nonetheless this cannot be conclusively determined given the imprecise nature of the literary evidence.

The horn players most probably performed on animal horns, though they may also have used wooden or bone chanters with horn terminal attached. As simple horns they could have been blown as signalling instruments, to make amusing noises or for playing melodies. They may have included instruments with fingerholes; these are depicted in medieval manuscripts and two such instruments have been recovered from sites in Sweden (Lund 1981, 260 and 1984, pl. 68, ex. 36).

The *Seanchas Mór* reference to the *áes airfitid*, who were consigned to the south-east corner of the king's hall, carries a gloss which explains them as *fedánaig*, literally, whistle players, which is again insufficient to determine the precise technology of their instruments. Were they identical with players of *buinne*? They may well have been interchangeable terms, in the same way as 'whistle' and 'flute' are still commonly applied to the same instrument. *Cuislennaig*, players of *cuisle ciúil*, on the other hand, appear, in some references at least, to refer to musicians of another order, which may suggest also that their instruments demanded greater skill, or were associated with more refined activities. There are two drawings in existence of an imaginary seating plan of the king's hall at Tara (*Teach Midchuarda*) – imaginary in the sense that they were written in the twelfth and the fourteenth centuries, and represent different schemas of a presumed eighth-century situation. Nonetheless it is possible that they were copied from older sources, and indeed they must reasonably be regarded as representative of contemporaneous society whose practices were long-established (cf. Buckley 1989).

In both drawings players of stringed instruments are placed at the top left-hand side, at the outer table by the wall, as described in the gloss, with *cornairí* and *buinnirí* diagonally opposite. A third group of musicians, not mentioned in either the older Laws or the later glosses, is also included on the inner left-hand table, i.e., in front of the string players to their right. This group is referred to as *cuislennaig*. These instrumentalists are very frequently mentioned in the literature also and clearly had aesthetic appeal of a similar order to that of the string players. They are associated with sweet and soothing sounds, with providing consolation and lulling to sleep of princes and kings, and in a few cases they are listed in tandem with the string players, which may indicate that they played in concert (cf. Ó Háinle 1976, 38; Buckley 1978, 62).

The term *cuisle* also refers to a vein, hence it also has connotations of narrowness and so does not help distinguish it organologically from *buinne*.

I. Quadrangular chordophone, 6 parallel strings:
Castledermot, North Cross, west face, north arm. 8th/9th century.

II. Quadrangular chordophone, 6 parallel strings:
Castledermot, South Cross, west face, north arm. 8th/9th century.

III. Quadrangular chordophone, 6 parallel strings:
Graiguenamanagh Cross, east shaft, lowest panel. 8th/9th century.

IV. Quadrangular chordophone, 6 parallel strings:
Ullard Cross, east face, south arm. 8th/9th century.

V. Psaltery (?) with 6 strings (left), bell and book:
Carndonagh, North and South Pillars, west face. 8th/9th century.

VI. Assymetrical lyre and single pipe:
Cross of Muireadach, Monasterboice, east face, south arm; triple pipes, north arm.
9th/10th century.

VII. Round-topped lyre: Cross of the Scriptures, Clonmacnois,
south shaft, centre panel. 9th/10th century.

VIII. Asymmetrical 6-stringed lyre and single pipe:
Durrow Cross, east face, south arm. 9th/10th century.

IX. Asymmetrical lyre:
Cross of Patrick and Columba, Kells, west face, head. 8th/9th century.

X. Single pipes: Cross of the Scriptures, Clonmacnois,
east face, north and south arms. 9th/10th century.

XI. Triple pipes: Cross of the Scriptures, Clonmacnois,
north shaft, centre panel. 9th/10th century.

XII. Round-topped lyre: West Cross, Kells, east shaft, fourth panel. Late 9th century.

XIII. Round-topped lyre: Kinitty Cross, east shaft, centre panel. Late 9th century.

XIV. Asymmetrical 3-stringed lyre (centre), bell and crozier: Shrine of the Stowe
Missal, dating from its refurbishment in 1381.

XV. Bowed lyre (or psaltery), 6 strings:
St Finan's Church, Lough Currane, Waterville, Co. Kerry, *c.*1200.

XVI. Triangular harp, 8 strings and 12 tuning pegs: Breac Maedóic, 11th century.

XVII. Triangular harp, 23 strings: Fiacail Phádraig, *c.*1376.

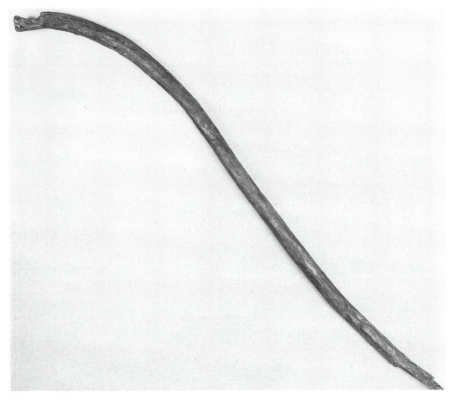

a. (approx. 60 cm long)

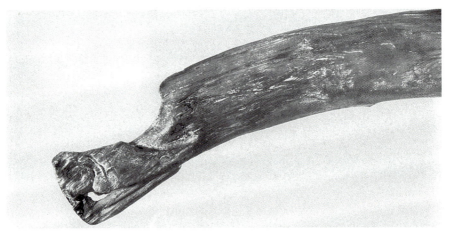

b. (approx. 16 cm long)

XVIII. Bow fragment (a) and detail of carved terminal (b)
excavated at Christchurch Place, Dublin, mid-11th century.

XIX. Hunting horn: Old Kilcullen Cross, west shaft, top panel. 8th/9th century.

XX. Fragments of a ceramic horn excavated at Wood Quay, Dublin, 13th century.

Plates I-XII, XV and XIX are published by permission of the Commissioners of Public Works, Ireland. Plates XIV, XVI-XVIII and XX are published by permission of The Director, National Museum of Ireland

Only the implied superior social status of players of this instrument suggest that it may have been more flexible in the technical and musical sense. Iconographic evidence does exist for association of chordophone and aerophone on the three scriptural crosses at Monasterboice, Durrow and Clonmacnois. On the first, a player of a single pipe is shown seated behind the player of an assymetrical lyre, suggesting that they are playing in concert to accompany the singing of the psalms, or more generally the praises of God, by the third figure who reads from a book. They attend upon the scene of Christ in Judgement, which is also depicted on the Durrow Cross with single pipe and lyre on the same arm. There the aerophone player is closest to Christ and no other company is in attendance. He could be interpreted as St Michael blowing the Last Trump since he appears to have wings, in which case the juxtaposition of the two players provides not musicological but ideological data: one blows the Trump to announce the Judgement while another plays his stringed instrument in praise and honour. The Clomnacnois Judgement scene is attended upon only by an aerophone player, and is therefore also open to both interpretations. A definite representation of the Last Trump is provided by an eighth-century Irish manuscript, St Gall MS 51, where Christ is seated in glory with an angel on each side playing an instrument resembling a trumpet while the faithful below look upwards at the celestial scene (cf. Henry 1965, pl. M).

The high cross instruments look alike, held in the mouth and pointed downdards, all of them showing a slight widening at the terminal suggesting a number of possibilities: the natural flare of the tibia (cf. examples in Brade, Buckley, Crane, Lund, Rimmer), a conical bore, or an attached animal-horn. This last would make it a hornpipe, like the Welsh *pibcorn*, the Scottish *stock-and-horn* and the German *Schwegelhorn*, a reed-pipe inserted into a horn. They could also represent conical reed instruments, made from bone or wood, with a single or double reed inserted in the mouth, or covered with a reedcap.

Of surviving instruments it is not always possible to determine whether they were used in this way in specific instances. A wooden tube with four fingerholes and with bevelling at both ends was recovered from a late Viking or early medieval site (*c*.850-1050) in Sweden (Lund 1981, 262, fig. 14; 1984, 25, pl. 63, examples 40-41). Because of the bevelling it must have had attachments at both ends and therefore have had a horn- or bell-shaped terminal and either a reed-cap or a bag at the top. Other reedpipes have been found in the Netherlands, dating between the ninth and eleventh centuries (Rimmer 1981, pl. 2e), in tenth/eleventh century Viking York (Crane 1972, 45-46, Hall 1984, 115-16), and most recently a find from Denmark of one of similar dating (Müller 1988). Of the objects from Irish sites housed in the National Museum, Dublin, a report was given by Galpin (1965, 128) of a small ornamented deerbone with nine (fingerhole?) perforations along its length, which may have been part of a hornpipe. This is suggested by the presence of pinholes at the larger end, or terminal, which could have served to secure a horn attachment. Theoretically it may also have been a bagpipe chanter, but without examining the object such a possibility cannot be explored. Unfortunately Galpin gave no account of the top of the pipe nor did he include a catalogue number or bibliographic source, making it now difficult to locate.[23]

Later iconographic evidence for hornpipes has not been noted in Irish sources. The earliest bagpipe depictions date from the sixteenth century[24] and no information of a specific nature exists for its earlier use in Ireland or, for that matter, in Wales or Scotland. This instrument is commonly depicted in west European manuscripts and sculpture from the thirteenth century onwards, and so far there is no evidence to suggest that bagpipes were used in north-west Europe before this date. Of other surviving aerophones none of them bears indication of having been used as a hornpipe or bagpipe chanter: no leather bag or fragments have so far emerged, nor are there traces of such on the terminals (cf. Müller 1988, 31, 35). Most of the Irish aerophones (Christchurch Place, Winetavern Street, High Street) appear to be block-and-duct or reed instruments and include examples without fingerholes, with two and with three fingerholes. They are made of birdbone and of yew wood. One fragment gives cause for special interest because of its unusually wide bore; this is the object from John's Lane which has one fingerhole remaining and the top half of a second.[25]

Only one other type of aerophone is depicted on the crosses, namely triple pipes which occur on two monuments, Muireadach's Cross and the Cross of the Scriptures. In the former the musician is seated to the left of Christ suggesting 'sinister', devilish, or secular association; the devil is often depicted with triple pipes in medieval iconography. The Clonmacnois instrument is on the shaft but not on the same side as the lyre-player. In both cases the instrument has three unequal conical pipes, that on the player's left being considerably longer than the other two, and with the familiar bell-shaped terminal. This could indicate simply that it had a wider bore – as in the case of the much more clearly discerned example in a twelfth century English bestiary of the Canterbury school, Oxford MS Bodley 602, f. 10 (cf. Becker 1966, 112, fig. 43). Roe (1949, 55) was the first to publish the Clonmacnois instrument which she described as a set of panpipes. This is most unlikely because the angle at which it is held shows it not to be rim-blown but offered right up to the mouth (as in the case of the Clonmacnois and Canterbury representations). In Schneider's opinion (1978, 163) the player's cheeks appear distended as though indicative of the effort required to blow a reed instrument. While this may be so it is difficult to be conclusive about such details from the lack of clarity in the stone carving; however the Bodley manuscript illustration suggests this feature with greater definition.

It is not possible to ascertain whether triple pipes were ever played in Ireland, or elsewhere in these islands, in spite of those illustrations and two others in

Scottish stone carvings of the ninth to eleventh centuries,[26] because iconography alone is an inadequate medium, given the range of its symbolism and the eclectic nature of its images. As far as knowledge of actual practice is concerned, triple pipes are known in the Arab world and in European culture only Sardinia, where they are called *launeddas*. Double pipes are widely used in Eastern Europe, in the Middle East and North Africa. Like our quadrangular harps, therefore, the question must remain open as to whether these are artist's imitations of Mediterranean Christian iconography or an account of local practices. If the latter, they are eloquent testimony to insular polyphonic music-making, as has already been commented by Münxelhaus (1982, 63-4). But this theory, while most likely a valid historical assessment of practice, may not conclusively be applied to triple pipes.

Contrariwise, despite lack of an Irish example we do have surviving panpipes from elsewhere in Western Europe, including one from tenth-century York, made of boxwood and discovered during the excavation of a Viking site (Hall 1984, 115-16, fig. 141). Panpipes from the Gallo-Roman period have been found in southern and eastern France (Homo-Lechner 1984; 1986, 160, fig.3). Since there is an abundance of iconographic evidence for such instruments in classical Greek (*syrinx*) and Roman (*fistula*) sources it is possible that this was their route into western Europe.

The remaining types of aerophones to be considered are all associated with more mundane, outdoor functions such as hunting, signalling, keeping watch, going into battle. The Irish words are *corn*, a horn, and *stoc*, an instrument of heralds and warriors, therefore either a horn or a trumpet. Both types are depicted on the thirteenth-century matrices of the seal of the Lord Mayor of Dublin: on one side the castle is shown with players of curved horns above the gate and a player of a straight trumpet in each of the towers, while on the other side a group of people in a boat are being watched over by horn players from the ramparts – indicating their function in the service of protecting the city.[27] In Old Irish, horns are referred to also as *corn buabhaill*, buffalo horns, and these were used as drinking horns and also as musical instruments. They were evidently much prized (a gloss in the Laws indicates a heavy fine for their theft) since they were imported objects, and thus rare and valuable (Ancient Laws V, 220-1). *Stoc* is most commonly referred to in the context of battle. There is also *stoc fógra* the function of which is obvious, though it could refer to 'messages' in the non-linguistic, 'musical' sense (i.e. where signals are given certain meanings) or to a tube being used as a voice-enhancer for linguistic messages, as in a megaphone.

Horns are depicted on two crosses: at Old Kilcullen for a hunting scene (cf. plate XIX), and on the base of the North Cross, Ahenny (eighth-ninth century) in a funeral procession. It is led by a group of whom the first figure is carrying a ringed cross, at the centre a horse bears a corpse, followed close behind by a horn-player. A hunting scene on the wall-painting of Holy Cross Abbey (fifteenth century) is still barely discernible to the naked eye; while this is a little late in date in the context of the present survey, it nonetheless provides useful additional evidence. No horns or trumpets of wood or bark have survived, which is not surprising in view of the fragility of their materials. However, the excavation of the thirteenth-century Wood Quay site in Dublin yielded fragments of a ceramic horn with its bell in the familiar green-glaze of Saintonge ware. The fragments include bell, mouthpiece and part of the body with a hole pierced in this and the bell sherd through which a carrying strap would have been inserted (cf. plate XX). Such an isolated example, and a foreign one at that, can provide no information on local use. Numerous ceramic horns survive from north-west continental Europe and probably served as signalling devices. Others were associated with pilgrimage and perhaps acquired at pilgrimage sites as a memento of the journey. Examples are those finds from Aachen known as *Pilgerhorn* (cf. Crane 1972, 60-1), also recovered from Netherlands sites (Rimmer 1981, 421). In this connection too, it is useful to note the references to bronze horns associated with saints in Ireland, according to the account of Gerald of Wales. He reported that a curse befell someone who blew St Brendan's horn, and mentioned another object which was venerated as the horn of St Patrick, which suggests that horns as well as bells could serve as sacred relics.[28]

In the wider European context oliphants or large ivory horns carried great social status. While some of them were used as instruments in the hunt, or as magnificent drinking horns, many were purely symbols of land tenure which exchanged hands along with the documents. This was the practice in Norman-French and Anglo-Norman culture and resulted from contact with the Arab world and the ivory trade. Whether this practice ever reached Ireland is not known.

It has been shown in this brief review that Irish social and cultural history should not be viewed in isolation when dealing with material survivals or iconographic representations of musical instruments. All of the objects excavated attest to an essential interconnectedness with Britain and continental Europe. Iconography is even more opaque involving as it does the enmeshing of theology, moral-didactic messages and cultural perceptions in a complex weave of artistic motifs requiring detailed and thoroughgoing investigation of Carolingian sources as well as materials from the north and east Mediterranean regions of the early Christian period. It is only when we understand the larger-scale patterns that particulars of this north-west European island can be properly assessed. Whether random imports, foreign models adapted and filtered through local perceptions, or specifically Irish forms, they represent, in their sum, an expression of regional character.

TABLE 1*

Organological Evidence from Iconographic Sources

CHORDOPHONES
Quadrangular   *8th/9th century*

Parallel (6)	Castledermot, North Cross, west face, north arm
Parallel (6)	Castledermot, South Cross, west face, north arm
Parallel (6)	Ullard Cross, east face, south arm
Parallel (6)	Graiguenamanagh Cross, east face, shaft, lowest panel

Psaltery (?)   *8th/9th century*

Parallel (6)   Carndonagh, North Pillar, west face

Assymetrical Lyres   *8th/9th century*

Splayed (?)   Cross of Patrick & Columba, Kells, west face, head

                               9th/10th century
Splayed   Cross of Muireadach, Monasterboice east face, south arm

Round-topped Lyres

Splayed	West Cross, Kells, east face, shaft, fourth panel
Splayed (?)	Killamery Cross, east face, head

                               9th/10th century
Parallel (6)	Psalter, British Museum MS Cotton Vitellius F. XI, f 2^r
Splayed (6)	Durrow cross, east face, south arm
Splayed	Cross of the Scriptures, Clonmacnois, south face, shaft, centre panel
Splayed (?)	Kinitty Cross, east face, shaft, centre panel

                               14th century
Splayed (3)   Shrine of the Stowe Missal

Bowed ?Lyre   12th century

Parallel (6)   St Finan's Church, wall

Triangular harps   *11th century*

(8-12)   Breac Maedóic

---

*   The details in the left-hand column refer to the arrangement of the strings and their estimated number, where possible. Shaft panels are numbered from the top down.

	14th century
(23)	Fiacail Phádraig

AEROPHONES

Horns	*8th/9th century*
	Ahenny North Cross, base, south side
	Old Kilcullen cross, west face, shaft, top panel
	13th century
	seal matrices of Lord Mayor of Dublin
Trumpets	13th century
	seal matrix of Lord Mayor of Dublin
Single pipes	*9th/10th century*
	Cross of Muireadach, Monasterboice, east face, south arm
	Durrow Cross, east face, south arm
	Cross of the Scriptures, Clonmacnois, east face, south arm
Triple pipes	Cross of Muireadach, Monasterboice, east face, south arm
	Cross of the Scriptures, Clonmacnois, north face, shaft, centre panel

TABLE 2

Contexts of Iconographic Depictions

	8th/9th century	
Crucifixion	quadrangular chordophone	Castledermot North & South Crosses
Crucifixion	quadrangular chordophone	Ullard
Independent	quadrangular chordophone	Graiguenamanagh
Loaves & Fishes	assymetrical lyre	Kells Cross of Patrick and Columba
Ecclesiastics	psaltery(?), bell & book	Carndonagh pillars
Ecclesiastic (?)	bell, book & crozier	Old Kilcullen
Hunting scene	horn	Old Kilcullen
Funeral procession	horn	Ahenny North Cross
	9th/10th century	
Christ in Judgement	assymetrical lyre & bird & single pipe & book; triple pipes opposite	Muireadach's Cross
Christ in Judgement	semi-curved lyre & single pipe	Durrow Cross
Christ in Judgement	single pipe	Cross of the Scriptures
Independent	triple pipes	Cross of the Scriptures
Independent	round-topped lyre	Cross of the Scriptures
Independent	round-topped lyre	Kinitty Cross
Independent	round-topped lyre	Killamery Cross
?	round-topped lyre	Kells West Cross

	11th-14th centuries	
Independent	triangular harp	Breac Maedóic (11th)
Independent	bowed lyre (or psaltery?)	St Finan's Church (12th)
City waits	horns & trumpets	Dublin Seal matrices (13th)
Ecclesiastics	plucked lyre & crozier & bell	Stowe Missal Shrine (14th)
Independent	triangular harp	Fiacail Phádraig (14th)

TABLE 3

Organological Evidence from Material Sources

CHORDOPHONES

Bow fragment	Christchurch Place, Dublin	mid 11th century
Tuning pegs	Christchurch Place, Dublin (3)	mid/late 11th century
	High St, Dublin	13th century
	Christchurch, Cork (3)	13th century

AEROPHONES

Wooden flutes

No fingerholes	Christchurch Place	*c.*1200
Fragment	Winetavern St	13th century
Fragment	John's Lane	13th century

Bone flutes

No fingerholes	High St	13th century
2 fingerholes	High St	13th century
Mouthpiece fragment	High St	13th century

Bone ?reedpipe

9 fingerholes	site unknown	date unknown

Ceramic horn

Fragments	Wood Quay	13th century

NOTES

1. *Amhrá Cholm Cille* 20. See entry under *céis* in DIL 1913-1975.
2. Cf. Mac Néill 1923, 280.
3. Cf. Binchy 1941, 23, 1. 590.
4. For an account of ecclesiastical bells see Bourke 1980 and 1985, and for jew's harps see Buckley 1983 and 1986.
5. For information on Old and Middle Irish literary references see O'Curry 1873, Fleischmann and Gleason 1965, Herbert 1976, Ó Fiannachta 1976, Ó Háinle 1976, Buckley 1977, 1978 and [1989]. I am in the course of preparing a full review of these sources to serve as a companion study to the present article.
6. In some early medieval depictions the presence of a forepillar is not always certain, leaving doubt as to whether the instruments concerned are harps or triangular (delta-shaped) psalteries. See discussion below.
7. These later crosses have until recently been dated to the early tenth century (Stokes, Roe, Henry) but this has recently been challenged by Harbison (1979) who has suggested a slightly earlier *terminus ad quem*. In view of the several elements which require detailed consideration (artistic style, details of representation, structural details of objects depicted), a systematic comparative and interdisciplinary study of all of these stone carvings would yield useful results.
8. Cf. Porter 1931 and Henry 1967 for further discussion of this question.
9. Another similar quadrangular chordophone which appears to have one straight and one curved arm may be seen in Steger 1961, *Dkm.* 1. I am not aware of further examples with a rounded stringholder, whether on one or both arms.
10. I wish to record my indebtedness to Catherine Homo-Lechner with whom I have had several very useful discussions on this and other topics relating to medieval chordophones, and who kindly allowed me to examine her iconographic catalogue. For examples of all manner of psalteries, quadrangular, triangular and other, cf. Panum 1971, 144ff; and possible psalteries, Steger 1961b, *Dkm.* 29, 33/7, 34/3, 39, 43; Bachmann 1969, pls. 26, 40, 42, 57. Many of these are reproduced also in Seebass 1973.
11. But cf. Steger 1961a who identifies the term *Rotte* with continental triangular psalteries; see also note 12 below. Page (1977, 305) states that there is no evidence that zithers of any kind (i.e. including psalteries) existed in Anglo-Saxon England, in other words up to the time of the Norman Conquest (1066).
12. Some writers (e.g. Roe 1949, 57-8, fig. 12.46 – mistakenly referred to as 12.45 in her discussion on p. 57) believed it contained a zoomorphic carving on the neck but from the photograph this appears to be a crack in the surface of the carving. It should be emphasized that Roe's illustrations are drawings and not photographic reproductions. Many of them are seriously inaccurate and so it is unfortunate that Steger reproduced them without examining the photographs if not the original carvings (cf. 1961a, 119 etc.; 1961b, 59-60). It caused him to suggest that the Shrine of the Stowe Missal could conceivably represent a psaltery (1961a, 125) because Roe's line-drawing incorrectly shows a triangular harp-like profile. For detailed discussion see below, p. 20.
13. For an account of problems and methods in the interpretation of music iconography cf. Seebass 1973.
14. In her discussion of harp and lyre iconography on early Christian monuments Rensch (1969, 19-38) states that Monasterboice and Kells South Cross most clearly resemble the triangular-shaped frame harp (p. 24). In my opinion Monasterboice has a four-sided (not three-sided) frame, the shortest of which is the base, and looks more like an oblique lyre

than any kind of harp, also suggested by the presence of a bridge in the lower section of the instrument. Such detail is no longer visible on the Kells carving, but its profile is similar to that of Monasterboice.

15. See De Geer 1985, 50ff. for useful organological maps of the region for the period under discussion.

16. Cf. Seebass 1987 for a recent survey of medieval harp terminology, iconography, social status.

17. I exclude from consideration here illustrations in older St Gall MSS, conceivably made by or for Irishmen, but which may have been produced under continental influence e.g., MS 23 (Psalter of Folchard, ninth century) p. 23 and MS 21 (tenth century) p. 5 (cf. Steger 1961, *Dkm.* 13 and 23, respectively), although both of these may well not represent harps but psalteries. Cf. the discussion above.

18. The carving was first published in Lynch 1908, 373. Cf. also the copy in Bachmann 1969, pl. 55, and Seebass 1973, pl. 29. Seebass (*ibid., Darstellungband*, 32-3) remarked that it resembles a psaltery since the strings appear stretched over an elongated table, though he does warn that the image is unclear. He nonetheless chooses to focus on the parallel strings and does not discuss the ridge at the lower end which appears to resemble a tailpiece rather than the continuation of the string band. At the very least, however, there is an incompatibility between the parallel strings and this narrow 'tailpiece': in order to be attached in this way, the strings would have to narrow towards their fixing point. Alternatively, this ridge might have been intended to represent the player's hand stopping the strings whose traces have long disappeared.

19. The oldest extant instrument continues to be the so-called 'Brian Boru' harp in the Library, Trinity College Dublin of *c.* fourteenth century date.

20. In the latter article Lawson fails to locate the sites or museum holdings from which these examples are drawn, but merely refers in the most general terms to 'medieval' and 'medieval and early post-medieval' England and Wales.

21. Unfortunately such cooperation between musicologist and scientific laboratory seems an unlikely prospect in Ireland at present owing to an evident lack of interest on the part of some of those who house the objects and undertake archaeological excavation and research. The monopoly of this field of enquiry by those who excavate leaves little room for the kind of collaboration with specialists in a whole range of other disciplines which fuller analysis of these artefacts demands. The situation is not at all helped by the lack of involvement of musicologists in (medieval) historical enquiry in general. Musicology, too often associated with performance and aesthetic pursuits, does not appear to be valued for its important role in social and cultural history. Musical instruments are just as much cultural artefacts as are implements for woodworking, weaving, cooking, and warfare. They are not mere *objets d'art* to be valued only for their sound-producing potential, as implied in an exhibition catalogue from the National Museum of Ireland in which a number of bone flutes are referred to as children's toys, presumably because they are of simple technology (cf. *Viking and Medieval Dublin*, Dublin 1973, 13). Whether they were used by children or adults (for whatever purpose) we shall probably never precisely know, but this is hardly a suitable basis for determining their value as historical artefacts, nor is it a criterion for estimating their capabilities or functions as sound-producers.

22. It is etymologically related to the Germanic word *Bein*, a leg, also *tibia.*

23. I should welcome any information which could assist in identifying this object. Baines (1960, 32) also reported Galpin's observations but does not seem to have pursued it any further. Galpin (1965, pl. 35) gives an illustration of the dismantled pipe of an eighteenth century *pibcorn* which demonstrates the structure of the instrument.

24. Cf. Breathnach (1977, 70) who unfortunately does not identify the source beyond saying that it is a manuscript in the collection of the Royal Irish Academy, Dublin.
25. See Table 3 below for further details. A preliminary report on the Dublin instruments may be found in Buckley 1988.
26. The two Scottish examples may be found on the Lethendy Slab, Perthshire (ninth/tenth century) and on the upright cross slab at Ardchattan, Argyll (tenth/eleventh century). Cf. Porter 1983, 258 for a photograph of Lethendy, and Allen 1903, III, 378, fig. 393, for Ardchattan.
27. The seals are discussed in Armstrong 1913, 124 and engravings of the images reproduced in [Anon] 1884, pl. XVIII.
28. See Buckley [1989] for bibliographic details.

REFERENCES

Allen, J. Romilly. *The early christian momuments of Scotland. A classified, illustrated, descriptive list of the monuments, with an analysis of their symbolism and ornamentation by John Romilly Allen with an introduction by Joseph Anderson.* 2 vols. (Edinburgh, 1903).

Ancient Laws. *The ancient laws of Ireland,* ed. W. N. Hancock, J. O'Donovan et al. 5 vols. (Dublin, 1865-1901).

[Anon.] *Rental of the estates of the Right Honorary the Lord Mayor, Aldermen and Burgesses of Dublin* (Dublin, 1884).

Armstrong, E.C.R. *Irish seal matrices and seals* (Dublin, 1913).

Bachmann, Werner. *The origins of bowing* (Leipzig, 1966). Trans. Norma Deane. (Oxford, 1969).

Baines, Anthony. *Bagpipes* (Oxford, 1960).

Becker, Heinz. *Zur Entwicklungsgeschichte der antiken und mittelalterlichen Rohrblattinstrumente* (Hamburg, 1966).

Binchy, Daniel A. *An Críth Gablach.* Medieval and modern Irish series 11 (Dublin, 1941).

Brade, Christine. *Die mittelalterliche Kernspaltflöten Mittel- und Nordeuropas* (Neumünster, 1975).

Breathnach, Breandán. *Folk music and dances of Ireland* (Dublin and Cork, 1977).

Bourke, Cormac. 'Early Irish hand-bells', *Journal of the Royal Society of Antiquaries of Ireland 110* (1980), 52-66.

____ 'A crozier and bell from Inishmurray and their place in 9th century Irish archaeology', *Proceedings of the Royal Irish Academy* 85 C 5 (1985), 145-68.

Bruce-Mitford, Myrtle. 'Rotte', *The New Grove Dictionary of Music and Musicians,* ed. Stanley Sadie (London, 1980), vol. 16, 261-5.

Bruce-Mitford, R. and M. 'The Sutton Hoo lyre, Beowulf and the origins of the frame harp'. In Rupert L. Bruce-Mitford, *Aspects of Anglo-Saxon archaeology; Sutton Hoo and other discoveries* (London, 1974), 188-197.

____ 'The musical instruments'. In *The Sutton Hoo ship burial* (London, 1983), III, 611-720.

Buckley, Ann. 'Notes on the tiompán in Irish literature', *Studia Instrumentorum Musicae Popularis* V (Stockholm, 1977), 84-90.

____ 'What was the tiompán? A problem in ethnohistorical organology. Evidence in Irish literature', *Jahrbuch für musikalische Volks- und Völkerkunde* IX (1978), 53-88.

___ 'Timpán/Tiompán', *The New Grove Dictionary of Music and Musicians*, ed. Stanley Sadie (London, 1980), vol. 18, 826, and *The New Grove Dictionary of Musical Instruments*, ed. Stanley Sadie (London, 1986), vol. 3, 586.

___ 'A note on the history and archaeology of jew's harps in Ireland', *North Munster Antiquaries Journal*, 25 (1983), 29-35.

___ 'Jew's harps in Irish archaeology, *Second Conference of the ICTM Study Group on Music Archaeology*, ed. Cajsa S. Lund (Stockholm, 1986), I, 49-71.

___ 'A ceramic signal horn from medieval Dublin', *Archaeologia Musicalis*, I (1987), 9-10.

___ 'A Viking bow from 11th century Dublin', *Archaeologia Musicalis*, I (1987), 10-11.

___ 'Musical instruments from medieval Dublin — a preliminary survey', *The archaeology of early music cultures. Third international conference of the ICTM Study Group on Music Archaeology*, ed. Ellen Hickmann and David W. Hughes (Bonn, 1988), 145-162.

___ [1989]. 'Music in ancient and medieval Ireland', *A New History of Ireland*, ed. F.X. Martin and F.J. Byrne, I (Oxford: forthcoming).

Crane, Frederick W. *Extant medieval musical instruments. A provisional catalogue by types* (Iowa, 1972).

De Geer, Ingrid. *Earl, saint, bishop, skald — and music* (Doctoral dissertation: Uppsala, 1985).

DIL. *Contributions to a dictionary of the Irish language*, ed. Myles Dillon et al. (Dublin, 1913-75).

Durham, Brian. 'Archaeological investigations in St Aldate's, Oxford', *Oxoniensa* 42 (1977) 83-203.

Fleischmann, Aloys and Gleason, Ryta. 'Music in ancient Munster and monastic Cork', *Journal of the Cork Historical and Archaeological Society* 70, part 2 (no. 202), (1965), 79-98.

Gaborit-Chopin, Danielle. *Ivoires du moyen âge* (Fribourg, 1978).

Galpin, Francis. *Old English instruments of music, their history and character*. Fourth edition revised with supplemental notes by Thurston Dart. (London 1965; repr. London, 1978).

Hall, R. *The Viking dig. The excavations at York* (Bristol, 1984).

Harbison, Peter. 'The inscriptions on the Cross of the Scriptures at Clonmacnois, County Offaly', *Proceedings of the Royal Irish Academy* 79 C 7, (1979), 177-88.

Harrison, Frank Ll. 'Celtic musics: characteristics and chronology', *Geschichte und Kultur der Kelten*, ed. K.H. Schmidt and R. Kodderitzsch (Heidelberg, 1986), 252-63.

Henry, Françoise and Geneviève. 'Remarks on the decoration of three Irish psalters', *Proceedings of the Royal Irish Academy* 61 C 2 (1962), 101-66.

___ *Irish art in the early Christian period to AD 800* (London, 1965).

___ *Irish art during the Viking period* (London, 1967).

Herbert, Máire. 'Ár n-uirlisí ceoil', Ó Fiannachta ed., *Léachtaí Cholm Cille* VII (1976) 21-30.

Homo-Lechner, Catherine. 'Une flûte de pan gallo-romaine au Musée archéologique de Metz', *Music Archaeology Bulletin* 3 (September, 1984) 10-12.

___ 'L'archéologie sonore en France: premiers résultats', *Second conference of the ICTM Study Group on Music Archaeology*, ed. Cajsa S. Lund (Stockholm, 1986), I, 157-61.

___ 'Les fouilles de la Rue de Lutèce à Paris', *Archaeologia Musicalis*, 1/8 (1988), 63-5.

___ 'Whistles and calls from the recent excavations at the Louvre', *The archaeology of early music cultures. Third international conference of the ICTM Study Group for Music Archaeology*, ed. Ellen Hickmann and David W. Hughes (Bonn, 1988), 163-73.

Hurley, Maurice. 'Wooden artefacts from the excavation of the medieval city of Cork', *Woodworking techniques before AD 1500*, ed. S. McGrail. BAR International Series 129 (Oxford, 1982), 301-11.

Lawson, Graeme (1978a). 'Medieval tuning pegs from Whitby, N. Yorkshire', *Medieval Archaeology* 22 (1978), 139-41.

___ (1978b) 'The lyre from Grave 22', *The Anglo-Saxon cemetery at Bergh Apton, Norfolk*, ed. B. Green and A. Rogerson. East Anglian Archaeology. Report no. 7 (1978), 87-97.

___ 'An Anglo-Saxon harp and lyre of the ninth century', *Music and tradition: essays on Asian and other musics presented to Laurence Picken*, ed. D.R. Widdess and R.F. Wolpert (Cambridge, 1981), 229-44.

___ 'Conservation versus restoration: towards a handling and performance policy for excavated musical instruments, with special reference to microwear studies and finds from the English warship Mary Rose (1545)', *Second Conference of the ICTM Study Group on Music Archaeology*, ed. Cajsa S. Lund (Stockholm, 1986) I, 123-30.

Lund, Cajsa. 'The archaeomusicology of Scandinavia', *World Archaeology* 12/3 (1981), 246-65.

___ *The sounds of prehistoric Scandinavia*. Musica Sveciae (Stockholm, 1984). [disc and booklet]

Lynch, Patrick J. 'Some notes on Lough Currane, Church Island, Co. Kerry', *Journal of the Royal Society of Antiquaries of Ireland*, 5th ser., 18 (1908), 368-81.

MacNeill, Eoin. 'Ancient Irish Law. The law of status and franchise', *Proceedings of the Royal Irish Academy* 36 C 16 (1923), 265-316.

McKinnon, James and Remnant, Mary. 'Psaltery', *The New Grove Dictionary of Music and Musicians*, ed. Stanley Sadie (London, 1980), vol. 15, 382-7.

Megaw, J.V.S. 'Bone musical instruments from medieval Exeter', *Medieval and post-medieval finds from Exeter 1971-1980*, ed. J.P. Allan. Exeter Archaeological Reports 3 (1984), 349-51.

___ 'The emperor's new clothes: the *new* music archaeology?', *The archaeology of early music cultures. Third International Conference of the ICTM Study Group for Music Archaeology*, ed. Ellen Hickmann and David W. Hughes. (Bonn, 1988), 343-53.

Müller, Mette. 'Reed-pipe of the Vikings or of the Slavs?', *The archaeology of eary music cultures. Third International Conference of the ICTM Study Group for Music Archaeology*, ed. Ellen Hickmann and David W. Hughes. (Bonn, 1988), 31-8.

Münxelhaus, Barbara. 'Der Beitrag Irlands zur Musik des frühen Mittelalters', *Die Iren von Europa im frühen Mittelalter*, ed. H. Löwe. (Stuttgart, 1982), II, 630-8.

O'Curry, Eugene. 'Of music and musical instruments in ancient Erinn', *Manners and customs of the ancient Irish*, ed. with introduction and appendices by W.K. Sullivan (London, 1873). Lecture, XXX, 212-409.

Ó Fiannachta, Pádraig, ed. *An ceol i litríocht na Gaeilge. Léachtaí Cholm Cille* VII (Maynooth, 1976).

___ An ceol sa tseanlitriocht, *Léachtaí Cholm Cille* VII, ed. Pádraig Ó Fiannachta (Maynooth, 1976), 5-20.

Ó Háinle, Cathal. 'An ceol san fhilíocht chlasaiceach', *Léachtaí Cholm Cille VII*, ed. Pádraig Ó Fiannachta (Maynooth 1976) 31-57.

Ó Ríordáin, Breandán. 'Excavations at High Street and Winetavern Street, Dublin', *Medieval Archaeology*, 15 (1971), 73-85.

Page, Christopher. 'Biblical instruments in medieval manuscript illustration', *Early Music*, 5/3 (1977), 299-309.

Panum, Hortense. *Stringed musical instruments of the middle ages*. Revd. and ed. Jeffrey Pulver (London, 1971).

Porter, Arthur Kingsley. *The crosses and culture of Ireland* (New Haven, 1931).

Porter, James. 'Harps, pipes and silent stones: the problem of Pictish music', *Essays in honour of Peter Crossley-Holland on his sixty-fifth birthday*. Selected Reports in Ethnomusicology, IV (1983), 243-67.

Rensch, Roslyn. *The harp. Its history, technique and repertory* (London, 1969).

Rimmer, Joan. *The Irish harp* (Cork, 1984).

___ 'An archaeo-organological survey of the Netherlands', *World Archaeology*, 12/3 (1981), 243-67.

Roe, Helen M. 'The David cycle in early Irish art', *Journal of the Royal Society of Antiquaries of Ireland*, 79 (1949), 39-59.

Schneider, Albrecht. 'Probleme der Periodisierung von Volksmusik und Folklore am Beispiel Irlands', *Musikethnologische Sammelbände* II (1978), 147-86.

Seebass, Tilman. *Musikdarstellung und Psalterillustration im früheren Mittelalter. Studien ausgehend von einer Ikonologie der Handschrift Paris Bibliothèque nationale fonds latin 1118*, 2 vols. (Bern, 1973).

___ 'Idee und Status von Harfen im europäischen Mittelalter', *Basler Jahrbuch für historische Musikpraxis*, 11 (1987) 139-52.

Steger, Hugo [a]. 'Die Rotte', *Deutsche Vierteljahrsschrift für Literaturwissenschaft und Geschichte*, 35 (1961), 88-147.

___ [b]. *David Rex et Propheta. König David als vorbildliche Verkörperung des Herrschers und Dichters im Mittelalter, nach Bilddarstellungen des achten bis zwölften Jahrhunderts* (Nürnberg, 1961).

The History of *The Lass of Aughrim*

HUGH SHIELDS

Few songs can have been so well transposed into another art form as the small fragment with which Joyce brings so striking a change of tone into the last story of *Dubliners*, 'The Dead':

'O, the rain falls on my heavy locks
And the dew wets my skin,
My babe lies cold. . . .'

The characters discuss the title of the song:

– Mr D'Arcy, she said, what is the name of that song you were singing?
– It's called *The Lass of Aughrim*, said Mr D'Arcy, but I couldn't remember it properly. Why? Do you know it?
– *The Lass of Aughrim*, she repeated. I couldn't think of the name.
– It's a very nice air, said Mary Jane. I'm sorry you were not in voice tonight.[1]

Perhaps Mr D'Arcy knew the whole song. His questioner was familiar with it, as the story will reveal. Yet there is not much evidence that it was a very well-known song, in Ireland or elsewhere. We are told later how D'Arcy's questioner had heard it, but not how the urbane tenor himself came by an old ballad of this kind. Popular tradition still knows it a little, though disobligingly it drops the older, more poetic title and labels the song 'Lord Gregory',[2] after its relatively inactive hero. It thus discards an evocative Irish toponym in favour of an unfamiliar personal name: a change which Joyce would surely have found unwelcome. Irishness obtrudes significantly into his story, and the narrator touches on the Irishness of the song:

Now that the hall-door was closed the voice and the piano could be heard more clearly. Gabriel held up his hand for them to be silent. The song seemed to be in the old Irish tonality.[3]

Was this an opinion of the author? Writing to Nora Barnacle some two years after finishing the story he particularly mentions the tune: 'the tears come into my eyes and my voice trembles with emotion when I sing that lovely air.'[4] He gives no clue as to whether he was aware – or would have cared – that the song had a Scots origin and is also known as the 'Lass of Roch Royal'. Its history has been partly explored.[5] Here my purpose is to delve into it more deeply, in a way which will promote particular reflection on the undoubted Irishness of this ballad of Scots origin. The subject will be of more interest to the history of the ballad form in Ireland than to Joyce or to his story. But at the same time it will allow some readers a degree of cultural 'interpenetration' which is unusual in the pluralist society we inhabit today. For not many get an opportunity to appreciate artists so different as the world author who happens to be Irish *and* a West Cork contemporary of his who might have been forgotten altogether had not a recent invention preserved an image of her beautiful singing of this song. Elizabeth Cronin was recorded on magnetic tape some thirteen years after Joyce's death: we shall return to her in the later stages of our 'history'.

FROM ROCH ROYAL TO AUGHRIM

The *Lass of Aughrim* first appears as 'Isabell of Rochroyall' in a Scots manuscript songbook of the early eighteenth century: a densely and at times obscurely charged narrative of 35 verses.[6] Despite obscurity – or circumstantial complexity – in this and other versions, the ballad has a simple dramatic action in the hero's or more usually his mother's rejection of a girl who has borne him a child. 'Annie' (*sic*) knocks for admittance to Lord Gregory's castle and is refused. His mother, speaking as if with his voice, requests tokens of her identity which she, deceived, provides by allusion to their former intimacies. She is still refused and goes away. Lord Gregory wakes from some kind of sleep in which he dreamt with foreboding about Annie. His mother tells him of her visit and receives his curse for not waking him. He goes in search of Annie and finds her and her child dead, usually drowned.

Its poetic style, as F.J. Child concluded, assigns the song without doubt to the strongly oral ballad form which first appears in the later Middle Ages. It was probably composed a good deal earlier than its oldest text was written: a fact made more plausible by parallels, in European ballads, to the scene in which the admission of a visitor is made conditional on a test by love tokens.[7] The probability of an early date would further weaken a hypothesis – which, anyway, has little to suggest that it is worth making – that the ballad was composed in Plantation Ireland. In view of its strong Scottish tradition this would mean in Ulster, where by the later seventeenth century there was indeed a solid presence of Scots settlers. But that is already late, and no ballads of the early genre have been recognized as of Irish origin, so that the pursuit of such a possibility seems vain.

It was, however, through Ulster – from Scotland – that the ballad reached Ireland: and by oral transmission. In view of the active trade in ballad sheets and their importation into Ireland, this may seem a bold statement. But the oldest sheets of this song to survive date only from the later eighteenth century – printed in London – and they seem moreover to comprise the only version of the ballad that was known in England (for it was from this version that the Northamptonshire poet John Clare knew it when he made an eccentric adaptation of his own).[8] Furthermore, the title 'Lass of Aughrim' and its analogues give interesting phonetic evidence of gradual transmission, when we look at the surviving Scots and Irish records.

Such toponymic reference to the girl occurs in the text exclusively at the weaker cadences of the unrhymed odd lines, with the first syllable of the toponym opening a bar. Of the eight Scottish texts in Child which come into question (A-G, 'M'),[9] four have forms of 'Roch Royal' (ADEF, cf. C). But 'Loch Royan/Ryan' is just as popular if we count Bronson's Scottish versions[10] (nos. 2, 3; Child 'M', cf. BG) and one other collected in 1826 in the western Scottish Lowlands.[11] Unlike 'Roch Royal', 'Loch Ryan' is an identifiable place and down to the present day a place of embarcation for Ireland. Rather than the form

Rough Royal [ˈrɔx rɔˈjal] $\frac{6}{8}$| ♩ ♪ ♪ ♩...   (Bronson, no. 4, from Buchan)

It appears to have been

Loch Ryan [ˈlɔx ərˈeiən] $\frac{4}{4}$| ♩. ♪ ♫...   (Bronson, no. 2)

which travelled over, perhaps/ in the form

Locharain [ˈlɔx ərˈen] $\frac{6}{8}$| ♩ ♪ ♩...   (Bronson, no. 3, Aberdeen)

to which we note an Irish form both geographically and phonetically close:

(Annie O') Lochran [ˈlɔxərˈɛn]   (North Co. Down, c.1850).[12]

This form derives from a report of an unrecorded version. Irish versions, as we move South, alter the name so that the lass becomes a lass of

Aughrim [ˈɔxərˈəm] $\frac{3}{4}$| ♩ ♪ ♩...   (John Reilly et al.)

Arem(s) (?) [ˈarˈəms] $\frac{3}{4}$| ♩ ♪ ♩...   (Eliz. Cronin)

Ormonds [ˈɔrˈməns] (3)| ♩ ♫♫ ♩...   (Ollie Conway)

Finally we note the change from Aughrim to

Ocram [ˈɔˈkrəm]

on the eighteenth-century ballad sheets. This sequence is illustrated on the
accompanying map,[13] where, of course, we conjecture a chronological sequence
though the extant versions do not illustrate chronology and geography moving
in unison. No doubt a steady geographical dissemination does not have to be
concluded; but the phonetic changes and the changes of toponym are so well
in accord that the ballad seems very likely to have spread through Ireland –
some two centuries or more ago – in a relatively simple movement from North
to South.

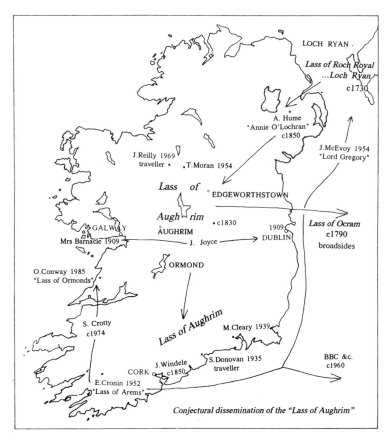

Conjectural dissemination of the "Lass of Aughrim"

Of special interest is the attachment of the English broadsides (and John
Clare) to the Irish tradition of the ballad: the only example I have noted of an
old Scots ballad evidently taking this devious route to England. Aughrim
(*Each-dhruim*: 'horse's back') is a small locality in Co. Galway and the site of
a traditionally remembered Williamite victory of 1691; less apt is the Co.
Wicklow 'Aughrim', and there appear to be no similarly named places in
Scotland. It was quite natural in this name for an English printer or performer

to substitute [k] for the phonetically foreign [x]. Other features shared by the London sheets and some or all of the Irish versions, while lacking in Scots tradition, are as follows:[14]

8.3, 11.3	*swaft, swapped* etc. (for *changed* or *gave*), H, JR, TM, SD;
8.1, 11.1, 14.1	*remember* (for *mind*), H, JR, TM, SD, MC, EC, Joyce;
16.2, 18.2	*close my hands* etc. (for *glove my hands*), SD *hold my hand*, EC *clothes on her hands;*
17.2, 19.2	*brown berry comb* (for *red river comb* etc.), H;
6.1-4	the first and second halves of this favourite verse are transposed, and the broadside reads:

> It rains upon my yellow locks,
>   and the dew falls on my skin,
> Open the gates, Lord Gregory,
>   and let your true love in – Cf. H, TM, JR, EC, SD, Joyce;

23.1-4	the song concludes with the lover's professed intention to withdraw to a solitary retreat: 'I will go down into some silent grove *etc*,' – see the concluding section below.

These details confirm what the London ballad sheets with their Irish-looking title simply suggest: that the broadside *Lass of Ocram* was undoubtedly derived from an Irish source. And since the readings noted are well scattered through its 23 verses, there is no reason to think that the text is not substantially, or wholly, from the same Irish source as the title. It is a long and thoroughly narrative text like the early Scots ones: the only such version from Ireland that is fully preserved. Probably from outside Ulster like the other Irish versions which use the name 'Aughrim', it provides further evidence that Scots ballads circulated little altered, except in their forms of language, in parts of Ireland untouched by Scots settlement.[15] Perhaps another long narrative version of this ballad was the source of a verse quoted by Maria Edgeworth, to support discussion of an Irish wake, in the notes of her *Castle Rackrent* (1800):

> Deal on, deal on, my merry men all,
>   deal on your cakes and your wine,
> For whatever is dealt at her funeral today
>   shall be dealt to-morrow at mine.[16]

The London broadsides do not contain the section with such a verse which concludes certain early texts; but their conjectured date agrees with that of the novel. These earliest datings of the ballad in Ireland are followed by scant nineteenth-century records of it: the allusion to 'Annie O'Lochran' already referred to, and a fragmentary text printed only in 1885 but from the recollection, by an Irish emigrant in the States, of a Co. Westmeath labourer's singing of over half a century earlier (c.1830).[17] Publications such as the *Lyric magazine*[18] of 1820, sold by Joseph Smyth of Belfast – for others may also have included a reprint of the ballad from a Scottish source – have not exerted any perceptible influence on Irish oral tradition. More interesting is the tune specification for a literary poem in a manuscript of John Windele of Cork (1801-65): 'Air, The Lass of Aughrim'. Evidently the ballad was familiar in the South to at least a few. The poem which follows fits the preserved Irish 3/4 airs well.[19] Among these early texts, fragments and reports, however, there is regrettably – though not surprisingly – no other musical information, and we must turn to documents of the last few decades to learn something of the tune, or tunes, one of which Joyce declared himself so moved by, though unfortunately not moved enough to secure a notation of it.

'THAT LOVELY AIR'

The relative rarity of the *Lass of Roch Royal* in the modern oral traditions of Britain or America left Bronson a yield of only 25 airs, most of which have no certain link with the ballad but belong to non-narrative songs whose derivation from it is conjectural. Four rather miscellaneous Scots tunes (nos. 1-4) make up the best part of the collection he assembled. It is not clear why he did not print at least two of the three Irish airs given below. Though Irish sources for traditional songs in English were not well known in the fifties and sixties these two had been recorded for the BBC and consigned to its archive: their existence could have been ascertained, especially as both had been published in print and one on disc.[20]

Eventually the American film director John Huston came, a little before his death in 1988, to make a film of James Joyce's story; regrettably, it was one of the Scots tunes that served him.[21] In a darkened cinema I jotted down a skeletal notation of it which, I later found, followed the Scots original closely except in tending to avoid closed cadences. Perhaps this was meant to evoke the 'Irish tonality' Joyce spoke of so vaguely? The Scots air is here given with variants of my cinema notation in small-head notes:

The preoccupations of film directors generally do not extend to certain sorts of authenticity. But since Irishness mattered to Joyce, it would have been nice if the air had been an Irish one. I know of only the three airs already mentioned:[22]

EC   2 'The rain— beats at my yel-low locks A - And the dew wets— me   still,

TM   1 'Oh—, the rain rains on my yel-low locks And the dew drops on my chin,

JR   1 'Let the rain r - ain, beat my yel-low locks, Let the dew a beat - e my skin -e

EC   The babe— is cold in   my   ar — ms, Lord — — Gre-gor - y, let me   in.'

TM   My ba - by is cold in my —   ar — ms, L - ord — Gre-gor - y, let m -e in.'

JR   Let the bon - ny lass of Au-ghe-rim And her— ba - by   come   in.'

These tunes are in modal contrast with one another and they vary in outline; it is difficult to perceive simple evolutionary links joining them. Nevertheless links probably exist, for the tunes agree in several features which cannot be all fortuitous: metre and its rhythmic content, including triple set against duple division, especially

$$\overbrace{\downarrow\downarrow\downarrow}^{3}/\downarrow\,\downarrow$$

recurrent motifs, sometimes transposed up an approximate fifth [EC, bars 1-2 and 4-5; TM, bars 0-1 and 4-5) or octave (JR, 0-1 and 1-2); partial melodic similarity within phrases (the beginning of TM and EC, the end of JR and TM); asymmetrical structure in short-line quatrains, and tending not to repeat phrases (EC, *ABCD*; TM, *ABCB²*; JR, *ABA²C*); pentatonic character in the choice of stressed notes or in whole phrases (first phrase of EC and JR) or in avoidance of a particular degree (6 in TM).

These features are all conventional enough in Ireland, and they might contribute to something which could be popularly called 'old Irish tonality'. But we have also to allow that the tunes may preserve features that came with the words of the ballad from Scotland, and that there may have existed for it an international melodic tradition comparable to the traditions which Bronson identified and described for many other old ballads. Moreover, melodic features cannot be too simply conceived as 'national'. Pentatonality, for example, is found in Ireland, but it is a more noteworthy Scots trait. The short-line quatrains that do not much repeat material suggest British ballad airs more readily than native Irish lyric. Whatever the extent of the melodic tradition, the Irish airs are remarkable among those preserved because they seem to be the only ones transmitted by traditional means which have survived in sound. As for Bronson's comparative study of the Scottish musical relics: he found the merest traces of mutual similitude in them (none of which recur in the Irish airs). Only in his appendix does he make a comparison of interest to the Irish airs, by printing a Scots text[23] of the song recognizably derived from Elizabeth Cronin's (which however he did not print), and by assigning to it a number (4.1) which relates its tune to an older Scots one from Buchan (4). The Buchan tune is as follows:[24]

Both Mrs Cronin's and – somewhat less – Tom Moran's tune have points of limited musical agreement with this Scots one – not however John Reilly's, except in its structural proximity. Probably John Reilly's is a native Irish replacement of an air of Scots origin which it partly resembled: Irish variants of his air may be found.[25]

Whatever the age of their 'Irish tonality', any of our three tunes could, given a proper context, be called a 'lovely air'. But beauty in traditional music is not experienced in the context of academic prose, nor indeed in any kind of writing. Joyce's generation was not particularly eager to appreciate this fact and was much given to literate modes of evaluation. Seeking musical criteria, they found nothing purely musical in traditional singing but the melody which, without analysing, they usually praised by means of a simple appeal to feeling. Sir Hubert Parry is typical in his naive judgment of the 'Londonderry air' as 'the most beautiful tune in the world'.

Now that popular song can be envisaged off the printed page, the singers can be better taken into account. These three, none of whom I ever met, were obviously people of talent, people who unlike their musical ancestors lived in a time of mobile recording units and portable tape recorders, and through these left us a little of themselves. Of the three, the woman has had the most influence, and particularly for the singing of this song. Tom Moran's fragmentary version, John Reilly's complete but unpublished one, are little known. But Elizabeth Cronin sang a full version which immediately caught the attention of professional collectors, who in turn transmitted it to a wider public. With its gentle *parlando* rhythm, homely accents that recall those of Irish, but lacking the melodic ornament of much singing in Irish,[26] her *Lord Gregory*, or *Lass of Arems*(?), was a stylistic understatement of a kind that often makes the best performance of traditional lyric and especially of the early ballad.

People of mainly urban background, lacking traditional formation but interested in the revival of popular musical tradition, were impressed by its demonstration of a strong but to most of them unfamiliar aesthetic. A little help from the media made the recording accessible, and within two years of the making of Mrs Cronin's recording Hamish Henderson deposited in the School of Scottish Studies a rendition learnt from it by Jock McEvoy of Glasgow, already mentioned (Bronson, no. 4.1). Ewan McColl seems to have used Mrs Cronin's air, altering it metrically, for a version he attributed to a travelling woman then living in England (Bronson no. 21). In 1966 Dolly McMahon, wife of the radio producer Ciarán Mac Mathúna, included the song on her record *Dolly*.[27] Yet for some time Mrs Cronin's own singing of the whole song remained difficult to obtain unless in pirated copies. Then in 1976, in Devon, Peter Kennedy published it on cassette (see note 20). Tim Lyons of Co. Limerick sang her song on a disc published in America in 1978.[28] In June 1974, I had heard a Co. Clare man, the late Sinie Crotty, sing it in Dublin; Ollie Conway, also of Clare, said – when he sang it for a cassette published in 1985 – that he learned the song from Sinie.[29] Joyce's centenary in 1982 had already occasioned other uses: Ted Hickey sang it in a radio programme from Belfast (see note 5) as did the late Joe Heaney on a mainly musical disc entitled *Bloomsday* and published in Toronto (see also note 5).

It need not be supposed that these documents and allusions are 'complete'. In any case a written record, however complete, still leaves unsounded the oral practice which the writing serves. Another disc gives a hint of widespread Irish familiarity with the song: paradoxically by containing only an instrumental rendition of it. Young members of a family recorded in 1978 in the Connemara Gaeltacht play on concertina, with fiddle, flute and mandolin, an air they call 'Lord Gregory': Mrs Cronin's version. The title is by no means conventional among players to indicate a slow air, nor is the tune commonly played as such; so we may conclude that these young players knew or had heard the song for which this title *is* conventional.[30]

It is difficult, and here impossible, to compare all this recent musical activity seriously to what is usually called the 'folk tradition' of the past. The influence of media has been important in both past and present; but the ballad sheets and written aids of the past seem relatively ineffective alongside today's audio accessories and the more massive uses of literacy which support them. Is it because of these that the versions which have used Elizabeth Cronin's verbal text have broadly adhered to it with what would formerly have seemed unnatural fidelity? That the tune, while perhaps more varying, remains similarly faithful? Other factors are significant, notably the size and dispersion of the 'folk' who practise the song; also their motivation – Joe Heaney's singing voice tells us that learning it was an assignment more than a craving – and the rapidity of its transmission: we know of only one intermediary (Sinie Crotty) between Mrs Cronin and any of her musical posterity. That she has such posterity however we do know, and if it seems a rather esoteric one in some respects, how can we say that it is thereby distinguished from the older oral tradition of this rather sparsely documented ballad? Perhaps the rare documents actually reflect rare usage. Neither England nor America has much to offer; but the *Lass of Aughrim*, as the Scots ballad became in Ireland, has a poetic character and an interest of its own: on which some concluding remarks remain to be made.

'DISTANT MUSIC'

Elizabeth Cronin is distanced from her followers in time and they from each other in space, but the phrase 'distant music' is from Joyce: an evocation of the heroine of his story, seen by her husband, as she listens to the ballad sung in a further room.[31] The impression this song made on Joyce, as well as his artistic use of it, has been more than once explored and need not be examined in detail. But its 'traditional' features interest us. The love tokens of the ballad narrative inspired him to have an 'ornament', as he wrote to her (actually a necklace), made for the distant Nora, then in Trieste:[32] a naive attempt, one might say, to make fiction real in his own life. The gesture becomes less surprising when we read of the recent deception perpetrated on him by a 'friend' who claimed to have slept with Nora himself: a claim soon shown to be false but not before Joyce had written her two reproachful letters.[33] Such tricks are surely more common in ballad villains than in 'friends'! 'The Dead', of course, was intimately based on Nora's past, and the song a memory of a young admirer, so that the story and the song reflected separately upon experience while artistically reflecting on one another. In the convention of traditional poetry, the story could in fact be conceived as an explanation of the song: what might be called its *údar* ('authority') if it were a song in Irish. A few words on this concept are worth while.[34]

Lyric song in Irish has not generally been narrative in the manner of the European ballad, yet it is often evocative, and celebrates events that may comprise a sequence. Such events provide the motivation for a song, but are not narrated with it unless the need to do so is evinced. The practice is so fundamental that this objective but implied narrative can take a great variety of forms, some improvised and unstable, others having more the character of an artefact.

A question, to which the answer is probably negative, is whether Joyce was particularly aware of such a practice. Another, more inscrutable, question is whether the 'Irishness' of the *Lass of Aughrim* was of a deep and unconsciously experienced kind in himself which resulted in his composing a framing narrative ('The Dead') in response to a song, as it might happen in an oral tradition of poetry and *seanchas*. From the literary point of view it is assumed that one perceives the 'Musical Allusions in the Works . . .' (see note 1) as somehow illustrating an author's works, more than these the music. But in Joyce's case the author's musical experience and sensitivity make a reversal of perspective interesting, and the allusion to the *Lass of Aughrim* is moreover quite a special one.

It may be wondered whether the *Lass of Aughrim* in its history underwent the kind of acculturation that is suggested here. Ballads in English were adopted in Ireland, easily and gratefully with the language itself, and they often took on a character which, arising from the Gaelic use of exegetical lore, varied from elaborate *chantefable* to briefly documented circumstantial history. We have no record of the *Lass of Aughrim* developing in such a way, but in the corpus of its verbal texts we find a number of developments which tend to give them the increased lyric density of Gaelic songs whose story is 'elsewhere'. Change of perspective is one feature which can help to produce this effect, but Mrs Cronin is the only one of our informants to begin with a shift from third to first-person narrative, 'I am a king's daughter . . .'. On the other hand, all complete Irish versions agree basically about the ending: a lament on the girl's death uttered by her lover and conceived as withdrawal into the solitude of nature. It is already found in the eighteenth-century broadsides:

> I will go down into some silent grove
>   my sad moan for to make. . .

The motif is much used in Irish song; it does not appear in non-Irish versions of the ballad, which is transformed by the motif in the last verse into a common Irish lyric type, a man's love song. The firmness of this transformation is signified by the variety of expression: 'range over valleys, o'er mountains so wide (EC, Jock McEvoy changes this to 'wild' and Ollie Conway transposes 'mountains' and 'valleys'), 'I'll walk by the shore' (JR), 'go down to yonder castle And I'll live there alone' (MC), 'Thro' this wide world I will wander And thro' some shady grove' (SD). In general, the intention of withdrawal replaces a narration of double death.

The lyric effect is also made more intense in some versions by using a suitable verse or verses as a kind of refrain which is repeated at least a few times during the song. The refrain is first found in the incomplete text which endeavours to recall a county Westmeath version of *c.*1830 (Child H): the verse 'The dew wets my yellow locks . . .' is indicated to be sung after each 'strophic' verse. This is the last of the three verses of Nora Barnacle's fragment, and the one quoted by Joyce in *The Dead*: the impression we get is that in this case too it may have recurred at intervals in the full text.[35] John Reilly has an interesting way of extending this four-line refrain to twelve lines: he adds the two verses of question and response 'Saying, Who'll shoe my bare foot . . .?', 'Saying, I'll shoe your bare foot . . .' and sings the resulting twelve-line refrain before every group of twelve 'strophic' lines (four times). Since the first three strophic sections comprise the cumulative iteration of the tokens, the whole effect is highly repetitious. On the other hand, Elizabeth Cronin makes a refrain out of the morally critical verse addressed by the disguised mother of the lover to the girl, 'Leave now those windows . . .', and uses it at irregular intervals: three or four times depending on renditions.

Verbatim repetition of verses is not unknown in ballads in Britain,[36] and this ballad also makes good use of incremental repetition; it is well suited to be adapted to a more lyrical mode. On the other hand the development of a refrain is striking because Gaelic love song is little inclined to use refrains: a somewhat uncharacteristic device is adopted in order to achieve a characteristic Irish effect. In other ways the ballad lends itself to re-composition. The refrain brings certain threatening images into prominence: rain and wind, deep sea. Erotic motifs, without figuring in a refrain, also receive prominence, and may even show parallels with songs in Irish, though there is no evidence that the ballad has been altered under the influence of these:

'Then who will shoe my bonny feet. . .   '*A chos deas i mbróig,*
And who will comb my yellow locks . . .?'   *Is corach casda do chúl . . .*'[37]

'O, don't you remember   *An cuimhin leat an oíche úd*
   that night on yon lean hill   *do bhí tú agus mise*
When we both met together   *Ag bun an chrainn chaorthainn*
   which I am sorry now to tell?'   *'s an oíche ag cur chuisne?*'[38]

The variously lyricized texts of the 'Lass' not of 'Roch Royal' or 'Loch Ryan' but 'of Aughrim' suggest an imperfectly constituted oecotype: that is, the ballad was evolving towards a distinctive Irish style which it never entirely achieved.

There remain those regional (Irish) qualities we have noticed in it, a lyric intensity which a recent public has been made aware of through Elizabeth Cronin, which Joyce experienced through Nora Barnacle's mother and seems to have thought he found particularly in the melody: a fact his critics have tended to overlook. But the associative power of music makes simple musical judgments impossible, especially in the case of song; Joyce, we may believe, was rationalizing many associations: personal ones no doubt yet not unlike the 'force' or 'meaning' or 'authority' which a Gaelic audience associates with its songs. The music of the *Lass of Aughrim* was 'distant' for him in evoking a past from which he was excluded';[39] it is distant for those who listen to Elizabeth Cronin in being sung by a voice from the past. Not one but many voices sang it in the past, and it is characteristic of all traditional music to evoke distance. One voice is rescued by audio technology, and insights are provided which are, after all, in some respects mere glimpses. Could it be that the best fate which might befall so fine a recording was that, after the song had been re-cycled by some excellent new singers, a cataclysm should destroy it? Such an event cannot be counted on: so it is profitable to reflect seriously on the best use that may be made of musical archives.

NOTES

1. The fragment is quoted from James Joyce, *Dubliners*, repr. Viking Press (New York, 1967, first ed. 1914), 210, dialogue from 212, cf. 218-19. The text of the song reads thus in the proofs of the 1910 (unpublished) edition, but an earlier undated MS by an amanuensis has the more traditional 'my yellow locks', and the incomplete third line reads quite differently: 'But if you are . . .' – see the facsimile in *James Joyce Archive. Dubliners* (New York and London, 1978), 541. Joyce obviously at first recalled – and misplaced – a half-line of the ballad and subsequently replaced it by a more appropriate half-line (cf. R. Scholes 'Some observations on the text of Dubliners', *Studies in bibliography*, 15 (1962), 191-205 at 194-5).

    Editions of versions of the ballad: F.J. Child, *The English and Scottish popular ballads* (Boston, 1882-98), 2: 213-26, 3: 510-12, 4: 471-4; cf. 2: 288, 4: 186, 5: 225, 294; B. Bronson, *Traditional tunes of the Child ballads* (Princeton, 1959-72), 2: 218-28, 4: 472 (24 versions). Bibliography and commentary: T.P. Coffin, *The British traditional ballad in North America*, rev. ed. with supplement by R. de V. Renwick (Austin and London, 1977), 73-5, 234-5.

    See also Z. Bowen, *Musical allusions in the works of James Joyce* (Albany, N.Y., 1975), 21-2.

2. This title was also in use in Scotland: see the version mentioned in note 11 below, and Child, 2: 213, 219. Burns used it for a poem inspired by the ballad which was printed without author's name on broadsides, for example, Cambridge University Library, Madden 16, no. 671.

3. Joyce, *Dubliners* (as n. 1), 210.

4. R. Ellmann, ed., *Selected letters of James Joyce* (London, 1975), 165; 164, five days earlier

he had written: 'She [Nora's mother] sang for me *The Lass of Aughrim* but she does not like to sing me the last verses in which the lovers exchange their tokens.'

5. M. J. Hodgart and M. P. Worthington, *Song in the works of James Joyce* (New York, 1959), 6, 190. D. MacDonagh, 'The "Lass of Aughrim" or the betrayal of James Joyce', *The Celtic master. Contributions to the first James Joyce Symposium*, ed. M. Harmon (Dublin, 1969), 17-27. G.L. Geckle, 'The dead Lass of Aughrim', *Éire-Ireland*, 9 (1974), 86-96, refers to Elizabeth Cronin but not to MacDonagh's article. 'James Joyce and the Lass of Aughrim', radio programme by Ted Hickey, producer Paul Muldoon, broadcast 6 June 1982 from N. Ireland BBC; the ballad is sung by Ted Hickey as learnt from E. Cronin's version. *Bloomsday. James Joyce and Nora Barnacle*. Songs by Joe Heaney and Treasa O'Driscoll. LP Aquitaine AQA 16, Toronto, 1962; the ballad is sung by Joe Heaney as learnt from E. Cronin's version.

6. Child (as n. 1), 2: 215-17, 5: 397.

7. Child (as n. 1), 2: 215; especially the French ballad 'Germaine', see C. Laforte, *Catalogue de la chanson folklorique française, 2: Chansons strophiques* (Quebec, 1981), 404-7, no. I-3.

8. Broadsides: Cambridge University Library, Madden ballads, 5: nos. 960, 961 (n.p.d., same printer); *Roxburghe ballads*, ed. J. E. Ebsworth, 6 (Hertford, 1889), 613-15 (J. Pitts), repr. Child (as n. 1), 3: 510-11; Cambridge University Library, Res. b. 1745, no. 142 (J. Pitts). Dr Robert Thomson dated the sheets printed by Pitts *c*.1800 and assigned those without printer's name to John Marshall, *c*.1790 (oral communication). The four texts have no significant variants; quotations in this article are from the first sheet listed above.

   Clare's MS text is printed, with a facsimile, by G. Deacon, *John Clare and the folk tradition* (London, 1983), 112-19.

9. See n. 1 above. 'M' indicates Child's version in 4: 471-4.

10. See n. 1 above.

11. *Andrew Crawfurd's collection of ballads and songs*, ed. E. B. Lyle (Edinburgh, 1975), 1: 39-42.

12. A. Hume in *Ulster journal of archaeology*, 6, 1st ser. (1858), 50; cf. *Ulster journal of archaeology*, 5 (1857), 102. The proposed phonetic notations adopt the International Phonetic Alphabet, and include stress marks and supplementary non-lexical vowels as these features would be used in singing.

13. For which cf. H. Shields and T. Munnelly, 'Scots ballad influences in Ireland', *Ceol Tíre*, 15 (Oct., 1979), 3- 22, repr. in *Lore and language*, 3, nos. 4-5 (1981), 81-100.

14. Verse and line numbers refer to the broadside *Lass of Ocram* and are followed by its readings and these by traditional Scots readings in brackets; sigla then indicate Irish texts which agree with the broadsides, as follows: EC, Elizabeth Cronin, see n. 20; H, Child version H, see n. 17 and its context; Joyce, see n. 1; JR, John Reilly, see n. 22; MC, Mary Cleary, Waterford, 1939, Irish Folklore Dept, University College, Dublin, MS 696, 378-9; SD, Sean O'Donovan, Dungarvan, Co. Waterford, 1935, ibid., MS 150, 537-43; TM, Thomas Moran, see n. 20. I am grateful to Tom Munnelly for references to MC and SD.

15. For general discussion of this topic see the article cited in n. 13.

16. Facsimile reprint of the London 1800 edition: *Ireland from the Act of Union (1800) to the death of Parnell (1891)*, ed. R. L. Wolff (New York and London, 1978), xliii. Edgeworthstown, now Mostrim, is about 40 miles from Aughrim.

   Valéry Larbaud translated a long version, 'The Lass of Lochroyan', into French, sub-titled 'Ballade Irlandaise' in *La Plume*, 15 August 1901 (information kindly supplied by Prof. Roger Little). Though later to become one of Joyce's translators, Larbaud did not know Joyce at that time and Joyce had not written 'The Dead'. Their common interest in the ballad perhaps reflects kindred spirits, but it is not an effect of influence of one on the other. Anyway, Larbaud's sub-title is incorrect: his model was a Scots version (cf. Child E). Perhaps he used an unreferenced Irish printing like the one in the *Lyric magazine* (see n. 18).

17. Child (as n. 1), 2: 224, 226.

18. See *Lyric magazine. A collection of popular songs and ballads, with some never before published*, 2 (July, 1820), 156-63.

19. Royal Irish Academy MS 12 F 30, 116. V.1: 'No longer I will languish on fantasie's burne No longer in anguish Thy coldness I will Mourn It is greatful to part, There is sweetness in Death, It will ease this slack heart It will end this regret.'

20. *Journal of the English Folk Dance and Song Society*, 8 (1956), 21-3, BBC recording RPL 18,759 (Elizabeth Cronin); id., 23, BBC RPL 22,016 (Thomas Moran); *Folk songs of Britain* 4, *The Child Ballads*, 1, Topic Records LP 12T 160, London, 1969, first publ. Caedmon Records, New York, 1961 (E. Cronin, part). In 1976 appeared the cassette *Classic ballads of Britain*, ed. Peter Kennedy, Totnes, Devon (E. Cronin and T. Moran), from which the tunes are noted below.

21. Blaikie MS, see Bronson (as n. 1), 2: 219, no. 2.

22. Singers' initials indicate: EC, Elizabeth Cronin, Ballyvourney, Co. Cork, see n. 20; TM, Tom Moran, Drumrahool, Mohill, Co. Roscommon, see n. 20; JR, John Reilly, a settled traveller living at Boyle, Co. Roscommon, recd. by D.K. Wilgus, 1969, who has deposited a copy in the Dept. of Irish Folklore, University College, Dublin. I am grateful to Prof. Wilgus for permission to use this unpublished recording.

23. Sung by Jock McEvoy, Glasgow, 1954, School of Scottish Studies, SA 1954/105/A4; Bronson (as n. 1), 4: 472 (repr. in his abridged ed., *The singing tradition of Child's popular ballads* (Princeton, 1976), 197-8).

24. Bronson (as n. 1), 2: 219, no. 4.

25. See for example *Ceol*, 1 no. 2 (1963), 6-10. A fuller notation would enhance this comparison but would also show moderately free variation in the structure of JR's tune. TM's tune somewhat resembles that of 'An cuimhin leat an oíche úd?' (see n. 38 for this song) as given by P.W. Joyce, *Ancient music of Ireland* (Dublin, 1873), 23, which is structurally twice as long: AA^2BA^2 with long-line phrases. TM's tune could be considered an incomplete rendition of this common Irish structure, with his first half as A, cadence of A^2 on 1, and his second half as B with cadence on 5.

26. EC's air, like TM's (see n. 25), could have been derived from a structure of twice the length: $ABAB^2$ (cadence of B^2 a fourth higher than B). But a non-repetitive short-line quatrain is characteristic of the old ballad genre.

27. Claddagh LP CC3, Dublin, 1966. The song was re-issued on *Claddagh's choice*, CC40, 1984.

28. *Easter snow*, LP Innisfree SIF 1014, New Canaan, Connecticut. Another disc, brought to my attention by Nicholas Carolan, has Treasa Ní Mhiolláin singing Mrs Cronin's song, which she introduces as a song about 'an Irish girl who was treated badly by an English lord': *The Third Irish Folk Festival in concert*, Intercord Int. 181.008, 1976, side 3.

29. *Early ballads in Ireland, 1968-1985*, ed. Tom Munnelly and Hugh Shields (Dublin, Trinity College).

30. *Irlande, 1: Héritage gaélique et traditions du Connemara*, Ocora LP 558 541 (Paris, 1978).

31. Ed. cit. in n. 1 above, 210. The phrase is from *David Copperfield*: see D. Gifford, *Joyce annotated* (Berkeley, California, 1982), 123.

32. Joyce, *Letters* (as n. 4), 2: 239, 241, 245-6.

33. Joyce, *Letters*, 2: 231-3; cf. R. Ellmann, *James Joyce*, rev. ed. (New York, 1982), 160.

34. H. Shields, 'Popular modes of narration and the popular ballad', in *Harvard English studies* (forthcoming).

35. Apparently missing. Ellmann, *Letters* (as n. 4), 240, gives without a source what he calls Nora's version:

> If you'll be the lass of Aughrim
> As I am taking you mean to be
> Tell me the first token
> That passed between you and me.
>
> O don't you remember
> That night on yon lean hill
> When we both met together
> Which I am sorry now to tell.
>
> The rain falls on my yellow locks
> And the dew it wets my skin;
> My babe lies cold within my arms
> Lord Gregory, let me in.

C.P. Curran in *James Joyce remembered* (New York, 1968), 41-2, a fellow-student of Joyce, gives seven lines in three scraps recalled imperfectly by Joyce's sisters from his singing, in which are noteworthy: a) the line 'What was my last gift to you?' (reflecting 'Tell me the *last* token', omitted above), and b) the fact that Joyce is said to have claimed to know 35 verses of the song. This is unlikely, but the oldest preserved version of the *Lass of Roch Royal* actually has 35 verses (see n. 6). Could he have meant to indicate it, and so have known of the ballad's Scots origin?

36. A verse verbally similar to the first of those just noted, 'For the rain rains owre my yellow hair' etc. occurs three times in a version of *Young Johnstone*, see Child (as n. 1), 2: 291.

37. *Lass of Ocram* broadside, see n. 8, and a fragment of *Bean an fhir rua* in G. Petrie, *Ancient music of Ireland*, 2 (Dublin, 1882), 48, 'Pretty foot in a shoe, Your tresses are twisting and sinuous'.

38. Nora Barnacle's fragment (see n. 35), and *An cuimhin leat an oíche úd?*, Petrie, *Ancient music* (as n. 37), 1 (Dublin, 1855), 142 (spelling modernized): 'Do you remember that night when you and I were at the foot of the rowan tree and the night was freezing?' For the air of another version of this song see above, n. 25.

39. The poem 'She weeps over Rahoon' is another expression of Joyce's preoccupation with those past events: *James Joyce Archive. Chamber music etc.*, ed. M. Groden (New York and London, 1978), xl; text, 241.

The Composition of
The Children of Lir

DAVID GREER

The story of how Hamilton Harty came to compose *The Children of Lir* has been well told by John Barry:[1] how the idea came to him while holidaying on the Antrim coast in 1936, when he saw the sculpture by Rosamond Praeger in the old school-house at the Giant's Causeway; how he completed the work two years later during a temporary respite from the illness that was to bring about his untimely end; and how he conducted its first performance by the BBC Symphony Orchestra on 1 March 1939, with Isobel Baillie singing the wordless soprano part. Canon Barry has also reflected on the significance that the tale of Finola and her three brothers had for Harty as he contemplated his own mortality.

John Barry's account is amplified by the recollections of the late James Moore, who as a young man accompanied Harty on his walks during that holiday of 1936. In 1979, the centenary of Harty's birth, Moore was interviewed in a televised programme which included a performance of the work. This is what he said:[2]

Interviewer:	How did his inspiration come about for *The Children of Lir*?
Moore:	Well, he was very fond of walking, and one day we were going on a walk round the Causeway headlands, the path that's now managed by the National Trust, and suddenly it struck me that he might be interested in a sculpture work in the Causeway School. It is a *bas-relief* of the Children of Lir; and the Sea of Moyle of course is just, as you know, beyond the Causeway; and [looking at the sculpture] this was Finola sheltering her swan brothers on a rock there. He seemed to be entirely taken over by it – he seemed to be in another world, and entranced. He came back and gazed at it many times. And then one day he said to me, 'Jimmy, you have started something – what was lying dormant for years has now come to the surface', he said, 'I can't get

away from it – I feel I am going to make it into an orchestral work.'

Interviewer: Now was there any other part of the coast which he brought into his work?

Moore: Yes, he was very interested in the wee church at Ballintoy, and he felt that this was the church where the first Christian bell rang that brought them back to life. I think he probably portrayed that in the final music of *The Children of Lir*.

Interviewer: So, in a way, before he started to actually write the composition, he had formed a complete picture in his own mind.

Moore: Oh yes, and I feel that during the two years that elapsed, with that long illness he had, he was really working at it in his mind, preparing roughly for what was to come.

Interviewer: Now the illness we know caused his death, was a sort of cancer in his brain, and during that time he actually lost an eye, didn't he?

Moore: He did, and he invited me to come to Rostrevor to celebrate – as he put it – the birth of the offspring. He put it in a most amusing letter, 'The offspring has arrived, the mother is well. Come and celebrate with us in Rostrevor for a week'. And I went there and had a very happy time with him. And then he invited me over for the first performance. I wasn't able to go, but I was in London just before that and he showed me this score [shows the manuscript full score], written in his own hand. Now can you imagine a man with one eye writing those notes?

Interviewer: It is very tiny – incredible.

Moore: It is amazing, yes, and the one place that seemed to me to be the climax of the work was here [points at the score] where the soprano voice, which represents Finola singing to her brothers, becomes very agitated and frenzied here, rising to a high C, when she actually yells – screams on a high C – and then – suddenly the first Christian bell rings and they are brought back to life again. This was the climax of the work, and I have a feeling, you know, that it was a sort of a preview of his own death. I feel the funeral music at the end there was really his own funeral march, if you like.

In this article I propose to discuss the genesis of the work, with particular reference to a portfolio of sketches that has recently come to light. To begin with, however, it is necessary to say something about the relationship of the work to the old legend which so absorbed Harty's thoughts in that summer of 1936.

The original Irish version of the legend is one of three tales known as *Trí truagha na scéalaidheachta* – The Three Most Sorrowful Tales of Erin, or literally, The Three Sorrows of Storytelling.[3] They are preserved in manuscripts in Trinity College, Dublin, and elsewhere, and were first edited with translations by Eugene O'Curry in the London periodical *Atlantis*, 3-4 (1862-3). O'Curry's text and translation of the *Lir* story were re-edited by R. J. O'Duffy and published by the Society for the Preservation of the Irish Language in 1883 as *Oidhe Chloinne Lir: The Fate of the Children of Lir*. A modern re-telling of the story in Irish only by J. P. Craig was published in 1901 as *Clann Lir* (Modern Irish Text series, 1), and Gerald Griffin the novelist included a less literal translation than O'Curry's in his *Tales of a Jury-Room* (1843). A shortened version of the story is given in T. W. Rolleston's *Myths and Legends of the Celtic Race* (1911). But the version that was most probably known to Harty was the translation in P. W. Joyce's *Old Celtic Romances Translated from the Gaelic*, published in 1879, the year of the composer's birth. It is perhaps significant that Joyce prefaces his translation with four lines from Thomas Moore's 'Silent, oh Moyle' (*Irish Melodies*), which Harty also quotes in his programme note written for the first performance (reproduced on pages 94-6). And we know that Harty was at least familiar with Joyce's writings, for he set some of his poems to music.

In the legend, the swan-children spend the years of their enchantment in three different places: three hundred years on Lake Darvra (Lough Derravaragh, Co. Westmeath), three hundred on the Sea of Moyle (the stretch of water between the Antrim coast and the Mull of Kintyre in Scotland),[4] and three hundred on the west coast, at Irros (Erris, Co. Mayo) and Inishglora, a small island about five miles west of Belmullet. It was on Inishglora that they first heard a Christian bell, were baptized, and died.[5] However, as Harty tells the story in his programme note, they do not go to the west coast: they remain on the Sea of Moyle, and it is there that they hear the bell and die.[6] It is not hard to understand why he adapted the story in this way: in performance the work benefits from the listener's imagination being focussed on one geographical area; but more importantly, the composer's imagination was fired by the Antrim coast where he saw the sculpture, and he thought of the church at Ballintoy as being the church whose bell signalled the swan-children's end. Indeed, one feels that this church, so prominently placed and looking out to sea, actually played a decisive part in determining the structure of the work. The Introduction, so the programme note tells us, 'illustrates the thoughts of one who stands on the Antrim cliffs on a day of storm and tempest, and recalls the sorrowful story of the enchanted children of Lir while gazing down on the turbulent Sea of Moyle'. Why then do we begin with a chorale? Because, as the note tells us, the onlooker (Harty) is actually standing beside the church: 'The last few pages are in the nature of a meditation on the "sorrowful story" by one who might stand in the little church enclosure . . .'. So the idea of the onlooker standing by the church forms a frame for the story, giving us the Introduction and Coda, while the story itself – as recalled by the onlooker – forms the main body of the work. However, with the sounding of the bell at cue 49 the church itself becomes part of the story, as the children are baptized and die there. This sort of flashback technique – with past and present linking up at the end – is familiar from the cinema, and Harty's vivid and precise portrayal of the story may have been influenced by this. And as we shall see later, the idea of a church looking out across the water had a further significance for Harty as he reflected not only on the legend, but on events in his own life.

A word should be said here about the artist whose *bas-relief* so fired the composer's imagination. Sophia Rosamond Praeger was born in Holywood, Co. Down, in 1867 and spent the whole of her life there apart from a period of study at the Slade School in London. Early in her career she illustrated children's books (some of which she wrote herself), but later on she concentrated on sculpture. Her most famous piece is *The Philosopher*, hundreds of copies of which were sold the world over. Other examples of her work can be seen in the Ulster Museum, Belfast, Belfast Cathedral, Sullivan Upper School, Holywood (where she was a pupil), the National Gallery of Ireland, Dublin, and elsewhere. When Harty's ashes were brought to Ireland after the second World War they were placed in the churchyard at Hillsborough under a bird-bath in Limerick limestone commissioned from her. She died in 1954.[7]

Praeger's representation of the Children of Lir (illustration 1) shows the swan-children on a rock, which we may take to be Carricknarone, where the legend relates that they often sought refuge from storms. Their enchanted state is represented by Finola being shown in human form and her brothers in their swan form. The grouping also owes much to the legend, according to which Finola always sheltered Conn at her right side, Ficra at her left, and Aed at her bosom. (At the end of the story Finola asks that they be buried in this position, no doubt upright, as was common among the Celts.)

1   *The Children of Lir*, bas-relief by S. Rosamond Praeger in the old school-house
at the Giant's Causeway, Co. Antrim

THE SKETCHES

Moore tells us that he saw the completed score two years later, in 1938, and we
may suppose that composition of it occupied Harty most of that time, with
interruptions as his illness took hold and periods of medical treatment became
necessary. Fortunately, many of the sketches – along with those for other works
by him – have recently come to light, and these offer many insights into the
processes by which he arrived at the definitive work.[8] To clarify some of the
points in the following discussion I have provided a synopsis of the thirty-
minute work in Table 1. The labels given to the themes are derived from the
programme note. In brief, the work has affinities with Sonata Form, with the
Sea and Swan-children themes constituting the First- and Second-subject
material, and with elements of Development and Recapitulation. Into this is
inserted a slow middle episode, and the whole work is framed by the
Introduction and Coda of which I have already spoken.

We can now consider the five substantial sketches for the work that are to be
found in the Portfolio.[9]

TABLE 1

Outline of *The Children of Lir*

cue*	
	Lento e con dignità. Chorale (A major), leading to Recollections (4, F sharp minor) and Rallying-call (6)
9	Allegro brioso ed animato. Sea (A minor), leading to *Con brio* (11) and whole-tone passage (8 bars after 14), culminating in tutti restatement of Sea (18)
20+5	Transition
22	Swan-children (C major), leading to 'playful' *scherzando* (G major) at 25
30	Transition (Evening)
33	Andante tranquillo. Finola (voice, G flat major)
36	Allegro brioso ed animato. Development of Sea and subsidiary ideas, leading to tutti restatement of Sea (A minor) at 39
42+12	Transition
43	Swan-children (F major), leading to 'playful' *scherzando* (44) and Finola (voice, 47), culminating in Church bell
49	Lento e con dignità. Chorale (Church), leading to Meditation based on Finola (A major) at 52

*As in the full score published by Universal Edition (London), 1939

A (Portfolio, pp.101-2): 47 bars of short score, from beginning to second statement of Rallying-call (cue 7). Undated

B (Portfolio, pp.97-100): 129 bars of short score, from beginning to cue 12. Undated

C (Portfolio, pp. 89-95): 188 bars of short score, from beginning to cue 16. Undated

D (Portfolio, pp. 105-8): 167 bars of short score, from Con brio (cue 11) to transition to Swan-children (cue 22). Undated

E (Portfolio, pp. 109-50): sketch of the entire work in short score, dated 'Aug 20. 1938' (illustration 2). Pages now missing were given to the parish church at Hillsborough, Co. Down (Harty's birthplace), by Harty's friend and executrix Olive Baguley, and are still to be found there. Photocopies of them have been inserted into the sketch.

To these should be added the manuscript of the full score (**F**), which is separate

2 First page of sketch **E**, the first complete draft of *The Children of Lir*, completed 20 August 1938

from the Portfolio and dated 'Nov. 1938'.[10] As far as this article is concerned this represents the definitive form of the work, though a few minor changes were made in the published full score, discussed on page 41-2.

Sketches **A-D** are undated, and the order in which they are given above is a speculative chronological arrangement based on their degree of closeness to the definitive score **F**, though this is not an easy matter to determine with complete confidence. On their actual dates there will be more to be said later on. Although the general arrangement of the thematic material in these sketches is broadly the same as in the definitive score, there are a great many differences in detail as Harty felt his way forward, and some substantial differences as he explored different possibilities. So we find that in **A** the phrases of the opening Chorale are separated by a solo bass clarinet passage. In **B** and **C** Harty tries bringing back the Chorale after the Rallying-call. In **C** and **D**, instead of the non-thematic whole-tone passage that we find 8 bars after cue 14 in the definitive version, there is a new melodic idea. He probably decided to abandon this not only because new thematic material is premature at this point, but also because it is somewhat similar to the second first-subject theme in the opening movement of the *Irish Symphony*. Even in **E**, the complete sketch dated 20 August 1938, there are still a great many substantial differences compared with the full score (**F**) completed only a few months later. For instance, there is no clarinet link before Recollections at cue 4; he is still struggling with the transitions into Sea (9), Swan-children (22) and Evening (30), and he has the voice enter with the woodwind at 31. The Recapitulation is much longer in **E** than in **F**, and – most striking of all – between 51 and 52 he launches into a 53-bar funeral march which is nowhere to be found in **F**.[11]

However, I have still to mention the most striking difference between sketches **A** to **C** on the one hand and **E-F** on the other, and that is that the opening Chorale is quite different.

THE CHORALE

Example 1(a) shows the opening of the Chorale in **E** (essentially the same in **F**), and 1(b) shows the Chorale in **C**, representing the earlier group. Yet another version of this 'old' Chorale is found on p. 85 of the Portfolio (**G**).[12] This is significant in that it shows Harty experimenting with setting it in irregular metre, which was to become a feature of the 'new' Chorale. But most interesting of all, the old Chorale turns up in sketches for two quite different works. One, pp. 195-205 (**H**), is an incomplete and undated sketch for an orchestral work which includes among its thematic material references to the Irish tune *The Wearing of the Green*.[13] The Chorale forms the introduction, preceded by a falling fifth on the basses and timpani – a forerunner, perhaps, of the timpani opening of

EXAMPLE 1(a)

(a) Sketch E

EXAMPLE 1(b)

(b) Sketch C

Lir. The other work, also incomplete, is on pp. 263-70 and is in full score (**I**). Again, the Chorale occurs at the beginning, preceded by a falling fifth in the basses. This sketch is also undated; however, some of the thematic material (though not the Chorale) occurs in yet another sketch for a work of over 600 bars on pp. 245-62. This is dated 'May 14 1912', and since **I** is on manuscript paper of the same type and apparently the same vintage, we may conclude that **I** also dates from about this time.

It would seem, therefore, that the Chorale was on Harty's mind for about quarter of a century before he embarked on *Lir.* As the idea for *Lir* evolved the old Chorale became attached to it, only to be ousted by the new one in sketch **E** of 1938. Of course, the old and new chorales are not completely unrelated: both begin with stepwise descending movement, which is repeated sequentially when the second phrase commences a tone (old) or semitone (new) lower. But the difference between them in terms of musical experience is enormous. The old Chorale is a relation of Tchaikowsky's Friar Lawrence, an affinity re-inforced by the scoring of its earliest version (**I**) for clarinets and bassoons. The new Chorale, with its fuller scoring and passing dissonances, has the elemental grandeur of Sibelius, whose music Harty had experienced on the conductor's rostrum in the intervening years.

The irregular metre of the new Chorale is of significance. From its tentative appearance in version **G** of the old Chorale it became an important feature of the new. For Harty it was a symbol of antiquity and devotion, no doubt from its association with the free rhythm of Gregorian chant. A similar irregularity characterizes the episode of the monks' procession at cue 18 in *The Mystic Trumpeter.* But once established in *Lir* it becomes a pervasive feature of the whole work, evoking the buffeting wind and waves of the tempestuous Sea of Moyle.

THE SEA THEME

An earlier version of this theme occurs on p. 87 of the Portfolio, along with two other unidentified fragments. First Harty penned the version shown in Example 2(a), and then under it he wrote the second version (Example 2(b)). The fact that these are in E minor suggests that at this stage he was not thinking of the theme in connection with *Lir.* Clearly (b) is an improvement over (a), the rising triplets imparting more character and thrust, and this version is more or less the form that he adopted for *Lir.* Example 2 also shows the theme as it appears in sketches **B**, **C** and **E** and the full score **F**. In **E** Harty seems to be thinking of it as a violin melody in octaves, rather than for the violas; however, in this sketch he does hit on the canonic treatment of the continuation, and this he carries over into **F** (Example 3). This use of canon at a close time-interval is characteristic

EXAMPLE 2

EXAMPLE 3

of Harty: he also uses it in one of the first-subject themes in the first movement
of the *Irish Symphony*.

The arrival of the Sea theme is heralded by the Rallying-call at the end of the
Introduction. The Rallying-call is present in **A, B, C** and **E** and its gradual
evolution is one of the bits of evidence that suggests a chronological order for
the undated sketches. The Sea theme was probably conceived before the

Rallying-call, but from the listener's point of view the Rallying-call heralds the Sea theme, anticipating its falling fifth and the rising triplets (Example 4).

EXAMPLE 4

FINOLA

In order of appearance the next theme for discussion is the one for the Swan-children, but for reasons that will become apparent I will leave this until I have dealt with Finola's music, that remarkable episode in G flat major in which her singing is represented by a wordless soprano 'placed some distance from the main body of the orchestra' (composer's note in score). Sketches **A-D** do not get as far as this into the work, so the only *Lir* sketch which concerns us here is **E**. As already mentioned, in this version Harty has the voice enter at the point corresponding to cue 31 in the published score, and there are other differences: the voice at cue 32 is more elaborate in **E** and from cue 33 there are differences in the division of the melody between voice and instruments as well as many small variants in melodic and rhythmic detail.

The Portfolio reveals that – like the Chorale – Finola's song (Example 5) had

EXAMPLE 5

been on Harty's mind for many years before the composition of *Lir*. It first appears in a sketch for an orchestral work in F major on pp. 81-4 of the Portfolio (**J**). The end of the sketch has become detached from the rest and is now p. 231 of the Portfolio. This bears the date 'Sept 8. 1914'. It may be that this was the work known as *The Tinker's Wedding* which was scheduled to be first performed at the Norwich Festival at the end of October, though the outbreak of war caused the Festival to be cancelled.[14] Finola's song appears fragmentarily in A minor in a Lento middle section (Example 6) and returns again just before the end (illustration 3).

EXAMPLE 6

The same theme occurs in a sketch for another orchestral work – this one in A major – on pp. 25-31 of the Portfolio (**K**). This one is dated 'Sept 1919'. Again the theme appears in a Lento middle episode (Example 7) and returns in the closing section.

EXAMPLE 7

Yet another sketch containing the theme is found on pp. 227-30 (**L**). This is for another orchestral work in F major and it embodies some material also found in **K**. Finola's theme again appears in a Lento section (Example 8).

It appears then that Harty's interest in this theme – like his preoccupation with the Chorale – amounted almost to an obsession. He thought of it as providing the central lyrical material in three works before *Lir* (**J, K, L**), and in at least two of them (**J, K**) the sketches show him bringing the theme back

3 Page from sketch **J** (1914) showing return of
Finola's theme (Lento) just before the Presto conclusion

EXAMPLE 8

in the closing section, just as he was to do in *Lir*. The theme itself does not change much, but the treatment it receives in the finished version of *Lir* – vocalised to an accompaniment of muted strings *divisi*, in the key of G flat, and with heart-stopping *portamenti* in the cellos and basses (tuned down to D flat) – is light years away from the sketches of 1914 and 1919.

Harty's decision to introduce a wordless soprano into the music at this point is of great importance. Of course there are several instances of this in the orchestral repertory that may have been at the back of his mind: one thinks of Nielsen's *Sinfonia espansiva* (1911) or Vaughan William's *Pastoral Symphony* (1921), for example. But it is probable that the work that influenced him at this juncture was much less well-known than either of these – Alfredo Casella's ballet suite *Le couvent sur l'eau (Il convento veneziano)*, composed 1912-13. One of the peculiarities of Harty's programmme-building during his conductorship of the Hallé Orchestra was his penchant for modern Italian composers such as Casella, Pizzetti, Busoni and Respighi, an interest that probably stemmed from his friendship with Michele Esposito. Harty included Casella's piece in a Hallé programme on 17 November 1921, an occasion which with hindsight gains added significance because it marked the début of the soprano Isobel Baillie (1895-1983) with the orchestra. In her autobiography[15] Dame Isobel recounts how, as a young singer, she was 'discovered' by Harty soon after he took over the Hallé in 1920, how she gave her first Hallé concert performing this work, and her feelings on finding that she had to sing from the back of the stage, and count bars like any orchestral player, some thirty yards from the conductor. This was the beginning of a friendship that lasted until his death. It was she who sang in the first performance of *Lir* on 1 March 1939 – once again from the back of the stage – and in her autobiography she wonders whether Harty remembered this effect from her début eighteen years earlier. This seems more than likely; the scene depicted in the Casella – of sounds floating across the water from a convent – is not so distant from that in *Lir*, with the water and the church and Finola's singing. It may well have sprung readily to the mind of an ailing man looking back on better times.

SWAN-CHILDREN

We can now retrace our steps to consider the Swan-children theme at cue 22. Sketches **A-C** do not get this far into the work, but **D** contains three different settings of the theme as Harty struggled to achieve a satisfactory transition into it. Example 9 shows the melody as it appears in **E** and **F**. The slight adjustment to the grace notes enhances the pentatonic flavour in **F**: this is not merely a matter of surface detail, for the adjustment strengthens the affinity that exists between this theme and Finola's theme, for it is clear that the two are closely related (Example 10). There are no pre-*Lir* sketches for Swan-children to indicate that it had an independent existence, and it seems likely that the theme grew out of Finola as Harty worked at the score. The affinity is even more marked when he brings back Finola's theme at cue 47, where changes of rhythm heighten the resemblance even more (Example 11).[16]

EXAMPLE 9

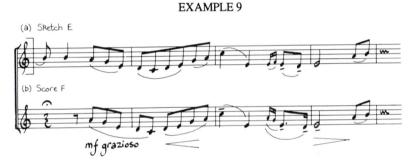

EXAMPLE 10

EXAMPLE 11

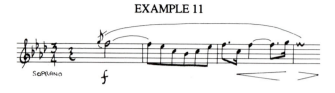

SOPRANO

THE COMPOSITION OF *LIR*

From a study of the Portfolio we learn that some of the principal thematic ideas in *Lir* pre-date the work for many years. The 'old' Chorale goes back to 1912, and Finola to 1914. Harty used them in sketches for other works which never saw the light of day. It may be that he had long harboured thoughts of writing a tone poem on the legend, which John Barry says he had known since his childhood.[17] But there seems no doubt that the determination to do so came from that day in 1936 when James Moore introduced him to the sculpture by Rosamond Praeger. His words, as remembered by Moore, bear this out: 'Jimmy, you have started something – what was lying dormant for years has now come to the surface . . . I can't get away from it . . . I am going to make it into an orchestral work'.

This means that undated sketches **A-D**, as well as the dated sketch **E**, all date from between Summer 1936 and Summer 1938. Since these all begin from the beginning[18] it might seem surprising that within this short period he kept going over old ground instead of pushing forward and getting the whole work mapped out. But this seems to be the way he sometimes worked: for instance, the Portfolio contains six drafts of the opening flourish of the Piano Concerto. And it is hardly to be wondered at if, at a time of illness, radium treatment and surgery, he had to re-enter the work from the beginning several times. In the circumstances the speed with which he worked is quite remarkable. The definitive full score **F** was completed in November 1938, only some three months after the completion of sketch **E**. As we have seen, sketch **E** – though complete – is still far from being definitive, so in that short space of time, as well as scoring the work, he subjected it to a further process of revision.

THE FIRST PERFORMANCE

During the 1936-7 and 1937-8 seasons Harty's illness forced him to cancel many concert appearances.[19] He conducted two studio concerts with the BBC Symphony Orchestra on 23 December 1938 and 1 March 1939, but his first public appearance since his illness was the first performance of *Lir* on 1 March 1939 in the Queen's Hall, with the BBC Symphony Orchestra. Harty conducted only his own piece; Boult conducted the rest of the programme, which consisted of Mozart's *Don Giovanni* overture, Beethoven's Third Piano Concerto (with Solomon) and Vaughan Williams' *London Symphony*. According to Nicholas Kenyon the programme was altered to accommodate the new work, a gesture which indicates the esteem and affection in which Harty was held.[20] The general goodwill towards him is amply borne out by the press comments which greeted the occasion, whatever the feelings of the critics towards the music. In the *Manchester Guardian* (2 March) Neville Cardus wrote that Harty

> . . . was given a tumultuous and affectionate welcome from a crowded Queen's Hall. And he at once lifted the occasion far above sentiment and goodwill by conducting with simply mastery a magnificent performance of a new work of his own and one of the most poetic compositions of any British composer of the last decade or so.[21]

Nevertheless, Cardus expresses uneasiness about the formal aspect of work, in particular the apparent musical necessity to recapitulate material when the narrative programme requires no such repetition. Other writers similarly mingle praise with criticism. 'Rathcol' in *The Belfast Telegraph* (3 March) also contemplates the nature of programmes music and finds this example guilty of 'looseness – not to say patchiness – of structure'. Other writers comment on its old-fashioned Romantic idiom: Scott Goddard in *The News Chronicle* (2 March) refers to its ancestry in Berlioz and Liszt while Edwin Evans in *The Liverpool Daily Post* (2 March) describes it as pre-Straussian and asks 'Does it really matter that it seems to hail from another era than our [own]?' The charge of anachronism, even irrelevance, was put most forcefully by *The Times* (2 March). Acknowledging the work's 'agreeable euphony' the paper continues:

> But this concern with old, unhappy, far-off things does not make a strong appeal to a generation which has its own share of present miseries. And it was made to appear even more old-fashioned by its juxtaposition with Vaughan Williams' twenty-year-old 'London' Symphony.

But the most damning comment came from Richard Capell in *The Daily Telegraph* (2 March): referring to the work's 'long-familiar style of expression' he continues, '. . . but magic is the essence of Sir Hamilton's chosen theme, and magic is precisely what this sure, craftsmanlike hand has failed to command'. In this respect Capell also compares the work unfavourably with the Nocturne movement of the *London Symphony*. On the other hand, J. A. Forsyth in *The Star* (2 March) admired the work for its tunefulness, while *The Irish Independent* (6 March) appreciated its Irishness, particularly as exemplified by 'Fionnghuala's caoine'. Almost everyone praised the beauty of its orchestration.

Before and after the first performance telegrams and letters flooded into Harty's home in St John's Wood from friends and well-wishers: from connections going back to his Hillsborough childhood like Sir William Thomson and Lady Arthur Hill; from musical colleagues of his early years in London like W. H. Squire; from former Hallé players like Arthur Catterall; from singers with whom he had worked such as Maggie Teyte, Roy Henderson, Norman Allin and Muriel Brunskill; from composers like Rutland Boughton and William Walton; from fellow conductors like Henry Wood, Julius Harrison and Clarence Raybauld; and from many others. Wood expresses the hope that Harty will direct the piece at 'my Proms'. Boughton firmly rejects Capell's charge of lack of 'magic'. James Moore wisely comments that the Irishness of the work grows out of the Irishness of its creator, and – referring to an older work by Harty – quips 'your geese are now all swans'. Rosamond Praeger is 'very proud of having my name even so slightly connected with so grand a thing'.

4   Sir Hamilton Harty in 1939

Miss F. L. Culver, proprietress of the Bayview Hotel at Portballintrae, where Harty had stayed during that summer holiday of 1936, expresses her pleasure at hearing the work on the wireless, as does a lady in Scotland who had made the acquaintance of Harty on that holiday.

For the first performance Harty conducted from the manuscript full score (**F**). He had signed a contract with Universal Edition (London) on 23 December 1938 but the printed score could not be ready in time for the hastily-arranged première. In preparing for the concert Harty marked up the score, and some of these markings – mainly additional expression marks – were incorporated into the printed score.[22] In the process of learning the score he also continued his habit of many years of marking off the bars according to phrase-lengths by means of the sign /4, /5. etc., and after the performance he inscribed on the title page '29¼ mins. 1/3/39 Conducted by the Composer'.When the printed score was published it bore a dedication 'To O. E. B.' – his friend Olive Baguley, who nursed him to the end.

Harty conducted a few more times after this concert. With the outbreak of war the BBC Symphony Orchestra moved to Bristol, from where he conducted a broadcast of *Harold in Italy* (with Lionel Tertis) on 14 February 1940 and a Tchaikowsky centenary concert on 22 May. But gradually the cancer renewed its hold. Ernest Hall, principal trumpet in the orchestra, has recalled Harty's last concert, on 1 December 1940:

> I was very distressed when Sir Hamilton conducted the BBC Symphony Orchestra for the last time. He was a very sick man after his operation, and while he was conducting this concert, his hair fell over one eye, so devoid of vision, he did not attempt to move it. It was very pathetic.[23]

Harty's frame of mind during these last months is conveyed on a postcard he sent to James Moore. The picture on the card is a reproduction of a painting by Peter Scott of geese in flight, and on the reverse he wrote, 'I wish I was going over with them too'.[24] A few months later his wish was granted.

But the music lives on. After its première, performances were few and far between, until the centenary year of 1979 when, on 4 December (Harty's birthday), the Ulster Orchestra gave the televised performance mentioned at the beginning of this article. Other performances followed, and in 1982 the work was issued on a gramophone record.[25] With the passage of time we can now appreciate *The Children of Lir* in perspective, as a late, but nonetheless powerful, Irish contribution to the tradition of the symphonic poem.

APPENDIX: Harty's Programme Note for the First Performance of *The Children of Lir* (reproduced from the programme booklet)

POEM for Orchestra   The Children of Lir   *Hamilton Harty*

Singer: ISOBEL BAILLIE

(First performance)
(Conducted by the Composer)

THE Fate of the Children of Lir forms part of the ancient Irish Sagas in which historical happenings and pure fantasy are inextricably mixed. This story, which was known as one of the "Three Tragic Stories of Erin", has to do with the four beautiful children of King Lir—Aed, Ficra, Conn, and their sister Fionnghuala (Finola, "white shoulder"). Aed and Finola, Ficra and Conn, were twins, and Lir's wife died in giving birth to the latter pair.

After a long time Lir married again, but his new wife became increasingly jealous of the beauty and fame of the four children, and of the great love felt for them by Lir. Making use of her magical powers, she caused an enchantment to fall upon them so that they were changed into white swans, and doomed to wander over the Irish waters for a thousand years. Not until the clang of the first Christian bell fell upon their ears would they return to their old shape. So for this long time did these four swans haunt the lakes and seas of Ireland, at the end coming to the Sea of Moyle, which is the tempestuous stretch of water between the Irish and the Scottish coasts. There, sometimes in sunshine and gaiety, oftener in storms and cold and privation, did they spend the greater part of their sentence, Finola always protecting and caring for her brothers. At night from the rocky islet of Carricknarone where they sheltered sometimes could be heard their sweet and sorrowful singing :—

Silent, O Moyle, be the roar of thy water;
Break not, ye breezes, your chain of repose;
While murmuring mournfully, Lir's lonely daughter
Tells to the night-star her tale of woes.

Thomas Moore

One morning as they swam off the wild and rugged cliffs of Antrim, the swan-children suddenly heard the sound of a bell from a little church on the cliff top. Immediately they were changed back into their human shapes, noble and beautiful still, but incredibly old. They were taken by the coast people to the little church and baptized, and as they were received into the Christian faith they died. They were buried in the little churchyard overlooking the sea, within hearing of the bell which had brought their tragic sufferings to an end—Finola lying in the middle with a brother at either side, and her favourite brother Aed

in her arms. For she had said "As I often sheltered my brothers when we were swans, so let us be placed in the grave, Conn at my right side, Ficra at my left, and Aed in my bosom".

Though this poem for orchestra is based on the above story (which is indeed printed in the full score) the composer has not followed it in detail, but rather taken from it for musical illustration certain scenes and moods to which the musical sections of the work correspond. These sections are not, however, definitely separated from one another, but fall naturally into place as the music proceeds. Through all runs the sound of the sea, sometimes stormy and boisterous, sometimes calm and subdued. The orchestra used is fairly large, and there is a soprano voice (behind the scenes) which represents the singing of Finola, when at night with her brothers she was used to seek shelter on the rocky islet of Carricknarone.

The introduction, *Lento e con dignità*, illustrates the thoughts of one who stands on the Antrim Cliffs on a day of storm and tempest, and recalls the sorrowful story of the enchanted Children of Lir while gazing down on the turbulent Sea of Moyle—a picture of heaving waters, clouds of spray, and screaming seagulls. In imagination he sees these four children in all their grace and dignity changed by an evil spell into the shape of swans, but facing their tragic future with bravery and defiance :—

lighter and more playful character, telling of calmer seas and bluer skies:—

This scherzando section is combined with the previous theme (No. 5) and the music rises to a climax of passion and defiance. The passages of a recitative-like character which follow suggest the approach of evening, and the music darkens in texture, calming down as it leads into a short intermezzo marked *Andante tranquillo (quasi un' notturno)*. Here the whole of the orchestra is directed to play "in a hushed and subdued manner", and to a gently rising and falling accompaniment Finola is heard (in the soprano solo) singing her plaintive song of weariness and of longing for the day of release:—

Except for slowly moving figures in the lower strings, like a long lazy ocean swell, or an occasional ripple in the flute and clarinets, like a thin line of foam, or the soft boom of the bass drum as the sea breaks on a distant beach, there is little to distract attention from Finola's lament.

This short section is followed by a resumption of the principal *Allegro* with its theme of the open sea (No. 3). The music follows its former course, but in a much shortened form, and most of the preceding themes are passed in brief review. There is a new note of urgency and anxiety in the music, for this is the last day of the children in their "swan" life, and though they are not actually aware of this they are conscious of something different, of something impending. Finola (as always the most spiritual and sensitive) becomes increasingly exalted and finally

These two themes with their stormy accompaniment gradually increase in intensity until they merge into a rallying-call, twice repeated, followed immediately by the next section—*Allegro brioso ed animato*—the principal theme of which typifies the free open sea:—

This appears frequently during the course of the work. For some time the music paints various aspects of this scene—the broad expanse of water, the tossing waves, the fresh winds:—

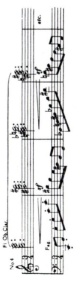

Eventually a more personal mood is introduced with the following theme, which embodies the passionate and sorrowful feelings of the swan-children as they remember the scenes from which they have been banished:—

But, as the story tells, they were not always sorrowful, nor was the sea always rough and tempestuous, and the music gradually assumes a

breaks into snatches of her song. As the music (and in imagination the
seas and winds) gathers more urgency and intensity, so does her voice
rise higher in pitch and sweep, until at the climax of passionateness there
is a loud cry from Finola, the orchestra breaks off suddenly, and the
clang of a church bell comes to the ears of the swan-children from the
high cliff edge of the coast towards which they are approaching. Immediately they are changed back into their human form again, "noble and
beautiful as ever, but incredibly old".

The last section of the music depicts the children being taken ashore
and being led up the rocky path to the little church on the cliff top,
where they die as they are baptized. The music, which has returned to
the mood of the opening introduction, illustrates these events, and the
slow procession to the spot where the children are finally laid to rest.

The last few pages are in the nature of a meditation on the "sorrowful
story" by one who might stand in the little church enclosure, and,
sheltered from the storm without, hear only the far away murmur of
the sea and the bells softly tolling in the church tower. Finola's song is
heard once more in the orchestra, and the poem ends quietly and softly,
except for a sudden outburst in the last bars—a last glance at the raging
Moyle, foaming and heaving far down below the cliff :—

NOTES

1. In David Greer (ed.), *Hamilton Harty: His Life and Music* (hereafter *HHLM*) (Belfast, 1978, repr. New York, 1980), 51-64. As with all my work on Harty, this article has benefited from conversations I have had with Canon Barry, particularly in connection with Harty's treatment of the legend.

2. Transcribed from a video recording now at The Queen's University, Belfast.

3. I am grateful to Mr W.G. Wheeler for the bibliographical information in this section.

4. 'Moyle' = 'Mull'.

5. There are extensive ecclesiastical remains on this island, and by coincidence an ancient bell was discovered in the church on the nearby island of North Iniskea.

6. *Belfast Telegraph*, March 1939: '"Telegraph" readers have already discussed the authenticity of the legend as Sir Hamilton treats it, but Sir Hamilton states that he has not followed the story in detail, but has taken certain scenes and moods suitable for musical treatment'.

7. There is a photograph of the bird-bath in *HHLM*, 61. For more information about Rosamond Praeger see John Hewitt, *Art in Ulster I* (Belfast, 1977), 180 *et passim*.

8. An inventory of the complete portfolio is given in David Greer, 'Hamilton Harty Manuscripts', *The Music Review*, 46 (1986-7), 238-52.

9. When it came into my hands the loose pages were in great disarray. The present ordering and pagination are my own and do not provide any evidence as to the chronology of the sketches.

10. All this material is in The Queen's University Library, Belfast.

11. This is the 'funeral music' that James Moore recollects from his visit to Rostrevor. He is mistaken in thinking that it is present in the full store.

12. Page 279 of the Portfolio is also related to this.

13. At one point Harty has written 'enter M^{rs} O'Shea' above a sustained chord, but the piece does not give the impression of being incidental music.

14. In 'Hamilton Harty Manuscripts' (as n. 8), 243 and 250, I suggest that items no. 42/3 in the inventory are the lost *Tinker's Wedding*. Now that no. 43, with its crucial date, has been identified as the conclusion of inventory no. 16 (=J in this article) that tentative identification must be transferred to nos. 16/43.

15. Isobel Baillie, *Never Sing Louder than Lovely* (London, 1982), 26-7. This book contains some useful information about Harty, who became something of an artistic mentor to her. Soon after the above-mentioned début with the Hallé he gave her her first 'big' *Messiah* (it was also the first broadcast *Messiah*). He also arranged for her to do a test recording for Columbia in February 1926, when he accompanied her singing Wakefield Cadman's *At Dawning* (not issued at the time, but transferred on to 33 r.p.m. in 1974 and issued on RLS 714). It was he who advised her in 1925 to go to Italy to have singing lessons with Guglielmo Somma, and in 1936 he suggested that some lessons with Plunket Greene might benefit her diction. He expressed his displeasure in letters when in 1928 she began to sing Wagner. Her American début was with Harty at the Hollywood Bowl in 1933. She last saw him at his St John's Wood home after a major operation, when at his request she sang *Across the Door*. The book contains some letters from Harty to her, and a photograph of Harty in America.

16. This affinity between Finola and Swan-children is reinforced still further when the first violins enter five bars later.

17. *HHLM* (as n. 1), 58.

18. Sketch **D** actually picks up from cue 11 but there seems to have been an earlier portion, now missing.

19. One of these, according to Nicholas Kenyon, was the first performance of his *second* Piano Concerto with the composer as soloist: see Nicholas Kenyon, *The BBC Symphony Orchestra: the First Fifty Years 1930-80* (London, 1981), 134 *et passim*. There is no trace of this work.

20. Kenyon, *The BBC Symphony Orchestra* (as n. 19), 150.

21. Queen's University has a file of press cuttings, letters and telegrams connected with the performance.

22. There are also a few minor changes, such as removal of slurs from the cellos and basses eight bars after cue 9, and removal of ties from the trumpet parts six bars before 30.

23. Note to Leonard Hirsch, copy at Queen's University.

24. Postcard in the possession of the writer.

25. Chandos ABRD 1051: Ulster Orchestra conducted by Bryden Thomson, with Heather Harper (soprano). See review in *The Gramophone*, 59 (1981-2), 1511.

Music at the Rotunda Gardens in Dublin, 1771-91

A CHANGE IN MUSICAL TASTE

BRIAN BOYDELL

During the eighteenth century, the promotion of concerts in Dublin for charitable purposes, which formed the core of musical performances in the city outside the theatre, was pursued by numerous musical societies; and their profits made a very considerable contribution to the founding and maintenance of at least eight Dublin hospitals. The most successful, consistent and long-lasting of these charitable efforts were the concerts initiated by 'Dr' Bartholemew Mosse in aid of his Lying-in Hospital, which was 'the first and only *Publick* one of its kind in his *Majesty's* Dominions'.[1]

Encouraged by the success of three annual performances of oratorios by Handel, first promoted in 1746, Mosse pursued more ambitious plans. Having secured in August 1748 the lease of an extensive plot of land bordering on Great Britain Street (now Parnell St), he laid out his New Gardens as a place of fashionable entertainment for the support of the Hospital in the style of London's Vauxhall. Furthermore, he attracted to the residential sites around the garden some of the most fashionable nobility of the city, creating what a contemporary traveller called 'a vortex of fashion'.[2] The New Gardens in Great Britain Street had distinct advantages over rival places of entertainment. Foremost was Mosse's enthusiasm and foresight which created this unrivalled 'vortex of fashion', and established a reputation of excellence in both music and performers. In addition, the concerts and entertainments were entrusted after Mosse's death in 1759 to a committee of devoted and informed 'Gentlemen of Approved Taste'[3] who clearly had influence in society and useful contacts with the musical world in London. Lord Charlemont and other members of this distinguished committee frequently spent extended periods in London, and would be requested by the Board of Governors of the Hospital to make enquiries about the possibility of engaging soloists of international repute for performances in the Gardens.[4] The imaginative planning of this venture culminated in the building of the 'Rotunda' concert hall, which was opened in 1767 and provided the name by which the Hospital and its Gardens became known.

From the time the Gardens were opened in 1749 there began a period of nearly half a century during which the Governors of the Hospital were the foremost and most consistent promoters of regular concerts in Dublin. After an initial period of uncertainties and rivalry, they employed a band of eighteen to twenty musicians who, with the best available soloists, presented approximately sixty 'concerts of vocal and instrumental musick' each year. For most of the period, these took place three times a week for about 21 weeks between April and September. The last short season organised by the Governors for the benefit of the Hospital consisted of merely eight subscription concerts given in 1791. Thereafter the Governors ceased to have direct control over the concerts, and benefited from letting out the premises to independent promoters.

Compared to the wealth of financial information concerning the remarkable total of over 2,400 concerts promoted for the Lying-in Hospital,[5] it is unfortunate that only a small proportion of the programmes have survived. These are to be found in newspaper advertisements, and are usually confined to a limited number of special occasions when the Gardens were illuminated in celebration of political anniversaries such as the birthday of royalty, or important military victories. On these occasions, of which there were usually about eight in the season, annual subscription tickets did not gain free admission, as they did to the ordinary run of concerts, the programmes for which were notified by bills posted in advance at the venue. None of the latter bills are known to have survived. The extent of advertising of programmes for the 'excepted' concerts varied from one period to another. A reasonable number are available for the first five years (1749 to 1754 inclusive); thereafter details are very scarce until the 1770s, when programmes become available for a sufficient number of concerts to be able to make an approximate statistical survey of the fashionable popularity of major instrumental works. The changes in musical taste revealed by this survey must be examined against the background of the previous period.

Although detailed programmes for the period 1749-70 are very scarce, an analysis of those few 'Rotunda' programmes taken in conjunction with other Dublin concerts make it clear that up to 1760 at least, Handel was the dominant composer in popular favour, followed by those who wrote in the Italian baroque style, such as Corelli, Vivaldi and Geminiani, along with the English composers Stanley and Mudge; with Boyce and Thomas Arne featuring prominently in vocal works. This general conclusion is confirmed by the list of orchestral material purchased by Dr Mosse from J. Walsh of London in 1754 for performance at his concerts, which includes:

> Handel   60 Overtures. 30 Concertos. The Water Music. 13 Sonatas.
>   12 Solos. Select Airs from the Operas. Songs from his
>   Oratorios.

Geminiani   54 Concertos. Sonatas.

Corelli   12 Concertos. 54 Sonatas.

Overtures and Concertos for Concerts by: St. Martini, Arne, Hasse, Dr. Greene, Ciampi, Stanley, Defesch, Ruge, Weidemann, Martini of Milan, Woodcock, Martini of London, Rameau, Bononcini, Castrucci, Locatelli, Alberti (22), Albinoni (18), Vivaldi (32), Tessarini, Veracini.[6]

That changes were about to take place in the regular musical fare that had satisfied the Dublin public for about half a century is shown by the first known introduction of the music of J.C. Bach, in 1769. It is announced in a frustratingly vague advertisement in *Faulkner's Dublin Journal* of 9-12 September 1769 which supplies interesting information concerning the Bach work, but little else:

> there will be a *Concert* in the Rotunda on Wednesday Evening next; the Vocal parts by Mr Savoi, and a young Lady, who has also offered to sing for the Benefit of the Charity. Mr Savoi will oblige the Publick with his most favourite Songs, and with the Serenata, composed particularly for his Benefit by Mr Bach . . .'.

A previous advertisement in the same paper adds that the words of the Serenata are by Metastasio.

During the last twenty years of the Rotunda concerts, the programmes are generally more complete and more frequently advertised. Up to 1788, the concerts were divided into three 'Acts'; and thereafter the custom of two Acts, as in present-day programming, was adopted. Examples (see Figure 1) show that the composers of major instrumental works are given,though the works themselves are seldom identified. Furthermore, different composers of the same name, such as Johann and Carl Stamitz, and the various Martinis are very seldom differentiated. Owing to the practice of announcing instrumental concertos in the form 'A concerto on the Violin by Mr X' the composer of the concerto cannot be identified; though in many cases it might be assumed from the practice of the time that the concerto was written by the soloist himself. The vocal items seldom give the name of the composer, though an intimate knowledge of the arias and songs from Italian and English operas and theatrical pieces popular at the time would lead to the source of many of them.

With the arrival of François Barthélemon in 1771 to conduct for two seasons (he was to return in 1784), a definite change from the dominance of baroque styles is noted, as both J.C. Bach and Stamitz make their appearance. Under the direction of the London-born Thomas Pinto, who was in charge in 1776 and 1777, and from 1779 to 1782, the change is more dramatic. The new music of the Mannheim composers along with that of the active Germans in London,

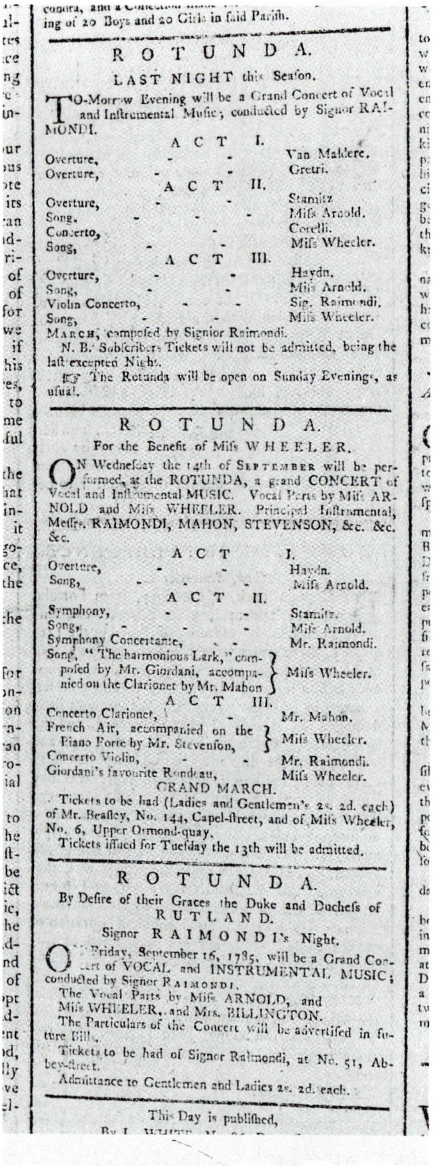

ing of 20 Boys and 20 Girls in ſaid Pariſh.

R O T U N D A.

LAST NIGHT this Seaſon.

TO-Morrow Evening will be a Grand Concert of Vocal and Inſtrumental Muſic; conducted by Signor RAIMONDI.

A C T I.

Overture,	Van Maldere.
Overture,	Gretri.

A C T II.

Overture,	Stamitz
Song,	Miſs Arnold.
Concerto,	Corelli.
Song,	Miſs Wheeler.

A C T III.

Overture,	Haydn.
Song,	Miſs Arnold.
Violin Concerto,	Sig. Raimondi.
Song,	Miſs Wheeler.

MARCH, compoſed by Signior Raimondi.

N. B. Subſcribers Tickets will not be admitted, being the laſt excepted Night.

☞ The Rotunda will be open on Sunday Evenings, as uſual.

R O T U N D A.

For the Benefit of Miſs WHEELER.

ON Wedneſday the 14th of SEPTEMBER will be performed, at the ROTUNDA, a grand CONCERT of Vocal and Inſtrumental MUSIC. Vocal Parts by Miſs ARNOLD and Miſs WHEELER. Principal Inſtrumental, Meſſrs. RAIMONDI, MAHON, STEVENSON, &c. &c. &c.

A C T I.

Overture,	Haydn.
Song,	Miſs Arnold.

A C T II.

Symphony,	Stamitz.
Song,	Miſs Arnold.
Symphony Concertante,	Mr. Raimondi.
Song, "The harmonious Lark," compoſed by Mr. Giordani, accompanied on the Clarionet by Mr. Mahon	Miſs Wheeler.

A C T III.

Concerto Clarionet,	Mr. Mahon.
French Air, accompanied on the Piano Forte by Mr. Stevenſon,	Miſs Wheeler.
Concerto Violin,	Mr. Raimondi.
Giordani's favourite Rondeau,	Miſs Wheeler.

GRAND MARCH.

Tickets to be had (Ladies and Gentlemen's 2s. 2d. each) of Mr. Beaſley, No. 144, Capel-ſtreet, and of Miſs Wheeler, No. 6, Upper Ormond-quay.

Tickets iſſued for Tueſday the 13th will be admitted.

R O T U N D A.

By Deſire of their Graces the Duke and Ducheſs of RUTLAND.

Signor RAIMONDI's Night.

ON Friday, September 16, 1785, will be a Grand Concert of VOCAL and INSTRUMENTAL MUSIC; conducted by Signor RAIMONDI.

The Vocal Parts by Miſs ARNOLD, and Miſs WHEELER, and Mrs. BILLINGTON.

The Particulars of the Concert will be advertiſed in future Bills.

Tickets to be had of Signor Raimondi, at No. 51, Abbey-ſtreet.

Admittance to Gentlemen and Ladies 2s. 2d. each.

This Day is publiſhed,

Figure 1 Some typical programmes from the 1785 season under Ignazio Raimondi, as advertised in *The Freeman's Journal*, 3-6 September 1785. The music of Haydn, first heard in Dublin in 1776, was beginning to challenge in popularity that of J.C. Bach and K.F. Abel, and the Mannheim composers. Mr [John] Mahon was the first named soloist to play concertos on the 'clarionet' since the 1740s; mention of the 'Piano Forte' reflects the vogue for this new instrument which began in the 1770s.

J.C. Bach and Abel, asserts its complete dominance.

It was in 1776 that the composer who was to dominate the scene for the last quarter of the century, as Handel had done before about 1760, was introduced for the first time in Dublin. On 8 August, Pinto programmed 'A New Overture, composed by Mr Hayden'.[7] The complete dominance of the new classical style of Haydn was to some extent tempered by Barthélemon's revival of Handel in 1784, and Charles Weichsell's enthusiasm for Corelli in 1786 and 1787. It was not until the final short season of eight subscription concerts (with the addition of six benefit concerts for the leading musicians) under Langrishe Doyle in 1791, that Haydn's name was significantly supplanted at the top of the list by that of the Paris composer, Pleyel, whose new style was becoming increasingly popular at London's Vauxhall Gardens, as a result of the promotion of Cramer and Clementi, who were challenging Salomon's championship of Haydn.

The up-to-date music of high artistic standard introduced during the later 1770s and 1780s was balanced for popular appeal by such pieces as 'A Grand Symphonia, expressive of a Hunt, with Echoes; interrupted by a Storm, composed by Mr Raimondi'[8]; and 'Rauzzini's Grand March' replaced 'The Duke's March' (from Handel's *Judas Maccabeus*), which had been the previous favourite as a rousing piece to end a concert. Such extraordinary gimmicks as 'a Duet upon two Flutes, by Mr Ashe, a Performance never before attempted in this Kingdom',[9] and extra-musical attractions such as the exhibition of a View of Mount Vesuvius at the concert on 12 August 1785 (see Figure 2) tempered the quite 'highbrow' appeal of the later Rotunda concerts. As at Vauxhall, the singers, who inherited a long tradition of appeal beyond that of pure music, assisted in diluting the more serious orchestral fare. It might be added that the sure way to attract a capacity audience was to engage a female vocal soloist of seductive appearance and dubious moral reputation. The notable success of Anne Catley's concerts in 1777 provide an example.

Dublin may have been geographically isolated, but as will be seen from the analysis of 'Rotunda' programmes, it was by no means cut off from the mainstream of new influences emanating from the Continent. The London connections of the committee who managed the concerts for the Lying-in Hospital resulted in the engagement after Claget's period in charge (1763-68) of a series of London-based conductors such as Barthelémon, Cramer, Pinto, Scheener, Weichsell and Salomon. The London musical scene in which these musicians were involved benefited from an influx of continental musicians seeking more favourable conditions than those which could be provided in areas disrupted by recent warfare. It was dominated between 1765 and 1781, in the subscription concerts organised for the exclusive upper-class audience, by J.C. Bach and Abel. These were succeeded by a similar series organised by Cramer and Clementi; Salomon's famous concerts (at which Haydn first appeared before a London audience in 1791) were launched in 1784. There were direct

Theatre.

R O T U N D A.

TO-MORROW Evening, being Friday the 12th of Au-
guft, will be a Grand Concert of Vocal and Inftru-
mental Mufic; conducted by Signior RAIMONDI.
 The Vocal Parts by Mifs ARNOLD and Mifs WHEE-
LER.

A C T   I.

Overture,	Abel.
Overture,	Bach.

A C T   II.

Overture,	Gretry.
Song,	Mifs Arnold.
Concerto,	Corelli.
Song,	Mifs Wheeler.

A C T   III.

Overture,	Stamitz.
Song,	Mifs Arnold.
Violin Concerto, in which will be in- troduced the favourite Air, " The Lake of Killarney," with Variati- ons, compofed and to be perform- ed by	Sig. Raimondi.
Song, " Sel Caro Bene,"	Mifs Wheeler.

MARCH, compofed by Signior Raimondi.
 The GARDEN will be ILLUMINATED.
 And between the fecond and third Acts of the Concert
will be exhibited a View of MOUNT VESUVIUS, defign-
ed by Mr. Kelly; the Fire-Work by Monf. Gayet, and the
Painting by Mr. Jolly.
 Subfcribers Tickets will not be admitted.

By the LORD LIEUTENANT and COUNCIL
of *I R E L A N D.*
A P R O C L A M A T I O N.
R U T L A N D.

WHEREAS we have received information upon oath,
that on Th———

Figure 2 An advertisement from *The Freeman's Journal*, 9-11 August 1785, reveals
Ignazio Raimondi responding to the growing demand for instrumental concertos featuring
variations, or a rondo, based on popular Irish melodies. The eruptions of Mount Vesuvius
were a favourite sight for those making the Grand Tour and were reproduced in firework
displays for the less fortunate.

contacts between these composer-impresarios and the latest developments on the Continent, particularly between what one might term the 'workshop' in Mannheim and the 'saleroom' in Paris. Cramer was indeed one of the second-generation Mannheim composers. The London pleasure-gardens such as Vauxhall, Marylebone and Ranelagh, upon which Dublin's Great Britain-street Gardens were modelled, featured the latest continental music introduced at the exclusive subscription concerts, diluted with songs and items of more popular appeal. In view of the adventurous taste of the English capital it is no surprise to find that as soon as the direction of the Rotunda concerts was entrusted to London-based musicians, a distinct change of policy in programme-content from the previous conservative attitude became apparent.

The occurrence of pieces with a specifically Irish flavour, especially among the vocal items, had been a feature of Dublin programmes since the 1740s, when 'Eileen Aroon' (spelt in many different ways) became an almost obligatory item in the repertoire of any visiting singer. Two sets of instrumental variations on this melody were published in 1743 and 1746. Although 'Eileen Aroon' was still a popular item in the programmes later in the century, its dominance was somewhat eclipsed by 'Gramachree Molly'. Besides being offered as a local compliment by many visiting singers, this air was 'made into a Rondeau, and performed by Mr Ritter on the Bassoon' on 1 July 1774;[10] and twice in May 1775 Signor Patria played 'a concerto on the hautboy with the favourite air of Gramachree Molly and Variations'.[11] Barthélemon used the melody in a similar way for a violin concerto in 1784. The use of traditional airs in concertos and solo keyboard pieces became increasingly popular towards the end of the century (see Figure 2). This tendency has sometimes been interpreted as a reflection of the increase in nationalist feelings that were apparent in the two decades before 1798, but an examination of London programmes during the same period reveals a similar fashion for the use of Scottish, Welsh and Irish melodies in instrumental works, particularly concertos. This would suggest that the fashion was not due to local nationalism but was encouraged in a more general context by the suitable role which such melodies could play in the post-baroque Rondo form so frequently used for the final movement of concertos, or as a theme for variations in the slow movement. The use of national melodies in this way might also suggest a prophetic hint of the habit of exploiting exotic or national colour, which was to become such a feature of romantic nationalism.

AN ANALYSIS OF THE PROGRAMMES, 1771-91

Before setting out in tabular form an analysis of the available programmes for the period 1771-91, certain comments and details concerning each season are presented here separately, since to include them in the analytical table would be detrimental to its clarity.The dates which follow refer directly to the table itself.

1771 and 1772: François Barthélemon was a leading figure in London's musical life as a violinist and composer. He moved there, at the instigation of the Earl of Kelly, in 1765, and remained for four decades. He was famed for his interpretation of Corelli's sonatas. He married Mary (Polly) Young the singer, who had been in Dublin in the care of her aunt Mrs Cecilia Arne between 1755 and 1762.

Among the vocal items in the programmes, arias from Piccinni's *La Buona Figliuola* and songs from the comic operas of Dibdin are common. Dibdin was a colleague of the Barthélemons, and his *Ephesian Matron* was performed at Dublin's Ranelagh Gardens in 1771.

1773: Unfortunately there are no published programmes for this season. it is presumed that the Revd Samuel Murphy, MusD, organist at Saint Patrick's Cathedral from 1770 until his death in 1780, was in charge at the Rotunda. No fee appears to have been paid to a conductor from overseas, and Murphy's responsibility for Rotunda music is inferred from the Minutes of the Board of Governors of the Hospital.

1774: Wilhelm Cramer had studied with Johann Stamitz and Cannabich, and joined the Mannheim orchestra about 1752. He arrived in London in 1772 after a short visit to Paris, and was encouraged to stay by J.C. Bach. Until the appearance of Salomon, he was considered England's foremost violinist.

George Wenzel Ritter was the foremost player of the bassoon of his time. He was a member of the Mannheim orchestra between 1764 and 1778.

1775: Pièrre Vachon was appearing frequently at the *Concerts Spirituels* in Paris in 1756 and 1758, and in 1761 secured a position as first violinist in the orchestra of the Prince of Conti. He went to London in 1772 for a short visit, and returned there in 1774 or 1775 where he remained for about ten years.

The Mr Arne who appeared several times as an organ soloist was Michael, son of Thomas, who made a feature of performing his father's organ concertos. The Mr Jones who was engaged to play on 21 nights for a fee of £20. 9s. 6d. was probably Edward, the Welsh harper, historian and composer, who started his career in London about 1774, and soon established himself as a player in the Bach-Abel concerts.

On 20 September, Mr Patria, the hautboy soloist, was advertised as playing 'a favourite Concerto on a new Italian Instrument never before heard in this Kingdom which imitates the human voice in the highest perfection'. Could this be the form of tenor oboe developed about 1750 in England and known as the *Vox Humana*? This is suggested by the item advertised for 8 August 1776, in which Mr Fischer is to play 'A solo on the Hautboy . . . (accompanied with a Vox Humane, by Mr Patria)'.

Songs from Thomas Arne's *Artaxerxes*, which had been performed with great success in Dublin in 1772, are prominent among the vocal items.

1776 and 1777: Thomas Pinto was born in London in 1714, his father having fled to England from Naples for political reasons. Thomas fled to Dublin in 1773 to escape his creditors, having lost £2,000 in a speculation with Dr Arnold in shares in Marylebone Gardens. He was accompanied to Dublin by his second wife, the singer Charlotte Brent, and his daughter, who was also a singer. He obtained the position of leader of the band at the Smock Alley Theatre in 1773, remaining at this post until 1779. During his regime at the Rotunda, which included the six seasons (with the exception of 1778) between 1776 and 1782, he introduced many of the Mannheim composers to Dublin for the first time. He is also due the credit for the first recorded performance of Haydn's music in Dublin: 'A New Overture, composed by Mr Hayden', on 8 August 1776.

In these two seasons, songs from Thomas Arne's *Artaxerxes* are still prominent among the vocal items. Anne Catley sang at six concerts in August, and her great popularity resulted in a notable increase in box-office takings on these occasions, which contributed towards the highest figure recorded for the net profit towards the Hospital charity.[12]

1778: Franz Lamotte was a violin virtuoso of the first rank with a reputation for astonishing technique in double-stopping, bowing and sight-reading. He went to London from Paris in 1776, and soon teamed up with Venanzio Rauzzini, the male soprano and composer, who accompanied him to Dublin. They were both in charge of the concerts at Bath from about 1777. Rauzzini had a younger brother, Matteo, who settled in Dublin as a composer and singing teacher about 1780. Some of the compositions attributed to Rauzzini may have been by Matteo.

1779-82: During Pinto's second extended period of directorship, the flautist Andrew Ashe, who was first engaged in 1780, began his long association with the Rotunda concerts. Born in Lisburn, Co. Antrim in 1759, he started his career learning the violin, but became increasingly interested in wind instruments, eventually developing the six-keyed flute from the prototype model of Vanhall, first flute at the Brussels concerts. On 31 May 1789 he performed 'a Duet upon Two Flutes . . . a Performance never before attempted in this Kingdom'.

Pergolesi's *Stabat Mater*, which retained its popularity in Dublin since its introduction by Pasquali in 1749, was given three performances in 1782.

Among vocal items, Master Stephenson (the future Sir John, the composer) appeared as a soloist singing Handel songs on 1 October 1779 in a programme which also featured catches and glees, and 'A New Song, written in Compliment to the Dublin Volunteers on the present Occasion'. On 30 July 1782, Mr Tuke sang 'An old French Song, the words and music composed by Theobald, King of Navarre, who was born in the year 1201. The translation of the words into English by Dr. Burney, with instrumental accompaniments . . . (by Mr Pinto).'

1783: Scheener (Schener or Schenner) is not listed in any of the standard reference books. His name is however given in a list of prominent London musicians in 1792 in London as a German violinist, by Joseph Haydn in his *London Notebooks*, Robbins Landon notes that Scheener (also Schenner) appeared for the first time in London in 1781.[13]

From this year until the end of the period under study, performances of works by Haydn outnumber those by any other composer.

After a loss of £83 was recorded in the *Profits to the Charity* in the Register's Accounts for 1782, the number of instrumentalists in the Rotunda band was reduced, and a saving of about £500 on the total expenditure on music is recorded for 1783. A military band was engaged on two occasions.

1784: Barthélemon, whose career has been described under the years of his previous visit (1771 and 1772), revived the music of the baroque composers, such as Handel, Geminiani and Corelli, which reflects his reputation for the interpretation of this style of music. On 9 June 1784 he followed the fashion of including 'the favourite Air Gramachree' with variations, in a violin concerto. Mrs Barthélemon frequently sang 'Aileen-a-Roon'.

On 24 August, Mrs Billington, best known as the leading English soprano of the time, played 'a Concerto on the Grand Piano Forte': possibly the concerto by Schroeter, which she played at the Smock Alley Theatre during the following year. Mrs Barthélemon also played a concerto on 'the Grand Piano Forte' on 3 August.

Note that in this season only, Carl and Johann Stamitz are differentiated in the published programmes.

Apparently the appeal of the military band, which was engaged on two occasions in 1783, encouraged the increase of such engagements in this season to fourteen.

This is the last year for which detailed accounts for the running of the concerts are available. The continuation volume of the Register's Accounts, which one would expect to find in the Hospital archives, is missing.

1785: Ignazio Raimondi was a Neapolitan violinist and composer who went to Amsterdam in 1762, and then to London, where he settled in 1780. he became well known for his programme symphonies as well as his concert performances. His 'Battle Piece' was a favourite concluding item during this season; and his 'Grand Symphonia, expressive of a Hunt, with Echoes; interrupted by a Storm' was repeated several times.

Philip Cogan, who was to earn a name as the most distinguished Irish composer for the keyboard of his time, performed an organ concerto of his own 23 March, and a Sonata for the Piano Forte on 2 March.

John Mahon (Mahone, Mahoun or Mahoon), the first named clarinet soloist in Dublin since 'Mr Charles' introduced the instrument in 1742, was one of a family of musicians of Irish origin who lived in England during the eighteenth century. He did more than anyone to popularise the clarinet in England during his time, making his debut in the Oxford Music Room in 1772 with a clarinet concerto. As a violinist, he played at the 1784 Handel Commemoration, and led the orchestra at the Oxford Music Room for many years. He retired to Dublin in 1825, where he died in 1834.

1786-1788: Charles Weichsell Junior (usually spelt 'Weichsel' in Rotunda programmes) was born in London, the son of Carl Weichsell the oboe player. He first appeared in Dublin on 6 December 1783, playing 'a solo concerto on the violin' as interval music at the Smock Alley Theatre. His father and his sister, who became the famous and somewhat notorious soprano Mrs Billington, probably arrived at the same time. Charles was in charge of the band for the production of Gluck's *Orpheus* at Smock Alley by Tenducci's company in January 1784. Carl had obtained a position as oboist in the theatre band. Weichsell's high placing in the list of composers most frequently performed is largely due to the popularity of his 'Battle Piece', 'Chace and Thunderstorm' and 'Grand March'. Undoubtedly many of the violin concertos were composed by him.

It is interesting to note that among the glees, which were now more frequently featured in Rotunda programmes, Michael East's 'How merrily we live' was a popular item. In the programme for 1 September 1786 it follows 'A favourite Quartetto for two Violins, Tenor and Bass' by Haydn.

1789: Johann Peter Salomon, born in 1745, was the son of a court musician at Bonn. Settling in London in 1781, he soon was playing a leading part in English musical life, devoting much of his energy to concert promotion, which culminated in the two famous visits of Haydn. The small proportion of published programmes available for this season reveal the first known performance of a work by Mozart in Ireland: a 'New Overture (manuscript)'. (Note that the terms 'Overture' and 'Symphony' or 'Sinfonia' are loosely applied in this period). The programme for 14 July featured a quintet for clarinet and string quartet; and on 26 June a quintet by Boccherini was performed.

1790: Only two complete programmes for this season have been traced. One is a benefit for Sperati the cellist, held at the Rotunda on 26 June; the other was held at the Exhibition Room in William Street on 18 May. The 34 (?) regular concerts organised for the benefit of the Rotunda Hospital are covered only by general announcements. It appears that these were conducted by Ashe the flute-player, John Abraham Fisher, DMus, and William Heron the Dublin organist, on a shared basis.

The Freeman's Journal of 7-9 October 1790 published the following critical comment:

> Within three or four years, that the Rotunda Garden and its surrounding ornaments and building, have undergone a very great change for the better, let it not be attributed to the usual resort of the fashionable and gay, to have given support for such improvements. On the contrary, the parliament gave its aid, by a tax on sedan chairs &c. The iron railing was erected by the joint contribution of the genteel inhabitants of Rutland Square, and the late ever to be revered Duke of Rutland gave a donation of £400 towards building the new rooms; and private contributions, with some parliamentary countenance, have sprung out of other additions.
>
> All this time, the visiting company has every year been thin, owing to want of incitement in the performers, and the neglect of employing vocal and instrumental performers of novelty and merit; and while this continues, we shall venture to say, that the whole, like a sumptuous monument may be admired, but the contents will continue like a *caput mortuum*, until the Governors shall judge it more wise to recur to the old system of entertaining the ears as well as the eyes of the usual visitors of public places.

1791: Dr Langrishe Doyle was organist at Armagh Cathedral, 1776- 80, and then at Christ Church Cathedral in Dublin 1780-1805. In the announcement for what proved to be the last series of concerts run directly for the benefit of the Rotunda, his name appears as the conductor; though it does not appear when the individual detailed programmes are announced.

This final series consisted of eight subscription concerts between 4 March and 6 May. In addition, there were six benefit concerts for the soloists. A total of ten programmes are available for analysis.

The preponderance of Pleyel is interesting in view of his promotion by Cramer and Clementi in London, and the composer's presence there in 1791. The equivalent figures for Haydn and Pleyel at Vauxhall Gardens in 1791 were 61 items by Haydn and 29 by Pleyel.[14]

Pergolesi was represented during this season by a performance of his *Stabat Mater*.

Explanation of the Analytical Table summarising Programmes from 1771-91[15]

The statistical analysis of the frequency of performance of works by named composers is confined to major instrumental pieces. The composers of instrumental concertos are seldom identified, but they are often undoubtedly by the soloist himself in the role of composer-virtuoso. A figure is given for unidentified concerto performances, which would have a bearing on the statistical analysis of instrumental works as a whole. No attempt has been made to identify all the songs contributed by the vocal soloists; the analysis does not therefore include vocal items.

With the exception of the 1784 season, no indication is given in the programmes as to whether Johann or Carl Stamitz is the composer concerned. The same applies to 'Martini' throughout.

The first column in the table gives the date of the season followed by the name of the conductor in charge. The last figure denotes the number of concerts given in the season.

The second column gives the names of the soloists employed and their instruments.

The third column gives the number of programmes which have been analysed, followed by the number of very incomplete programmes which have been taken into account. This last figure is given (in brackets).

The fourth column presents a statistical analysis of the frequency of performance of works by composers of instrumental pieces; and the final column notes the number of performances of unidentified concertos and final items.

The following abbreviations are used:

Vln:	Violin	Fl:	Flute
Vla:	Viola	Ob:	Oboe (Hautboy)
Vcl:	Violoncello	Fg:	Bassoon (abbreviated from *Fagotto*)
Pfte:	Pianoforte		
Voc:	Vocal soloists	Clt:	Clarinet ('Clarionet')
Org:	Organ		

Season Conductor	Soloists	Programmes analysed	Instrumental works		Unidentified Concertos etc.	
1771 Barthélemon 63	Barthélemon (Vln) Fischer (Ob)		Barthélemon J.C. Bach Stamitz	5 1 1		
	Voc:	4	Lord Kelly	1		
1772 Barthélemon 62	Mrs Barthélemon Mr & Mrs Gervasio, Rosselini, Passerini, Miss Shewcraft, Miss Jameson		Jomelli Corelli Gugliemi, T. Arne	1 1 1 1		
1773 S. Murphy 63	Vincent (Ob) Rossellini and Master Tuke (Voc)	0 (1)				
1774 Cramer 69	Vincent (Ob) Ritter (Fg) Voc: Sra Salvagni, San Giorgio, Miss Shewcraft, Mrs Hatton	13 in 1774 & 1775	T. Arne (Organ concertos) Cramer Fischer (Oboe concertos) Handel (Coronation music)	5 3 2 2	'Some favourite concertos'	
1775 Cramer 63	Vachon (Vln) M. Arne (Org) Crossdill (Vcl) Patria (Ob) Jones (Harp) Voc: Sra Salvagni, San Giorgio, Anne Catley, Mrs. Arne		Ritter (Fg concerto)	1		
1776 Pinto 59	Pinto (Vln) Fischer (Ob) M. Arne (Org) Voc: Miss Pinto, Mrs Arne, Miss Jameson	30 (9) in 1776 & 1777	Stamitz Abel J.C. Bach Cannabich Richter Esser	22 17 16 16 10 10	Ob Vln Marches	8 8 13
1777 Pinto 58 + 5			Schwindl T. Arne Toeschi Fischer Pugnani Haydn Borghi (Vln concerto) Giordani, Giardini, Vanhall, Handel, Geminiani: 1 each.	7 6 5 4 3 2 2		

Season Conductor	Soloists	Programmes analysed	Instrumental works		Unidentified Concertos etc.	
1778	Lamotte (Vln)	6	J.C. Bach	7	Ob	5
Lamotte	Voc: V.Rauzzini	(1)	Abel	6	Vln	4
63	du Bellamy,		Rauzzini	3		
	Master Mansergh		Stamitz	2	Marches	4
	Miss Jameson		Jomelli	2		
			Corelli, Esser,			
			T. Arne, Schwindl,			
			Galuppi, Martini,			
			Lord Kelly:			
			1 each.			
1779	Pinto (Vln)	41	Abel	32	Ob	33
Pinto	Patria (Ob)	(3)	J.C. Bach	16	Vln	14 +
63	Carnevale (Vla, '79)		Philidor	22	Vcl	10
	Ashe (Fl, '80)		Cannabich	20	Fl	8
1780	Del Oca (Vcl, 82)		Stamitz	19		
Pinto	Voc: Mrs Connor,		Van Maldere	19	Marches	22
	('79 & '80), Miss		Esser	16		
1781	Palmer ('79), Johnstone		Grétry	16		
Pinto	('80); Tuke ('80 & '81)		Schwindl	16		
57	Mrs Kennedy (3 nights		Rauzzini	7		
	in '80); Miss Jarrett		Martini	7		
1782	('81 & '82); Urbani ('82)		Lord Kelly	7		
Pinto	Castini ('82); Miss		T. Arne	5		
	Phillips (4 nights in		Pugnani	5		
	'82)		Richter	4		
			Urbani	4		
			Handel	3		
			Vanhall	3		
			Toeschi	3		
			Meder	2		
			Lamotte	2		
			Borghi	2		
			Haydn, Fischer,			
			Stanwick, Jomelli,			
			Rush, Raimondi; 1 each			

Season Conductor	Soloists	Programmes analysed	Instrumental works		Unidentified Concertos etc.	
1783 Scheener 57	Scheener (Vln) Voc: Leoni (Counter-tenor), Miss Jameson, Mansergh	10 (2)	Haydn Stamitz Abel Vanhall Esser Grétry Richter Pugnani Philidor J.C. Bach Van Maldere Schwindl, Toeschi, Tenducci, Kotzwara, Giordani, Cannabich, T. Arne: 1 each. Anon. 3.	10 9 6 5 4 4 4 3 3 3 2	Vln Fl Org Marches	8 3 1 3
1784 Barthélemon 38	Barthélemon (Vln) Ashe (Fl) Voc: Duffy, Mrs Barthélemon, Miss Jameson, I. Corry, Mrs Billington	18	Haydn Handel Barthélemon Geminiani J.C. Bach Corelli Abel Van Maldere Vanhall C. Stamitz J. Stamitz Philidor Esser, Grétry, Richter, Rauzzini, Giordani, Clementi, Schroeter, Pugnani. 1 each.	21 20 11 9 7 7 6 5 4 4 3 2	Vln Fl Pfte. 'Full Piece'	7 2 2 1
1785 Raimondi ?	Raimondi (vln) Ashe (Fl) Mahon (Clt) Voc: Miss Wheeler Mrs Arnold, Mrs Billington	11 (1)	Stamitz Raimondi Haydn Corelli Abel, J.C. Bach Grétry Esser, Van Maldere, Philip Cogan: 1 each.	14 13+ 11 6 5 2 2	Vln 'Clarionet' Fl Marches etc.	4 3 1 5

Season Conductor	Soloists	Programmes analysed	Instrumental works		Unidentified Concertos etc.	
1786	Weichsell (Vln)	23	Haydn	31	Vln	20
Weichsell	Ashe (Fl)	(2)	Corelli	19	Fl	21
?	Voc: Waterhouse (86)		Stamitz	8		
	Miss Langrishe (86)	0 for 1788	Richter	8	Marches 18	
1787	Bannister ('86)		Weichsell	6+		
Weichsell	Arrowsmith ('86); Miss		Pugnani	5		
?	Wheeler ('87) Miss Brett		Vanhall	4		
1788	('87); Brett ('87 & '88);		Toeschi	4		
Weichsell	Mrs Arnold (88)		J.C. Bach	4		
1 per week			Grétry	4		
(18?)			Abel	3		
			Lord Kelly	3		
			Martini	3		
			Philidor	2		
			Wagenseil	2		
			Esser, Lamotte, Geminiani, Handel, Cannabich, Jomelli: 1 each.			
1789	Salomon (Vln)	3	Mahon	3+	Vln	1
Salomon	Sperati (Vcl)	(1)	Salomon	3	Clt	1+
24?	Kotzwara (Vla)		Haydn	2	Concertante 1	
	Mahon (Clt & Vln)		Rosetti	2		
	Ashe (Fl)		J.C. Bach, T. Arne,			
	Voc: Miss Brett		Devienne, Mozart			
	and Mrs Arnold		Boccherini: 1 each			
1790	Ashe (Fl)	1	Mahon	2+	Clt	1
Ashe	Mahon (Clt)	+1 (elsewhere)	Haydn	2	Vln	1
Fisher			Pleyel	2	Fl	1
and			Jomelli	2	2 Flts	1
Heron			Ashe	1		
34?					Marches	2
1791	J. Reinagle (Vcl)	10	Pleyel	11	Vcl	7
Langrishe	Mahon (Clt & Vln)		Haydn	7	Vln	8
Doyle	M. Gautherot (Vln)		Gerowitz	5	2 Vlns	1
	Ashe (Fl)				Fl	4
	Erskine (Ob)		Corelli, Rosetti,		Clt	3
8 + 6	Voc: Small;		Pergolesi		Ob	3
	Madame Benda.		1 each.			

NOTES

1. From the handbill advertising the first Irish performance of *Judas Maccabeus* in aid of the Lying-in Hospital, on 11 February 1748.
2. C.P. Curran, *The Rotunda Hospital; its Architects and Craftsmen* (Dublin, 1945), 29.
3. Minutes of the Board of Governors of the Rotunda Hospital, 17 February 1769.
4. For example, Minute of 6 April 1764.
5. The financial aspects will form an important part of a detailed study of the Rotunda concerts between 1749 and 1791, for which this paper could be regarded as 'work in progress'. It will be published by the present author shortly.
6. The original invoice, which is in the archives of the Rotunda Hospital, is quoted in full and accompanied by a facsimile of a portion, in Brian Boydell, *A Dublin Musical Calendar, 1700-1760* (Dublin, 1988), 201.
7. Programme advertised in *Freeman's Journal*, 1-3 August 1776. Note that the terms 'Overture', 'Sinfonia' or 'Symphony' were loosely applied during this period. Haydn's 'London' Symphonies were billed as 'Overtures'.
8. 16 September 1785. Advertisement in *Freeman's Journal*, 3-6 September 1785.
9. 31 May 1780. Advertisement in *Hibernian Journal*, 26-29 May 1780.
10. Advertisement in *Freeman's Journal*, 28-30 June 1774.
11. *Freeman's Journal*, 23-25 and 27-30 May 1775.
12. The Register's Accounts, 1760-1784, in the Rotunda Hospital Archives.
13. *The Collected Correspondence and London Notebooks of Joseph Haydn*, ed. H.C. Robbins Landon (London, 1959), 265. I am indebted to Michael Taylor for pointing out this reference to Scheener.
14. C. Cudworth: 'The Vauxhall "Lists"', *Galpin Society Journal*, xx (1967).
15. I am grateful to Gundhild Lenz for assistance in noting details of programmes published in the Dublin newspapers.

The Creative Process in Irish Traditional Dance Music

MÍCHEÁL Ó SÚILLEABHÁIN

Most studies in Irish traditional music tend to focus on product rather than process (Breathnach, 1971; O'Boyle, 1976; Ó Canainn, 1978; are representative examples). While there have been some attempts to look at systems of performance technique (Bodley, 1973; Shields, 1975; McCullough, 1977), the difficulty of tackling such issues as improvisation and the creative process in general in a music which offers little in the way of theoretical terminology and verbalised concepts has tended to encourage historical and documentary studies rather than studies of the music as a form of creative expression. With the increasing number of Irish oral-tradition musicians studying musicology at university level, however, it seems more and more likely that such studies will emerge in the future – and, furthermore, that the obvious advantages of viewing the tradition from within will in turn offer fresh and important insights into the generative and regenerative process which informs this vibrant musical genre. Any insights in this paper are offered in the same spirit, in that they stem directly from the subjective experience of performing traditional dance music over the past two decades. They do, however, develop some points outlined in an earlier study on improvisation within Irish traditional dance music, as well as being directly related to a study on the highly creative fiddler Tommie Potts (Ó Súilleabháin, 1987a and 1987b).

THE FRAMEWORK

Irish traditional dance music, with very few exceptions, is constructed from basic eight-bar units which, in the standard piece, are made up as follows:

8 bars	8 bars	8 bars	8 bars
A	A	B	B

These units form an important part of the conceptualisation of the musicians and are referred to as 'parts'. The concept of bar has little or no significance as far as the musicians are concerned and is only used by those who are musically literate (still a minority) and, even then, mostly in the context of notation. If such is the case, how do traditional musicians sense the unit in question? In my opinion, the part is perceived on two interactive levels – through the feeling of eight main rhythmic pulses, and through the melodic framework pointed by tonal cadences.

The standard dance-tune consists of two different parts, each being 'doubled' (i.e. repeated with or without some modification). Occasionally in certain pieces, the parts are 'singled' (i.e. not repeated) but this is very much the exception and applies mainly to reels. Furthermore, in a relatively small number of cases, dance-tunes are found with three or more parts. Regardless of the number of parts, however, by playing through the entire piece once the musician covers what he calls one 'round'. A round, therefore, may be thirty-two bars in length (if the parts are doubled in a standard two-part piece) or sixteen bars (if the parts are singled). Similarly, the length of the round increases with the addition of extra parts which can normally reach a total of no more than six.

In a standard two-part piece with the parts doubled, the thirty-two bar round is perceived by the musicians as being in two distinct sections: the first half (covering the first part and its doubling) which is called the 'tune', and the second half (i.e. second part and its doubling) which is called the 'turn'. The tune is normally contained within the lower octave, while the turn usually breaks into the higher octave. There is an ambiguity here in the folk terminology in that the word 'tune' can refer to the first half of a round, and also to the piece itself in its entirety.

At the present time, the norm in traditional performance is that two rounds of a piece be covered and that the player then moves onto a second piece where he again covers two rounds. This can vary greatly, however, depending on the formality or informality of the performance situation, the type and length of tune selected, and the individual approach of the musician in question. At any rate, the overall structure of the round with its constituent parts reflects an understood socio-musical agreement among the musicians which has its origins in the past interaction between music and dance in the Irish tradition. Such a structure is the basic element in an agreed language for music-making of an informal and spontaneous kind.

Figure 1, therefore, is a graphic representation of the framework of a standard two-part piece with the parts doubled. Example (a) is a linear representation while example (b) is a circular one.

THE PROCESS

The concept of 'turning a tune' is widespread, particularly among the older

Example (a)

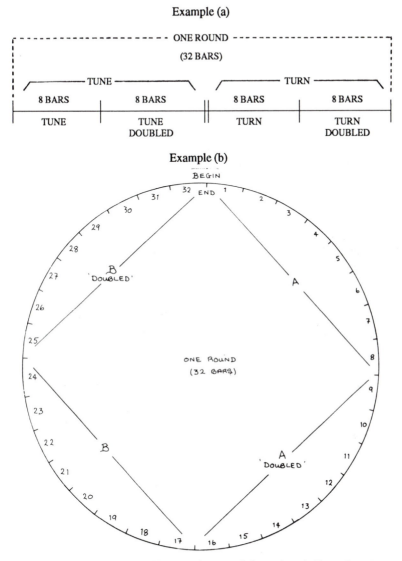

Example (b)

FIGURE 1: The standard thirty-two bar round shown here in linear (Ex. a) and cyclic (Ex. b) forms

musicians at the present time, and it reflects similar usages in Irish such as *ag casadh cheoil* ('turning' music) and *cas amhrán* ('turn' a song). In this way, 'turning' has a wider meaning which could be taken as synonymous with the creative process itself. One further folk-term which deals with something other than the framework of a piece, may provide us with another clue to this process: the term 'setting' as it is used by musicians to denote a particular version or

variant of a dance-tune. The word 'setting' itself implies a process whereby
something which is fluid or moving becomes in some way static, and it is to
this process that we must now turn our attention.

In so doing, I wish to trace a common thread through four improvisatory
aspects of the music – those of phrasing, rhythm, pitch, and structure. This
common thread concerns the creative tension between the inaudible and the
audible in musical performance – the totally or partially inaudible model on the
one hand, and the fully audible 'surface sound' on the other.

1 The Phrasing Dimension: Natural Phrasing   Since breaking the eight-bar
structure of the part is taboo, any setting which takes place must occur within
the part. It is obvious that merely remaining within the structure of the
round/tune/turn/part in no way guarantees an acceptable performance, and that
the musical essence is clearly within the form rather than being the form itself.
We must examine, therefore, those constituent elements within a normal part
which are not verbalised by the musicians. It is indeed possible to break the
eight-bar unit into smaller non-verbalised elements which the musicians are
aware of on a purely musical level. Illustration 1 shows how the standard
eight-bar part may be logically broken into two four-bar segments and even
further into two-bar segments. While we might view these segments as
representing the 'natural phrasing' (not a folk term) of the piece, the reality of

ILLUSTRATION 1: The 'natural phrasing' in the first part of a double jig (untitled)

traditional performance shows how the musician interacts with this 'natural
phrasing' in such a way as to express his own musical thought through a
selective phrasing of his own design. Illustration 2 shows a brief example of
this in a flute performance with bodhrán accompaniment. Phrasing, in this
instance, can serve to mark one aspect of what we refer to as the 'style' of a
player. Where that style is shared by others in a particular locality, we are
dealing with a recognisable regional style. While such regional styles form an
interactive base against which the individual creativity of the musician may be
measured, the generative force which gives rise to regional styles in the first
place is obviously that of the creative energy of the individual as manifested in

ILLUSTRATION 2: Variation of the 'natural phrasing' in the flute playing of J.P. Downes (accompanied by Marcus Walsh on Bodhrán). From Ó Súilleabháin (1984: 13)

this case within the dimension of phrasing. In making the choice between one phrasing length rather than another, the performing musician is concerned with that which is most human in music-making. In this way the music comes alive and justifies its existence. Such justification occurs on many levels, of course, and all of these levels are interactive. Out of this complex web of decision making we will next single out the particularly vital one of rhythm.

2 The Rhythmic Dimension: Motor Rhythm   While all commentaries on Irish traditional dance music content themselves with definitions of the various tune-types in terms of time signatures, for the musicians themselves such categories as double-jigs, single-jigs, slip-jigs, reels, hornpipes and the variety of forms used to accompany set-dancing, are identified themselves primarily in terms of the rhythmic flow. Thus to a traditional musician a piece with an underlying motor rhythm normally expressed in literate terms as:

is a double-jig. The fact that the written symbol does not allow for the elongation of certain notes need not concern us here. What is relevant at this point is that even when this basic flow of more or less even beats is absent, it nonetheless manifests its presence within the meaning of the music. Thus, a double-jig which begins is not merely meaningful in terms of what it is, but also carries a meaning in terms of its relationship with what it is not, i.e., it is not the double-jig motor rhythm which lies at the base of all such pieces in this category. Here is yet again another aspect of the creative process at work whereby the musician interacts with a given rhythmic flow in such a way as to allow his own musical thought free rein within the traditional norms of rhythmic possibility.

The rhythmic diversity of a player's style will be closely allied to the particular instrument he is playing. The basic press-and- draw of the ten-key melodeon, for example, leaves its rhythmic mark through the interaction of the bellows with the musical flow. A long note may be desirable just as much for the reason of inflating the bellows as for any purely musical one. This particular instrument-based rhythmic characteristic has found its way into some two-row button accordion styles and in this way has contributed towards shaping an identifiable Irish style of 'box' playing. The single-action piano accordian, however, does not have this physical limitation of a directional change in the bellows for each note and this has given rise to constant difficulties which this instrument has experienced in being widely accepted as 'traditional'. There are, of course, many other stylistic aspects of box playing which contribute actively to the acceptance/rejection process – notably the harmonic one – but in this instance we can see how the question of rhythmic choice can be integral to an instrument's traditional identity.

It might be mentioned in passing that ornamentation within the dance music tradition is largely a rhythmic rather than a melodic one: the aptly named 'cut' (single upper grace note), for example, has articulation as its prime function, while the piping 'cran' is a dramatic development of this involving a sucession of cuts on the low D or low E of the chanter in such a way as to produce a rapid triplet/quadruplet/quintuplet depending on the dance meter in use.

What is important in this instance, however, is the manner in which the player varies the basic motor rhythm in order to achieve the desired rhythmic effect. This effect is frequently referred to by traditional musicians as 'lift'. My own experience has been that this quality of 'lift' is achieved in any one of two ways – or through a combination of both. On the one hand, the desired rhythmic vitality can be achieved through the actual process of variability within the many possible rhythmic cells. In this case the lift seems to be generated through the actual process of decision-making which takes place at a rhythmic level. It would be wrong, however, to accept the common notion of the primary importance of the variability of durations (the cells out of which all rhythm is itself constructed). There are many instances of players who are highly respected for the feeling of lift which they generate in their playing and yet who vary the durational/rhythmic aspect of the music to a surprisingly small degree. In these cases, the generative factor appears to lie in the handling of accentuation in such a way as to achieve the desired effect. In simple terms, the feeling of lift is an invitation to dance – hardly a suprising one considering the strong dance basis of this tradition. The body gestures of the musicians along with the sympathetic body gestures of the listeners in any session event (performance context) is a visible manifestation of the point under discussion. Here again, therefore, the musician is at his most human in taking musical options on a separate though related level to the phrasing one previously discussed.

3 The Pitch Dimension: Set Accented Tones   What Adams (1976) describes as 'the rather elusive concept of melodic contour' has frequently beeen used in analytical procedures. While it can lead to some interesting insights in the case of Irish traditional dance music, it is, I believe, of less importance to the musicians themselves than the idea of set accented tones (not a folk term) which I now wish to introduce.

Within a performance, the musician would appear to be holding on to certain individual tones which occur at important accentuated points. It is the occurrence, or deliberate non-occurrence, of these tones which appears to provide the necessary point of reference for the performer. Illustration 3 shows a typical setting of the opening of the four bars of the double-jig 'The Old Grey Goose' (example (a)) with the eight set accented tones boxed. In order to demonsrate that these tones are at the heart of the tune's identity, and that any extended interference with them is in the nature of a contradiction of the tune itself, I have included five projected variants of my own (Illustration 3, examples (b) to (f)) which progressively disturb the set accented tones. Where these tones are retained in the variants, I have boxed them accordingly.

In example (d) we have three new succesive tones which comprise a variation sufficient to begin to move the tune away from its basic nature towards a new one. The immediate return to the standard tones, however, reinforces the original tune's identity. If the position of the set accented tones slips further – as it does in example (e) of Illustration 3 – a new tune emerges as far as traditional musicians are concerned. Example (f), however, exists somewhere between examples (d) and (e) and may still be identifiable as 'The Old Grey Goose'. It is the total context of the full piece, however, which would decide its identity one way or the other.

These set accented tones, of course, are the stepping stones of a piece's melodic contour, and the question arises whether this contour is ultimately of greater significance than the tones themselves. Without denying the importance of contour as a force within musical thought in this tradition, it would appear that as far as conscious musical perception goes, the set accented tones are the more important element. What I mean is that the musicians are frequently aware of several different settings of a piece where these settings can be seen to share largely the same set accented tones but with certain tones altered to such anextent as to merit the designation of a different setting by those musicians.

ILLUSTRATION 3: Set Accented Tones in the opening four bars of 'The Old Grey Goose'
with variants

As against that, in instances where the melodic contour is retained but within a
different mode – i.e. where the set accented tones are disturbed through the
alteration in the tone/semitone intervallic relationship which typifies each mode
– then the pieces are perceived by the musicians as being separate. In my
experience, even when this relationship in contour is pointed out to the
musicians, it is still perceived as existing between two different tunes rather
than between two settings of the same tune.

An excellent example of this is found in two very well-known reels which
share to a great extent the same melodic contour but are in different modes: 'My
Love is in America' and 'The Dunmore Lasses'. Both pieces are shown in
Illustration 4 while some of the contour relationships are shown in Illustration
5.

A final example of these set accented tones at work may be seen in Illustration
6 where transcriptions from the fiddle playing of Patrick Kelly of Cree, Co.
Clare show the relative stability of the accented tones. Interestingly enough, the

ILLUSTRATION 4: Outlines of typical settings
4(a)

4(b)

occurrence of the quadruplets in this example points to the possibility of retaining the set accented tones while shifting to a different meter. The phenomenon of dance tunes of different metrical types being related was originally pointed out by O'Neill (1913) in a chapter entitled 'The Development of Irish Folk Music'. A similar relationship can exist between non-metrical airs

ILLUSTRATION 5: Some of the contour relationships between 'My Love is in America' and 'The Dunmore Lasses'.

ILLUSTRATION 6: Extracts from transcriptions of the playing of 'Banish Misfortune' by the fiddler Patrick Kelly of Cree, Co. Clare.

and various forms of dance tunes. When one examines the relationship between such dance tunes in the light of our discussion on set accented tones, it is immediately evident that it is these tones which lie at the heart of that relationship. A single example will suffice: Illustration 7 shows the opening of three related tunes of this sort with the relevant tones boxed – a set dance in hornpipe meter, a double-jig and a reel.

Just as the creative player counteracts the 'natural phrasing' with the phrasing of his own choice, and just as on the rhythmic level he balances the underlying motor rhythm with a diverse array of rhythmic devices of his own choosing, so within the dimension of pitch the set accented tones provide an underlying framework for a form of pitch-play which takes place largely between these set tones but which may at times disturb the tones themselves. In this way the regenerative process from which new tunes emerge out of old is set in motion.

ILLUSTRATION 7: Three related dance times in different metres
(from the fiddle playing of Paddy Glackin).

4 The Structural Dimension: Interchangeable Segments   The detailed structure or form of these dance-tunes is made up of a complex web of relationships existing at every level of musical performance. I wish to draw attention here to one definable aspect of the structural dimension of the creative process by showing how certain melodic segments are at times interchangeable within a piece. Furthermore, it would appear that while certain segments remain consistently untouched, others have a ratio of flexibility in terms of their interchangeability. 'The Old Grey Goose', already quoted in part in illustration 3, is a good example of this. This six-part double-jig was originally published by O'Neill in his *Dance Music of Ireland* (see illustration 8). Illustration 9 shows the set accented tones of a typical current setting of the piece. Alternate groups of four set accented tones are given in some instances in Illustration 9, and those segments with a high rate of interchangeability are linked by arrowed lines. Notice how the final two bars of each part remain virtually untouched in contrast with the flexibility of other segments. The settings in Illustration 9 are an amalgam of the improvisational possibilities which I have heard in this double-jig as performed by many players over the past fifteen years.

ILLUSTRATION 8:
'The Old Grey Goose' as printed in O'Neill's *Dance Music of Ireland*

ILLUSTRATION 9: Interchangeable segments within the six-part double-jig
'The Old Grey Goose'.

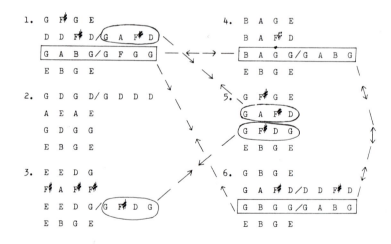

Finally, as an example of both set accented tones and interchangeable segments operating simultaneously within a specific traditional performance, Illustration 11 shows a transcription of the second part and its doubling of 'The Rambling Pitchfork' as played by Patrick Kelly of Cree. In this instance, bars 1, 3, 5, 9, 11 and 13 could be in all cases an exact repeat of bar 1, and this basic structural approach is shown in Illustration 10. Kelly, however, who was known for his individual settings, improvises instead around the set accented tones of D and F, while in bar 13 he inserts a repetition of bar 12, achieving a kind of musical climax which signals the end of the piece.

ILLUSTRATION 10: The basic structural format of the turn (and its 'doubling') of the double-jig 'The Rambling Pitchfork' (author's reconstruction).

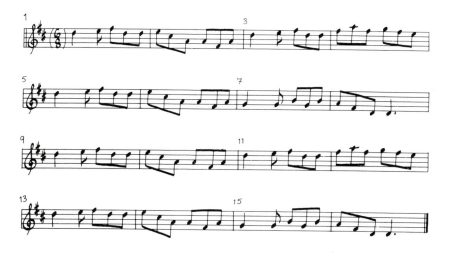

ILLUSTRATION 11: A transcription of the final playing of the turn (and its doubling) of 'The Rambling Pitchfork' as played by Patrick Kelly of Cree, Co. Clare.

The reconstructed basic structural format shown in Illustration 10, therefore, is the partially inaudible structural model against which the player improvises. By making full use of the allowed traditional techniques between the set accented tones – and on occasion altering the set tones themselves – an overall musical architecture is worked out which the player finds pleasing. Where the new format achieves something of a permanence through repetition, the result is referred to as a 'new setting'.

Here then is our fourth and final example of the creative process as it manifests itself in four musical dimensions. In the case of all four, I have singled out the common thread of an existing tension between the inaudible and the audible within the music. Just as the round itself is inaudible and yet informs every aspect of traditional dance music performance, so the fully or partially inaudible elements outlined here – natural phrasing, motor rhythm, set accented tones, and basic structural format – serve as an essential basis for a creative and individual selection of musical options whereby the player manifests firstly his musical idiolect, secondly his musical dialect, and finally the musical language itself which we identify as Irish traditional dance music.

REFERENCES

Adams, Charles R., 'Contour Typology', *Ethnomusicology*, 20, no. 2 (1976), 179-215

Bodley, Seóirse, 'Technique and Structure in Sean-Nós Singing', *Éigse Cheol Tíre / Irish Folk Music Studies*, 1 (1973), 44-63.

Breathnach, Breandán, *Folk Music and Dances of Ireland* (Dublin., 1971).

McCullough, Lawrence E., 'Style in Traditional Irish Music', *Ethnomusicology*, 21, no. 1 (1977), 85-97.

Ó Boyle, Seán, *The Irish Song Tradition* (Dublin, 1976).

Ó Canainn, Tomás, *Traditional Music in Ireland* (London, 1978).

O'Neill, Francis, *Irish Minstrels and Musicians* (Chicago, 1913).

___ *The Dance Music of Ireland* (Chicago, 1907).

Ó Súilleabháin, Mícheál, 'Gnéithe de Cheardaíocht Phádraig Uí Cheallaigh', *Comhar*, 38, no. 10 (1977) 26-27.

___ *The Bodhrán: A Practical Introduction* (Dublin, 1984): Ó Súilleabháin 1984.

___ 'Tourner Un Air: L'Improvisation dans la Musique Traditionnalle Irlandaise', *L'Improvisation dans les Musiques de Tradition Orale*, ed. Bernard Lortat-Jacob (Paris, 1987): Ó Súilleabháin 1987a.

___ *Innovation and Tradition in the Music of Tommie Potts* (PhD dissertation, The Queen's University of Belfast, 1987): Ó Súilleabháin 1987b.

The Function of Strokes in Sixteenth-Century Sources of English Keyboard Music

DESMOND HUNTER

The application of grace signs in the form of oblique strokes is one of the most striking features of early English keyboard music and yet still one of the most puzzling aspects of its notation. Only one sign, the double stroke, enjoyed widespread currency. It appears in virtually every source of English keyboard music of the virginalist era but surprisingly is not explained by any contemporary English theorist. Thomas Morley's references to keyboard music, in his treatise of 1597, concentrate on definitions of the various genres popular in England at the end of the sixteenth century.[1] Although Charles Butler refers to the 'Ornaments of Melodi and Harmoni', he does not in fact deal with embellishment.[2] In a much later treatise John Playford makes a brief reference to keyboard graces:

> But as for the true Fingering and severall graces used in the playing on this Instrument [the virginals], it cannot be set down in words, but is to be obtained by the help and Directions of the Skilfull Teachers, and the constant practice of the Learner.[3]

Almost one hundred years earlier, in 1565, an important Spanish tutor was published: Tomás de Santa María's *Libro llamado arte de tañer fantasía*. One chapter of this work is devoted to ornamentation and the author gives directions on how and where to execute ornaments.[4] There are contributions to the subject by other Spanish theorists, notably Bermudo (*Declaración de Instrumentos musicales*, 1555), Venegas de Henestrosa (*Libro de Cifra Nueva*, 1557) and Correa de Arauxo (*Facultad Orgánica*, 1626).[5] Although ornament/grace signs in contemporary Spanish keyboard music are rare, the wealth of information on keyboard ornamentation in the treatises, particularly in Santa María's work, provides a stark contrast with the almost total lack of information in contemporary English sources. This does not mean however that the English attached little or no importance to the art of ornamentation. On the contrary, it suggests that they may have been very conscious of the importance of preserving the improvisatory nature of ornamentation, a point which is underlined by Roger North, writing around 1700:

> It is the hardest task that can be to pen the manner of artificiall Gracing an upper part; It hath bin attempted, and in print, but with woefull Effect . . . the Spirit of that art is Incomunicable by wrighting, therefore it is almost Inexcusable to attempt it.[6]

Evidence of the emergence of the double-stroke sign as an indicator of embellishment in English keyboard music can be found in several sources dating from around the middle of the sixteenth century. The earliest continental source to make use of the double stroke is Susanne van Soldt's Book (London, British Library[Lbl] Add. 29485), which according to Alan Curtis may have been written mainly in Antwerp around 1570.[7] It appears that additions were made after the book was brought to England, probably by the English music master of Susanne van Soldt.[8] Furthermore, there is a strong possibility that all the grace signs were added to the manuscript after its arrival in England. The signs in the main part of the manuscript are in a different colour of ink to the music and appear to be in the same hand as those given in the pieces which were added at the end of the book. It seems clear therefore that the use of oblique strokes in keyboard music to indicate graces originated with the English.

The earliest use of strokes in English keyboard sources however was not in connection with embellishment. Indeed, during the sixteenth century the signs fulfilled several functions and it was only towards the end of the century that they became associated primarily with embellishment. The period from around 1530 to around 1570 is therefore an important one in the history of the signs; and the main purpose of this essay is to trace the changing function of the strokes during this period. The sources relevant to this study are listed in the table given below; and in the discussion which follows application in each source receives separate treatment.

TABLE OF SOURCES[9]

Siglum	Shelf-mark/Title	Date
Lbl	Roy. App. 56	c.1530
Lbl	Roy. App. 58	c.1530
Eam	Evesham Abbey Bible	c.1540
Lbl	Add. 29996 (early layers)	c.1548 – c.1555
Lbl	Add. 15233	c.1550

Obr	156	*c.* 1550
Lbl	Add. 5465 (The Fayrfax Manuscript)	*c.* 1550
Lbl	Add. 60577	*c.* 1550
Lbl	Add. 30513 (The Mulliner Book)	main part *c.*1550 additional layer *c.*1570
Och	371	*c.*1560
Och	1034A	*c.*1570
Dtc	410 (The Dublin Virginal Manuscript)	*c.* 1570

During the sixteenth century the form of notation used for English keyboard music was subject to considerable variation; this is most evident perhaps in the composition of staves, particularly in the sources which date from the first half of the century. In the early layers of *Add. 29996*, staves vary in composition from five to nine lines and a composite staff, ranging from ten to fifteen lines, is used occasionally. A composite staff is used also in the early part of the *Mulliner Book*. In the *Evesham Abbey Bible* the copyist drew mainly seven- and eight-line staves. The configuration which became the norm for virginalist music, consisting of six-line staves (the so-called 'Anglo-Dutch' format), was used in *Och 371* and *1034A*. In view of notational inconsistencies it is not surprising that the meaning of the signs (given mainly in the form of single and double strokes) also varied to some extent. Clearly copyists did not always use the signs with similar intent. It should be noted however that there is little variation in the positioning of the signs in the sixteenth-century sources. The strokes tend to be attached to the notes affected:

i) either drawn through or positioned at the end of the stem of a note-value lower than a semibreve;

ii) drawn through the note-head of a semibreve.

Lbl Roy. App. 56

This manuscript has been described as 'the oldest extant source of keyboard plainsong settings'.[10] It is also the earliest surviving source in which single- and double-stroke signs are used. Single-stroke signs drawn horizontally through the stems of notes are used on fol.1ᵛ as a visual aid, to clarify the movement of a voice in the middle of the texture as it moves between the staves. The main function of the single stroke however is as a correction sign; and in this form it identifies notes which were notated in error at a level too low. On fol. 2 for instance, the sign is drawn horizontally through the stem of a crotchet indicating that the note-value should be read as a minim. This method of correction was not associated exclusively with keyboard music; it was applied, where necessary, in the vocal music recorded in the contemporary manuscript, *Roy. App. 58*. The only use of the double stroke in *Roy. App. 56* appears to be as a cancellation sign, in which form the number of strokes drawn was probably arbitrary.

Lbl Roy. App. 58

Several of the keyboard pieces recorded in this source are of considerable interest from the point of view of style: 'A hornepype' by Hugh Aston, 'My lady careys dompe' and 'The short mesure off my lady wynkfylds rownde', the latter two given anonymously. Apart from occasional use of the single stroke as a correction sign, single and double strokes are used to cancel notes drawn in error: on fols. 38ᵛ and 39, in Aston's 'A hornepype' (✗ , ✗ , ✗), and on fol.47, in 'My lady careys dompe' (✗). In view of the limited function of the signs in the early decades of the century the copyist was able to adopt this method of cancellation without ambiguity. Cancellation was not always effected in such a controlled manner; elsewhere in *Roy. App. 58* the scoring out of copying mistakes is somewhat less elegant.

EAM EVESHAM ABBEY BIBLE

A copy of the first edition of the Matthew Bible of 1537, which was the property of Evesham Abbey before the Dissolution of the Monasteries, contains music on three pages: on the reverse of the title-page, the page before 'The Prophetes in Englysh' and the page preceding the Gospel according to St. Matthew. The music was entered and probably composed by one John Alcester around 1540.[11] Two of the pages contain pieces intended for performance on the keyboard. The piece entitled 'for the Regallus the Virginallus and the Dulcemers', which could not be managed by one performer, includes two single-stroke signs: one is drawn horizontally through the stem of a crotchet indicating a correction of the notated value; the other is drawn obliquely through a semibreve (see Example 1b). Clearly this latter sign is related to neither correction nor cancellation. It seems likely that it was used in this context as an abbreviation, indicating a division similar to that notated in the preceding bars. A similar passage occurs earlier in the piece (see Example 1a); and a comparison of bars 28 and 52 suggests that the single stroke in the latter should probably be realised as a dotted minim f" followed by quavers e" and f".

EXAMPLE 1: 'For the Regallus the Virginallus and the Dulcemers' / Alcester *Evesham Abbey Bible*

(a) bars 25-29

(b) bars 49-53

There are two pieces on the final page of music: 'Non Exspextat' and 'The Trompetts'. There are three double-stroke signs in the first piece, each of which graces a minim (see Example 2). The application suggests that the sign is possibly an abbreviation for the form of division notated in bars 1-3 and in bar 6. The *schneller* in bar 5 deserves comment. This form of embellishment is only rarely notated in early English keyboard music (there is another example in

EXAMPLE 2: 'Non Exspextat' / [Alcester?] *Evesham Abbey Bible*
(a)

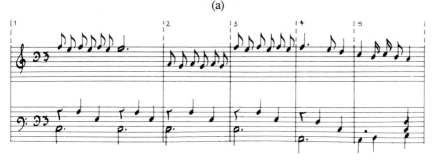

Add. 60577; see below); however, it may often be indicated by a grace sign. An interesting parallel may be drawn with Ammerbach's *Mordanten*.[12]

Lbl Add. 29996

The keyboard music in this large, composite manuscript was entered at different stages between around 1548 and around 1650 by various copyists including Thomas Tomkins. In examining the signs in this source it is important therefore to distinguish the sections. The sixteenth-century sections consist of i) fols. 6-48 (*c*.1548) and ii) most of the music on fols. 49-71 and 158-183 (*c*.1555).[13]

i)

The copyist(s) of this section made frequent use of the single stroke as a correction sign. The sign served other purposes however, and on fol. 41 a single stroke which is drawn through the note-head of a semibreve appears to indicate the merging of two voices (see Example 3). Application of the sign on fol. 43 is puzzling (see Example 4). John Caldwell suggests that mordents may be

EXAMPLE 3: 'Felix namque' / ap Rhys *Add. 29996*, fol. 41

EXAMPLE 4: 'Veritas mea' / Coxsum *Add. 29996*, fol. 43

implied.[14] It seems unlikely however that the sign relates to embellishment, particularly in view of the fact that nowhere else in the sixteenth-century sections of the manuscript is a single stroke used as a grace sign. It is possible that there is a connection between the application of the sign in this context and the notated rhythm on the lower staff, the sign serving as a visual aid.

The double stroke makes its first appearance on fol. 10 and is used intermittently throughout the section to grace minims. It has been suggested that the double stroke functions as an abbreviation for a simple division in this section of the manuscript.[15] This would not appear to be a convincing explanation for every occurrence. In the passages quoted at Example 5 the order of the division and the corresponding sign is reversed. In these instances it would seem

EXAMPLE 5(a): 'Felix namque' / Redford *Add. 29996*, fol. 40

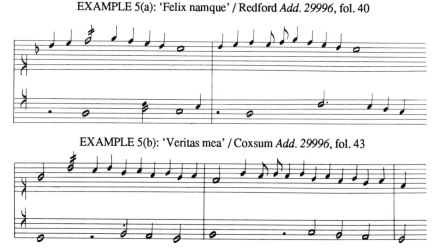

EXAMPLE 5(b): 'Veritas mea' / Coxsum *Add. 29996*, fol. 43

appropriate to realise the double stroke in a way which provides some variation of the repeated figuration. It is possible however that the sign is used elsewhere as an abbreviation. On fol. 18 there is a close similarity between the contexts of the double-stroke sign and a notated turn (see Example 6). The turn is given in the penultimate bar of a piece by John Redford, 'A solis ortus cardine', which concludes in the first system of the page. In the anonymous 'Corus nove ierusalem', which begins in the second system, the copyist possibly adopted the time-saving measure of using signs to indicate turns. It should be noted that the figuration in Example 6b is persistent throughout the piece. Furthermore, the turn is a frequently notated division in sixteenth-century keyboard music.

Application of the double stroke on fol. 40ᵛ is striking (see Example 7). The sign is drawn through the note-head of each of four consecutive semibreves. This is the first occurrence in the manuscript of the sign being applied to a note-value other than a minim. It is possible that a form of embellishment is implied by each of the signs, but it is conceivable that there is a connection with

EXAMPLE 6(a): 'A solis ortus cardine' / Redford *Add. 29996*, fol. 18

EXAMPLE 6(b): 'Corus nove ierusalem' / [anon.] *Add. 29996*, fol. 18

EXAMPLE 7: 'Felix namque' / Redford *Add. 29996*, fol. 40ᵛ

the notated rhythm on the lower staff (see above for a reference to similar application of the single stroke).

ii)

In the second section of the manuscript the single stroke continues to function as a correction sign. One single stroke, which is drawn obliquely through a crotchet stem on fol. 168ᵛ however, appears to indicate an inflection (the note affected is b' and b'-flat seems to be implied). Several double-stroke signs appear to relate to embellishment and possibly indicate shakes (the notes graced are minims). Possible additional functions of the double stroke in this section are to point imitative entries (see fol. 162ᵛ) and to underline a sequence (fol. 177ᵛ).

Lbl Add. 15233

This source contains keyboard music by one composer: John Redford. There are very few occurrences of the single- and double-stroke signs. Indeed, apart from the occasional application of the single stroke as a correction sign, the double stroke is given only at the beginning of an untitled setting of 'Felix namque' (see Example 8). This piece is preserved also in *Add. 29996* (fol. 42) but the opening is not graced in this source. The treatment for such openings recommended by Correa, who was 'more or less in touch with the English style',[16] is of some interest:

> Y aduiertase que siempre que entrare la derecha con sola na voz, a de ser . . . con el dedo tercero, y con quiebro en el organo, y redoble en el monacordia.

> (And observe that always when the right [hand] enters with only one voice, it is to be . . . with the third finger, and with a quiebro on the organ and a redoble on the clavichord.)[17]

EXAMPLE 8: ['Felix namque'] / Redford *Add. 15233*, fol. 6ᵛ

Although Correa distinguishes between the type of embellishment appropriate to the organ and the clavichord, he nevertheless advocates that the opening should be graced. Even when three voices enter together Correa recommends taking two with the left hand so that the right hand may be free to perform a *quiebro* or *redoble*.[18] This tendency to embellish openings may have been conventional in England and the signs in Example 8 may be indicative of such a practice.

Lbl Add. 30513 (The Mulliner Book)

The importance of this source is clearly stated by Denis Stevens:

> Three quarters of the total number of pieces . . . are unique: there are no copies of them anywhere, and if the manuscript had not been so well looked after the largest single source for the instrumental music of Redford, Blitheman and Tallis, would have been lost. And countless authorities would have to state that no organ music by Shepherd, Farrant, Newman, Shelbye and Heath had come down to us.[19]

The main section of the *Mulliner Book* (fols. 6ᵛ-115) dates from the middle of the century. The pieces at the beginning of the manuscript were entered at a later date. This later section appears to be contemporary with the *Dublin Virginal Manuscript* with which it has an important feature in common (see below).

Mulliner i) Single-, double-, triple- and quadruple- stroke signs are used in this source. The single stroke is used only as a correction sign. A principal function of the other signs is to clarify the part-writing when the parts cross. (Occasionally the application seems to have been necessitated because of careless copying.) In the passage quoted at Example 9 the strokes facilitate the reading of the highest parts. Triple-stroke signs are used occasionally elsewhere to identify the merging of two parts; in *Add. 29996* the copyist used a single stroke for this purpose (see above).

EXAMPLE 9: [untitled] / [anon.] *Mulliner Book*, fol. 17

There is interesting application of the signs on fol. 12 (see Example 10). The double stroke is applied to crotchets in the midst of a busy quaver line. A triple stroke is used also but it may not carry a different meaning. The bass line in the piece in question has mainly quaver movement and Mulliner could be forgiven for copying the third last bass note in the bar quoted as a quaver rather than a crotchet. Mulliner may have realised his error and added a correction sign; and it is conceivable that, in view of his own error, he decided to identify clearly all the crotchets in the bar by drawing two or three strokes through their stems. The angle at which the final sign is drawn (somewhat less acute than the others) would support this interpretation.

EXAMPLE 10: ['Miserere'] / Redford *Mulliner Book*, fol. 12

Double- and triple-stroke signs are used occasionally in connection with embellishment. Robert Donington suggests that the double stroke is used in the *Mulliner Book* as an abbreviation: 'the sign tends to appear where space is cramped but the written-out convention [a shake] where space allows'.[20] This view cannot be supported; indeed, it is seriously weakened by the fact that the copyist occasionally created more space by extending stave lines into the margin of a page. There is similar extension of stave lines in other sources, usually to accommodate a written-out shake.[21] On fol. 8 a pair of double-stroke signs is given on the penultimate beat of a piece (see Example 11) and in view of the cadential context some form of decoration would seem appropriate. It might be conjectured that the sign is used to indicate a more rapid form of the preceding four-note division.

EXAMPLE 11: ['Audi benigne Conditor'] / Carleton *Mulliner Book*, fol. 8

The only passage in which the triple-stroke seems to relate to embellishment is at the beginning of the first 'Gloria tibi Trinitas' setting by Blitheman (see Example 12); and a parallel may be drawn with the context of the written-out *schneller* in the *Evesham Abbey Bible*. It cannot be assumed that the triple stroke implies a more elaborate embellishment than the double stroke. The addition of a stroke may be analogous with the addition of a tail to a note-value; that is to say, it may have durational significance, implying a short, crisp grace. David Wulstan associates Blitheman's triple stroke with rapidity of execution.[22]

EXAMPLE 12: 'Gloria tibi trinitas' / Blitheman *Mulliner Book*, fol. 88

Mulliner ii)   To return to the three pieces at the beginning of the manuscript, which are representative of a later style, the double stroke is used in the second and single- and double-stroke signs in the third; in every case the strokes appear to be used as grace signs. The single strokes in the third piece grace triads; and either three single-stroke signs are used simultaneously or two are combined with a double stroke (see Example 13).[23] The gracing possibly implies elaborate arpeggiation of each triad. There is one further occurrence in this piece of a

EXAMPLE 13(a): ['Galliard'] / [anon.] *Mulliner Book*, fols. 4-4ᵛ

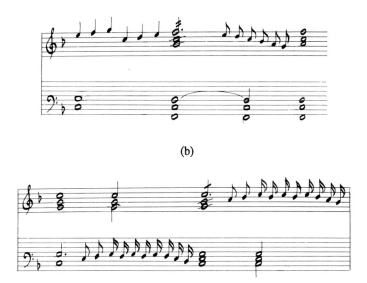

(b)

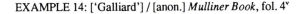

triad graced with a combination of signs, as in Example 13a; in each case the note graced with a double stroke is part of a line which then descends to a point of rest. Where the gracing is a combination of single-stroke signs only, there is no linear continuity. In view of the context of Example 13a, and the similar occurrence (on fol. 4ᵛ) referred to above, the reason for this application may have been to ensure that the elaboration of the triad would conclude with the sounding of the note graced with the double stroke. Not all triads are graced, and one on fol. 3ᵛ is graced with only one sign: a double stroke, which is drawn through the stem of the highest note. Elsewhere, the double stroke possibly indicates a short shake. In the passage quoted at Example 14 the application of the signs suggests realisation involving alternation with the lower-auxiliary note. In this connection it should be noted that an undershake is notated at the beginning of the first piece (see fol. 3 and *Musica Britannica*, vol. i, no. 0).

EXAMPLE 14: ['Galliard'] / [anon.] *Mulliner Book*, fol. 4ᵛ

The use of the single stroke in this section of the *Mulliner Book* can be paralleled in the contemporary *Dublin Virginal Manuscript* (see below).

Och 371

This is the earliest source for Byrd's keyboard music and it contains also the earliest keyboard piece based on the hexachord, a setting by White. Furthermore, there are early examples of the 'In nomine' genre, by Tallis and Strowgers. Apart from the conventional use of the single stroke as a correction sign, double-stroke signs are given on fourteen pages. Not all of the double strokes are the work of the original copyist; those in a different hand appear to have been added later, possibly much later.

The gracing at the opening of the anonymous 'Miserere', which begins on fol. 14ᵛ, is typical of the consistent application throughout this piece (see Example 15). The positioning of the sharp sign before the first note on the lower staff is interesting. It is not unusual of course for a sharp sign to precede the note to which it refers by several beats; there are numerous instances of this in the *Mulliner Book* (see Example 9). In the piece under consideration however all the chromatic signs except the first one are positioned immediately before the notes to which they refer. It is possible therefore that the chromatic sign at the beginning provides a clue to the realisation of the first double-stroke grace sign in the lower part; that is say, the implied grace may be an undershake with the lower-auxiliary note sharpened. Elsewhere in the piece, realisation of the double stroke as a short shake seems likely.

EXAMPLE 15: 'Miserere' / [anon.] *Och 371*, fol. 14ᵛ

The meaning of the application on one particular page would seem to be fairly clear (see Example 16). The form of quaver figuration which prefixes the graced e' in bar three often precedes a written-out shake; and in this context a similar form of embellishment is probably implied. It appears that the copyist notated part of bar two incorrectly and the notes were subsequently scored out. The sequential writing suggests that the quaver figuration in bar two should be followed by minims c'-sharp and d'. Similar figuration is given in bar four; and perhaps the sign given on the first note in the upper part in bar five has been misplaced and should in fact grace the final note in the upper part in bar four.

EXAMPLE 16: 'Upon ut re my fa sol la' / Strowgers *Och 371*, fol. 20

On fol. 13 there is what at first glance appears to be a quadruple-stroke sign. John Harley interpreted this as 'a pair of double-stroke signs'.[24] There is however a more convincing explanation for the application in this context. Close examination reveals that the graced note was written originally a third lower. Although this was erased and repositioned, it appears that the original double stroke was left, virtually sitting on the new note-head, and a new sign was drawn through the extended part of the stem. It seems likely therefore that this is simply an instance of untidy work on the part of the copyist, and it would be unwise to attach any particular significance to it.

Only a brief reference need be made to *Obr 156* and *Add. 5465* (The Fayrfax Manuscript). The two folios which make up the former contain portions of anonymous liturgical settings for keyboard in two-part counterpoint. A single stroke is used once but only as a correction sign. *Add. 5465*, an important Tudor song-book, contains a fragment of a keyboard piece, untitled and anonymous, on fol. 2. Although the ink is badly faded there is no evidence that any of the signs under consideration was used.

Lbl Add. 60577

A number of keyboard pieces were added to the *Winchester Anthology* by one of its sixteenth-century owners, William Way.[25] Way made use of the single stroke as a correction sign. In each case his error was the same: notating a minim instead of a semibreve. The context of a pre-beat *schneller* is similar to that of identical figuration in the *Evesham Abbey Bible*.

Och 1034A

The substantial piece by John Ambrose recorded in this manuscript contains six double-stroke signs. Three of these signs are included in the passage quoted at example 17. The figure which is bracketed in Example 17 occurs elsewhere in the piece (see for instance the bass part at the beginning of Example 17). This is the only time it is expressed in note-values other than minims, which may suggest that, in this context, the function of the signs is to underline the crotchet statement. Of the remaining signs, one is given on a crotchet and two on minims; and clearly a short embellishment, possibly a simple shake, is implied.

EXAMPLE 17: [untitled] / Ambrose *Och 1034A*, fol. 1ᵛ

Dtc 410 (THE DUBLIN VIRGINAL MANUSCRIPT)

The music recorded in this 'secular counterpart to the *Mulliner Book*'[26] consists mainly of Pavan/Galliard pairs and arrangements of popular tunes. The only composer's name given in the manuscript is that of 'mastyre taylere', who evidently was the composer of the 'Pavan' which begins on fol. 5ᵛ.

The single stroke is used as a correction sign on several pages. Although the sign is drawn at an oblique angle in the passage quoted at Example 18, the purpose of the application of the single stroke in this context is in all probability to effect correction. Nowhere else in the manuscript are grace signs of different types used together and it seems likely that the alto notes in Example 18 were intended to match those in the bass.[27]

A number of the double-stroke signs are cancelled; this cancellation is effected by the drawing of vertical strokes at either end of the sign. This method

EXAMPLE 18: ['Passing Measures Pavan'] / [anon.] *Dublin Virginal Ms*, fol. 2

of cancellation occurs frequently in later sources but the *Dublin Virginal Manuscript* appears to be the earliest source in which it is applied (see fols. 1, 16-18, 29ᵛ and 30).

Single- and double-stroke signs are used as grace signs. The application of single strokes is of some interest because the signs are given in pairs (see fols. 7 and 10). Although most grace thirds notated on the upper staff, other intervals are also affected (see Example 19). The application is similar to that in the pieces at the beginning of the *Mulliner Book* (see above). In both sources a single-stroke grace sign is never used on its own. It might be conjectured that the use of a pair of single strokes in the *Dublin Virginal Manuscript* is to distinguish the sign from a correction sign (one single stroke). Whatever the explanation, there is a suggestion that the implied embellishment should be realised within the interval graced: where the signs grace the interval of a third this may be a slide; but on the graced sixths (see Example 19), possibly some form of arpeggiation is implied.

EXAMPLE 19: ['Pavan'] / [anon.] *Dublin Virginal Ms.*, fol. 7

There are double-stroke signs in a number of pieces and on fols. 7 and 10 pairs of double strokes grace notated thirds. On fol. 10 six consecutive thirds are graced thus (see Example 20). Presumably the implied realisation is different to that suggested by the pairs of single-stroke signs; and it is possible that in each case the implication is a rapid alternation of the two graced notes in a form of shake. Italian musicians were familiar with this form of shake (with a third): Sylvestro Ganassi discusses shakes made with a third, a whole tone and with a semitone.[28] In later sources of English keyboard music double-stroke signs are applied in pairs occasionally, usually gracing either a third or a sixth,

EXAMPLE 20: '[Variations on the romanesca'] / [anon.] *Dublin Virginal Ms.*, fol. 10

and it is possible that the meaning of this application is the same as that suggested above. In view of the fact that oscillating quaver/semiquaver figuration (involving thirds, fourths, fifths and sixths) was not an unusual division for a composer to employ,[29] it might be deduced that a more rapid variety is represented by a pair of double- stroke signs.

It is clear that the association of the single- and double-stroke signs with embellishment developed only gradually during the sixteenth century. Apart from what appears to be exceptional usage of the single stroke, in the *Evesham Abbey Bible*, this sign undoubtedly was associated primarily with correction. Indeed, it retained that function during the seventeenth century and not surprisingly perhaps its role as a grace sign was limited. It has been shown that where the single stroke is used as a grace sign in the *Mulliner Book* and in the *Dublin Virginal Manuscript* it is given only in combination with at least one other single stroke, possibly to avoid any confusion with correction.

Evidently the double stroke had wider application in connection with embellishment much earlier. Already in the *Evesham Abbey Bible* and in *Add. 29996* it appears to function as an abbreviation/grace sign. In addition, it was used along with triple- and quadruple-stroke signs as a visual aid. By the end of the period which this group of manuscripts spans however, the sign appears to have become associated primarily with embellishment. It is possible that the double stroke was introduced first as an abbreviation for various divisions and only gradually acquired its freer association as a grace sign. In this latter form the main meaning of the sign was undoubtedly a shake, a meaning which continued to be associated with the sign throughout the seventeenth century. The emergence of the double stroke as the most important grace sign in English keyboard music of the virginalist era (often the only grace sign used in a manuscript) is not surprising and an interesting parallel may be drawn with lutenist practice. In his *Harmonie Universelle* (1636) the French theorist Marin Mersenne describes seven graces for the lute including the *tremblement* [shake] which is indicated by a comma. He notes that the comma is generally used to serve for all graces:

> Or celuy qui est formé en cette facon , s'appelle vulgairement tremble-ment, & la plus part ne se servent point d'autre charactere pour en exprimer toutes les differentes especes.[30]

> (Now that which is notated in this manner , is commonly called shake, and most people use no other symbol to express all the different sorts.)

The varying contexts in which the double stroke is used in keyboard sources suggest that it too carried different meanings.

Application of triple- and quadruple-stroke signs in the *Mulliner Book* represents exceptional sixteenth-century usage. The triple stroke functions largely as a visual aid; only at the beginning of a piece by Blitheman is it used as a grace sign. Use of the triple stroke as a grace sign continued to be exceptional in the seventeenth century. In fact, apart from usage in the *Mulliner Book*, the sign does not reappear in English keyboard music until around 1620, and then its application is confined to a small number of occurrences in a few sources, two of which were associated with Benjamin Cosyn.[31]

In conclusion it should be noted that the refinement in the application of the strokes in seventeenth-century English keyboard sources was to some extent a logical outcome of sixteenth-century usage. Although the single stroke continued to be used as a correction sign, correction ceased to be its primary function, and whereas in the *Mulliner Book* and the *Dublin Virginal Manuscript* the sign was used only in combination with at least one other single stroke to indicate embellishment, in *My Ladye Nevells Booke* (1591) and later sources it functions as a grace sign in its own right. The copyist of *My Ladye Nevells Booke*, John Baldwin, used the single stroke quite freely as a grace sign; however, several of his single strokes were subsequently altered to double strokes by a corrector, conjectured to be William Byrd,[32] the sole composer represented in *Nevell*. The long association of the single stroke with correction may have been an influential factor; and only rarely during the first half of the seventeenth century was this sign used with any frequency.[33] Clearly composers and copyists were content to express embellishment largely in the form of the double-stroke sign and in this respect followed a practice which had been established in the sixteenth century.

NOTES

1. See Thomas Morley, *A Plaine and Easie Introduction to Practicall Musicke* (London, 1597; facsimile, Amsterdam and New York, 1969), 181f; ed. Alec Harman (London, 1952), 296f.
2. See Charles Butler, *The Principles of Musick* (London, 1636; facsimile, New York, 1970), 55.
3. Musicks Hand-maide (London, 1663), *Lbl K.1.C.1* [Preface].
4. Tomás de Santa María, *Libro llamado arte de tañer fantasía* (Valladolid, 1565; facsimile, Farnborough, 1972); fols.46'ff.
5. See Charles Jacobs, 'The Performance Practice of Spanish Renaissance Keyboard Music' (diss., New York University, 1962), 151ff.
6. *Lbl Add. 32533*, fol. 106'; *Roger North on Music*, ed. John Wilson (London, 1959), 149.
7. See Alan Curtis, *Sweelinck's Keyboard Music* (2nd edn., Leiden and London, 1972), 205.
8. See *Dutch Keyboard Music of the 16th and 17th Centuries*, ed. Alan Curtis, *Monumenta Musica Neerlandica*, iii (Verenining voor Nederlandse Muziekgeschiedenis, 1961), xi.
9. Identification of location is by *RISM* sigla with the exception of Eam: Evesham, Almonry Museum.

10. John Caldwell, 'British Museum Additional Manuscript 29996' (diss., University of Oxford, 1965), 51

11. For a discussion of the bible and the music see M.D. Knowles and Thurston Dart, 'Notes on a Bible of Evesham Abbey', *English Historical Review*, lxxix (1964), 775ff.

12. See *Elias Nicolaus Ammerbach: Orgel Oder Instrument Tabulaturbuch (1571/1583)*, ed. Charles Jacobs (Oxford, 1984), lxvii and lxxxvii.

13. See Caldwell (as n. 10), 54 and 146ff for a detailed examination.

14. Caldwell (as n. 10), 68.

15. See Caldwell (as n. 10), 68 and David Wulstan, *Tudor Music* (London, 1985), 126.

16. Thurston Dart, *The Interpretation of Music* (London, 1954), 120.

17. Text (Correa de Arauxo, *Facultad Orgánica [Alcalá de Henares, 1626], fol. 15ᵛ*) and translation taken from Jacobs (as n. 5), 152.

18. Correa, fol. 16ᵛ, quoted in Jacobs (as n. 5), 166.

19. Denis Stevens, *The Mulliner Book: A Commentary* (London, 1952), 23.

20. Robert Donington, 'Ornaments', *The New Grove Dictionary of Music and Musicians*, ed. Stanley Sadie (London, 1980), xiii, 858.

21. See for instance *Lbl Add. 30485*, fols. 35-78 *passim* and *Pn Rés. 1185*, 52-107 *passim*.

22. See Wulstan, (as n. 15), 144.

23. These combined signs have not been reproduced in *Musica Britannica*, i.

24. John Harley, 'Ornaments in English keyboard Music of the seventeenth and early eighteenth Centuries', *The Music Review*, xxxi (1970), 195.

25. See *The Winchester Anthology: BL Add.MS 60577* (facsimile, Cambridge, 1981), Introduction by Edward Wilson and Iain Fenlon, 43.

26. *The Dublin Virginal Manuscript*, ed. John Ward (Schott, 1983), xii.

27. The literal transcription in Ward's edition (see footnote 26) is confusing (see no. 1, bar 34).

28. See *Sylvestro Ganassi: Opera Intitulata Fontegara* (Venice, 1535), ed. Hildemarie Peter (Berlin-Lichterfelde, 1959), 87.

29. See for instance 'Les Buffons' / Bull in *Musica Britannica*, xix, 101, bars 97ff.

30. Marin Mersenne, *Harmonie Universelle* (Paris, 1636; facsimile, Paris, 1965), *Traité des Instruments a cordes*, ii, 79.

31. *Lbl R.M. 23.1.4* and *Pn Rés. 1185*.

32. See Margaret H. Glyn, *Elizabethan Virginal Music and Its Composers* (London, 1924), 37ff, Alan Brown, *A Critical Edition of the Keyboard Music of William Byrd* (diss., University of Cambridge, 1969), 36ff, and Oliver Neighbour, *The Consort and Keyboard Music of William Byrd* (London, 1978), 22.

33. Apart from exceptional usage of the single stroke in *En 9447* (Duncan Burnett's Book), in which source single strokes outnumber double strokes by c.2:1, the incidence of single strokes is high in *Lbl R.M. 23.1.4* (Cosyn's Virginal Book) and in *Pn Rés. MSS 1185* and *1186*.

The Flageolet in Ireland

ASPECTS OF THE REPERTOIRE, THE INSTRUMENT AND ITS MAKERS

BARRA BOYDELL

The purpose of this paper is to survey the repertoire published in Ireland for the English flageolet, of the type popularised by William Bainbridge and other early nineteenth-century makers, together with some observations on the development of the instrument and on Irish flageolet makers. The survey of the repertoire is based on the music holdings of the National Library of Ireland,[1] in which sheet music from the later eighteenth to the mid nineteenth centuries predominates, corresponding with the period of the flageolet's popularity.

The exact identity of the type of flageolet referred to in printed music is seldom explicit. The name 'flageolet' was used for a number of related but distinct instruments popular at different periods and in different countries. For this reason a discussion of the identity of the English flageolet and some aspects of its development is appropriate.

The English flageolet can be defined as a duct-flute with inverted conical bore and with six or seven fingerholes in front and one thumbhole behind, to which additional keys were often added. A windcap with ivory mouthpiece is a feature of the instrument, with a sponge chamber inside to absorb the moisture from the player's breath. English flageolets were frequently made in the form of 'double flageolets' with two parallel pipes. In this case the left pipe had the six or seven fingerholes and thumbhole of the single flageolet, while the right pipe had three or four fingerholes and additional keys, enabling the instrument to play melodies with an accompaniment predominantly in thirds. Either pipe on the double flageolet could be stopped by using a wind-cutter key, cutting off the supply of air at the lip. Rarer examples of 'triple flageolets' also survive, in which a third pipe with thumb keys provided a variable drone.

The English flageolet is first defined in a patent taken out by William Bainbridge, *Certain Improvements on the Flageolet or English Flute . . .* dated 2 May 1803.[2] The flageolet described here is distinct from the flageolet popular in England and elsewhere in the seventeenth and early eighteenth centuries. This earlier form, familiar through publications such as Thomas Greeting's *The Pleasant Companion, or New Lessons and Instructions for the Flageolet*

(London 1661 and subsequent editions) and *The Bird Fancyer's Delight* (London, 1717), had four fingerholes in front and two behind, and went out of fashion in England during the eighteenth century. Mersenne, in his *Harmonie Universelle* of 1636/7, attributes the invention of the flageolet to Le Sieur Juvigny in the later sixteenth century. It had however been known in various forms since at least mediaeval times. The French association explains the name 'French flageolet' sometimes used in England; in France, with the addition of chromatic keywork, it was to remain popular into the late nineteenth century as the 'Quadrille flageolet'.[3]

It appears from Bainbridge's patent of 1803 that the 'flageolet or English flute' referred to was not altogether a new invention. The reference to 'improvements' is amplified by comments such as 'to admit of a regular fingering from D below the lines, up to A above the lines, which was not the case before, as the two F-sharps, and the D on the fourth line were cross-fingered on the old flagelet' and 'by lifting up the large key I make F above the lines, a note which was never made before on the octave flagelet'.[4] With the occasional use of a more rounded than beak-shaped mouthpiece for the recorder from the mid eighteenth century[5] and the decline in the popularity of the recorder around the same period, there would have been little in principle to distinguish recorders with such mouthpieces from what we can later identify as the English flageolet. It may be noted too that English flageolets were sometimes made with a form of 'mouthpiece' covered by the windcap analagous to the recorder's, so that they could easily be blown directly without the windcap, just like a recorder.[6] The transition between the recorder and the English flageolet is thus an area that needs to be looked at more closely.[7]

An analysis of woodwind instruction books suggests that the name 'flageolet' was revived in the English speaking world for the newer 'English' flageolet after the seventeenth- and early eighteenth-century form of the instrument had fallen out of use. Thomas Warner[8] records an average of two flageolet tutors or other instruction books published in England in each decade between 1660 and 1720. These all refer to the earlier or 'French' flageolet with four fingerholes and two thumbholes. There is then a complete absence of recorded instruction books for the flageolet in England and other English speaking countries until the appearance of the anonymous *A Scale for the Flageolet* published in Philadelphia in 1797, followed by the *New & Complete Pocket Preceptor for the English & French Flageolets . . .* published by George Astor in London *c.*1800[9] Occasional publications which, though not specific for the instrument, contain references to the flageolet had appeared during the intervening period on the continent. Here, particularily in France and Germany, the flageolet begins to be the subject of an increasing number of tutors and other instruction books as we move into the nineteenth century, as was also the case in English speaking countries.

While the form of flageolet concerned often cannot be determined from the titles of these publications alone, two facts emerge clearly: firstly that, as shown already in the title of George Astor's publication of *c*.1800 (as in a number of later publications),a distinction was made in England between the English and French forms of the instrument; and secondly, that the fashion for using the flageolet in the seventeenth and early eighteenth centuries for teaching tunes to singing birds[10] survived in France, as is indicated by the *Principes de Flageolet . . . pour instruire les sereins[!] et autres oiseaux* published by Frère in Paris, *c*.1805.[11]

In the early nineteenth century the increasing number of tutors for the English flageolet reflects the instrument's rapid climb to popularity. Warner lists five separate tutors published in England in the first decade of the nineteenth century, and six between *c*.1810 and 1815, after which the number reduces somewhat up to 1830, the final year covered by his survey. A parallel situation existed in France and Germany, in both of which countries the publication of flageolet tutors and instruction books peaked in the first decade of the century. In these countries the distinction between the French and English forms of the flageolet is, however, less clear.[12]

Of the tutors covering the flageolet published in England in the first decade of the century after Astor, the most significant, because of the authors' close connection with the development of the instrument, is Bainbridge and Wood's *Flageolet Tutor . . .* of *c*.1805.[13] William Bainbridge describes himself here as 'inventor and patentee (late principal oboe, flute and flageolet player at Ashley's Theatre and Sadler's Wells)' with a note '. . . his knowledge (from a regular apprenticeship to the turning business aided by constant professional practice) has enabled him to offer a patent flageolet, he presumes, at once excellent in point of make, tone and ease of fingering'. The patent referred to is, presumably, that of 1803 (see above).

One of the more distinctive features of the nineteenth century English flageolet was its appearance as noted above in double and triple forms, enabling the player to perform duets on the one instrument, with an additional drone in the case of the triple flageolet. The practice of combining two separately fingered pipes in the one instrument goes back at least to the Ancient Greek aulos. The application of this principle to the flageolet in the early nineteenth century draws primarily on the element of novelty or curiosity, for the flageolet was essentially a drawing room instrument rather than an instrument for serious music making. The novelty element of playing a solo duet on wind instrument(s) in the period immediately preceding the appearance of the double flageolet is anticipated in an advertisement for a concert at the Rotunda, Dublin, in 1780:

on Wednesday evening the 31st of May, instant, will be a grand concert of vocal and instumental music, conducted by Mr Pinto; in which will be introduced a solo concerto on the German flute, and also a duet upon two flutes, by Mr Ash, a performance never before attempted in this kingdom.[14]

Amongst the patents taken out by different makers for the English flageolet,[15] the earliest to refer to a double form is that of Thomas Scott of Middlesex, dated 10 January 1806, for an invention of

> a musical instrument called a flageolette, English flute, or an instrument on the flageolette principle, so constructed as a single instrument that two parts of a musical composition can be played thereon at the same time by one person.[16]

On Scott's double flageolet the notes on the second pipe are operated entirely by keys worked by the thumb of the right hand and the little finger of the left 'without the least interference of the fingers which are used for playing the primo on the other part of the instrument'. While the main pipe has a full chromatic range of two octaves plus a major third from middle C, the second pipe has a range of seven notes from D above middle C up to C natural, with an F sharp rather than an F natural. By sacrificing middle C on the main pipe, the little finger of the right hand can operate a wind-cutter key 'at the pleasure of the performer, for the entire purpose of introducing the second [pipe] to the air he may be playing'. Scott describes the fingering of his double flageolet in detail, that of the main pipe closely following the recorder with some changes in the upper part of the range. He also specifies that the lowest two holes are double (two small holes) as on many baroque recorders.

The double flageolet had already been referred to in instruction books prior to Scott's patent. Warner cites a *Méthode pratique pour le flageolet double et simple* by Metzler, published by Schott in Mainz *c.*1800.[17] Whether this double flageolet was of the French or English type must remain unresolved: no extant copy of this book is recorded and, while it was noted above that flageolets of the English type were certainly made on the continent at a later date, the French title of this publication suggests that it was written for a French market where, as far as is known, the English flageolet was not used at this early period.

In England the earliest instruction book recorded by Warner to specify the double flageolet was published by Bainbridge and Wood in *c.*1810.[18] The full title emphasises the appeal of the flageolet to the amateur, including the musically semi-literate:

> The Preceptor, or a Key to the Double Flageolet, for learning that fashionable and sweet-toned instrument, rendered easy to every capacity, even to those unacquainted with notes, several duetts being figured,

whereby any person will immediately learn them. The same plan will likewise considerably facilitate the learning of this instrument, to those acquainted with music, as they will only have to apply to the figures for learning the scale of the instrument. London, printed for Bainbridge & Wood, 35 Holborn Hill, the only place this instrument is manufactured.

The final comment is of interest: what had become of Scott's patent of 1806? Bainbridge, with his partner James Wood, was to become by far the major producer of flageolets, single and double (not to mention triple), but interestingly, the first patent taken out in Bainbridge's name specifically to refer to the double flageolet did not appear until 1819.[19] This patent outlines four 'improvements'. Firstly,

> to make two English flutes or flageolets of the same pitch as a concert German flute, or nearly so, in order that a person may be enabled to perform on each of them with one hand only, and produce notes, the production of which would require the use of two hands on an instrument constructed with the usual distances of the holes in flutes of the same pitch; besides which one person is enabled to play duetts on these large instruments.

He also describes making the double flageolet in such a way that it can be held 'in the manner of holding a German flute', ie. transversely, a practice he had already patented for the single flageolet on 13 June 1807.[20] Secondly, the 1819 patent covers the use of various keys to enable notes which normally require two hands to be sounded using the fingers of one hand only (B and C above the lines and E in the top space, on the left hand or main pipe), thereby facilitating the playing of both pipes together. Thirdly, the range of the flageolet is increased downwards to B natural (or the equivalent note on instruments of other sizes) through the addition of an extra key.

Examples of double flageolets by Bainbridge survive in which the two pipes are bored out of a single piece of wood.[21] Instruments of this type usually have few keys, and the 1819 patent may relate to the development of the more familiar form of double flageolet with two separate pipes mounted in the stock or head joint, these usually (though not always) having a greater number of keys. However, there are also examples of double 'flute flageolets' by Bainbridge which superficially resemble two transverse flutes, but being blown through a lateral mouthpiece connecting both pipes and having a windway and tongue as on the normal flageolet or recorder, a type which may lay greater claim to being the subject of this patent of 1819.[22]

English flageolets appear to have been made in relatively large numbers up to at least the middle of the nineteenth century with Hastrick, who continued Bainbridge's business from the same address from 1835 to 1855 and often stamped his instruments 'late Bainbridge, Inventor', and John Simpson, (a pupil of Bainbridge active between *c*.1826 and 1869) being the two most prominent makers. It is not clear how late into the nineteenth century flageolets were made in England. Baines cites a catalogue by the English makers Lafleur from *c*.1870 in which French flageolets are featured and the 'English Flageolet (same fingering as Piccolo or Flute) with or without Flute head' is also listed. Baines also illustrates instruments from a German catalogue *c*.1890 which includes a single flageolet.[23] As will be seen from the survey of the repertoire below, however, the flageolet does not appear in the musical sources noted up to such a late date.

THE REPERTOIRE

The dating of music from the period under investigation is often uncertain, since dates were only rarely included in publications. However, by a combination of publisher's addresses, watermarks and other indications, including the titles of popular songs and dances which refer to topical events, the dates of individual publications can often be narrowed down to within a few years.

The earliest music recorded for the flageolet published in Ireland is typical of what is to form the bulk of the flageolet's repertoire, namely arrangements of popular songs and dance tunes of the time. An arrangement by T[homas Simpson] Cooke of *Nobody Coming to Marry Me. A ballad sung by Mrs T. Cooke with unbounded applause* . . . was published by Jacob Goodwin at his 'Music Shop and Circulating Music Library' at 20 Sackville Street, Dublin. Goodwin is only recorded at this address between 1805 and 1806, when he moved to 47 Henry Street.[24] Thomas Cooke (born Dublin 1782, died London 1848) was a singer, instrumentalist, and prolific composer of operas, songs and piano arrangements.[25] The format consists of a song with piano accompaniment, with a separate part for 'flute or flageolet' which reproduces more or less exactly the vocal line, except that it is transposed from B flat major to D major. The absence of a transposed piano part here as elsewhere in equivalent publications aimed at the amateur market suggests that the flageolet (or flute) may be thought of as playing the melody unaccompanied; or was transposition a widespread practice amongst amateur keyboard players at the period?

A number of publications by Goulding, Phipps, D'Almaine & Co. of 117 New Bond Street, London, and 7 Westmoreland Street, Dublin, can be dated to the period 1806 to 1808 by the combination of the London address with the absence of the name Knevett from the Dublin address.[26] These include a second arrangement of *Nobody Coming to Marry me, a favorite ballad sung by Mrs Jordan* . . . again with a part transposed from B flat to D major for 'flageolet or flute',[27] and a song by Joseph Mazzinghi (1765-1844), the London composer who by this date had turned from opera to shallow keyboard and other music for the amateur market: *Flora's Wreath, a pastoral ballad, as sung by Mr Philipps, with universal applause at the Dublin Theatre, and at the public and private concerts,composed by J. Mazzinghi. Arranged for the voice and piano forte, with a flageolet, or German flute accompaniment ad. lib.*[28]

Also published by Goulding, Phipps, D'Almaine & Co. of London and Dublin between 1806 and 1808 are two items of greater interest: firstly, *The Nightingale: a favorite military rondo, arranged for pianoforte with an accompaniment for the octavo flute or flageolet. By J. Marsh Esqr.*[29] This is a more extended work in which the flageolet (or flute) plays together with the piano. Although the flageolet part is essentially no more than a more ornate version of the right hand of the piano, it features trilled notes to suggest a nightingale, a reminder of the association of the flageolet with birdsong. This same 'favorite military rondo' will be the subject of a more elaborate arrangement specifically for flageolet and piano by John Parry published between 1810 and 1820 (see below). The second item of interest published between 1806 and 1808 by Goulding & Co. in London and Dublin is an anonymous tutor: *The English & French Flageolet Preceptor or the whole art of playing the flageolet, rendered easy to every capacity, wherein every instruction relative to these instruments is elucidated in the most clear and simple manner and by which anyone may learn to play with taste and judgement in a short time[.] To which is added a valuable selection of favorite airs, song tunes, duets &c. many never before published in any book of instruction. The airs, &c, are adapted for the German flute or violin.*[30] We note here the coexistence of the English and French flageolets in the title.

The Dublin publisher Smollet Holden produced two volumes of *A Collection of old established Irish slow & quick tunes, arranged for the harp, piano forte, violin, flute, flageolet or bagpipes* from his address at [26] Parliament Street,[31] from where he was active from 1806 until his death in 1813. The business was then continued by his widow at the same address until *c.*1818. However, the indication on the titlepage that these were 'selected by' Smollet Holden indicates publication during his lifetime, i.e. between 1806 and 1813.

A date of *c.*1810-1812 can be assigned to *The Fairy Bower, a favorite new ballad, with an accompaniment for the piano forte . . . dedicated to Miss Alexander . . . by James May (Londonderry)* with a transposition from D major in the vocal part to F major, specifically for the flageolet.[32] This was published in Dublin by Paul Alday 'late Rhames 16 Exchange Street'. Alday succeeded Francis Rhames at this address in 1810 where he remained until 1815. The reference to Rhames suggests that this particular publication might be dated to the earlier part of the period 1810-1815.

Johann Bernard Logier of 27 Lower Sackville Street, Dublin, produced a series of *Collections of Country Dances* between 1812 and 1815, a number of which include the flageolet in the-title.[33] The dating is helped sometimes by the inclusion of a date in the title, sometimes by the names of the dances in each collection. Logier used an identical titlepage for the first four volumes in the series, thus: *Logier's Collections of Country Dances for the pianoforte or harp. These dances are so arranged that the[y] may be play'd by one or two performers on the piano forte; in the former instance, the middle line is suppressed; in the latter one of the performers plays the subject on the upper line an octave higher & the other the accompaniment. The same effect is produced by playing the upper line on the flute, violin or flageolet. The publisher considers it unnecessary to point out to the public the great variety which will result from these arrangements as it will produce all the effect of a duet or trio . . . Dublin. Published at I.B. Logier's Music Saloon 27 Lower Sackville Street.* Volume 1 in this series (the individual volume numbers are, when present, inked in on the titlepage) can be dated by the inclusion of a dance with the title *Eighteenhundred and twelve.* Volume 2 includes a dance *Lord Wellington* which confirms a date of around the same year.[34] Volume 3 has no titles which can help with the dating. The last dance in volume 4 is entitled *New Year 1813*, indicating a publication date of the end of 1812 or early 1813. Volume 5 marks a change in format, with no reference to flute or flageolet on the titlepage, but the dating is evident from the title *Logier's new Country Dances for the year 1813.* The remaining volume, *Logier's new Country Dances for 1815*, again only refers to the piano, and publication was shared by Clementi & Co. in London and by Logier in Dublin.[35]

The flageolet is mentioned in several other collections of national and other dances and melodies published in or associated with Dublin around this same period. *O'Farrell's pocket companion for the Irish or Union pipes, being a grand selection of favorite tunes, both Scotch and Irish, adapted for the pipes, flute, flageolet and violin . . . with some favorite duetts for the above instruments* was published by Goulding, D'Almaine, Potter & Co., 20 Soho Square, London, 'and to be had at 7 Westmoreland St. Dublin'.[36] While Goulding & Co. moved to 20 Soho Square in London c.1811, the comment 'to be had at' 7 Westmoreland Street indicates a date after 1816/17 when Gouldings closed their Dublin agency at this address, the premises being taken over by I. Willis. However, the inclusion of titles relating to the Napoleonic Wars, including *Wellington's Coming* and *General Graham's Waltz* (General Thomas Graham was Lord Wellington's right hand man from 1811)[37] would also indicate a date not much after 1817 since, as will be evident from the titles in the series of *Goulding & Co's Collection of . . . Country Dances* discussed below, titles relating to the Napoleonic Wars go out of currency around this same period.

Although not published in Dublin, mention may be made here of *O'Farrell's Collection of National Irish Music for the Union Pipes, comprising a variety of . . . tunes, set in proper stile [sic] and taste, with variations and adapted likewise for the German flute, violin, flagelet, piano & harp, with a selection, of favorite Scotch tunes, also a treatise with . . . instructions . . . for the pipes. To be had at Mr Gows 31 Carnaby Street, Golden Square & Mr O'Farrels*[sic] *65 Swallow Street.*[38] Humphries & Smith cite Gow at this address from *c.*1803-1815. The content of this collection is distinct from O'Farrell's *Pocket Companion* . . . noted above, and there are no titles which refer to topical events or persons to aid closer dating.

Of comparable content is John McLean's *The Amateur Companion being a rare selection of Irish and Scotch melodies arranged in a familiar stile* [sic] *for the pipes, flute, flageolet & violin to which are added a variety of country dances* which can be dated *c.*1816. Two editions of this are in the National Library:[39] one was published by MacLean 'at the Musical Commission Warehouse, 15 Essex Quay'; the second has identical contents but the titlepage has been changed in some details, including the address of the Musical Commission's Warehouse which is now 10 Bachelor's Walk, Dublin. The dating of *c.*1816 rests both on the inclusion of a *Waterloo Dance* in the contents, which provides a date post quem of late 1815, and the change of address. MacLean is recorded at 10 Bachelor's Walk from 1816-42. From 1813-16 he was at 19 Anglesea Street. The address in Essex Quay is not recorded elsewhere: whether it was a second address from which he operated while also in Anglesea Street, or an address occupied for a short period in 1816 remains to be resolved. Either way, the change in the titlepages to the Bachelor's Walk address indicates a date of *c.*1816 for these editions. The index at the back of the volumes describes each as *MacLean's 1st Pocket Volume for the Pipes, Flute, Flageolet and Violin*, expands the name of the Musical Commission's Warehouse to the 'Music and Musical Instrument Commission's Warehouse' and adds 'a variety of violins, flutes, flageolets etc, both new and secondhand. NB Music neatly engraved or copied'.

Power's Musical Cabinet for the German flute, flageolet or violin was published in several volumes jointly by William Power, [4] Westmoreland Street, Dublin, and James Power, 34, Strand, London, and includes a similar cross-section of song titles, marches and dances.[40] A date post 1810 is indicated by the change in that year of the name of the company at 4 Westmoreland Street from 'Power & Co' to 'William Power'. The brother, James, had moved in 1807 to London, where he operated from 34 Strand until 1838,[41] publishing in partnership with his brother in Dublin until 1820. Closer dating is however provided by the contents: while volume 1 contains no readily datable material, volume 3 includes *Lord Wellington's March* which is listed in John Parry's annual catalogue of dances for 1812 (see below), and *The Copenhagen Waltz* which Parry lists in 1814. A date of *c.*1812-1815 may therefore be suggested for Power's *Musical Cabinet.*

Three further collections of popular titles which refer to the flageolet and which, though not published in Ireland, have Irish connections, may be referred to here: *One hundred airs, (principally Irish) selected and composed by Lieut. Gen. Dickson, arranged for the piano forte, violin, flute, etc, by Mr Thomson, organist of St Nicholas, Newcastle upon Tyne. Dedicated . . . to . . . the Duke of Northumberland by Alexr. Monro Kinloch, dancing master. NB Most of these airs are also adapted for the flageolet & Irish pipes. London, Printed by Messrs Goulding & Co. for Mr Kinloch at his Music Saloon, Newcastle . . .*[42] This collection includes one topical title, *Badajoz*. The city of Badajoz was besieged and captured in 1811-12 during the Penninsular War, and it was there that Sir Alexander (later Lieut. General) Dickson came into military prominence, being in charge of the artillary under the immediate orders of Lord Wellington.[43] *Hannam's selection of celebrated Irish melodies, properly arranged either as solos or duetts, for the German flute, patent flageolet, violin or clarionet[sic].* *No[1]* was published in London by H.Hannam, 4 London Road, St. George's Fields, an address occupied from c.1816-28.[44] As with many other collections including Irish material, this draws on Moore's *Irish Melodies* which appeared from 1808 onwards.

A copy of *Monro's admired selections of popular country dances, waltzes, etc., carefully adapted for the harp, pianoforte, violin, flute or flageolet. No. 1 . . .* , published by J. Munro, 60 Skinner Street, Snow Hill, London, bears on the titlepage the seller's sticker: 'Sold by Elizabeth Attwood, No.4 Nassau Street, Dublin. Near Grafton Street', an address held from 1817-22.[45] Closer dating is provided by a 'List of New Publications' on the back page which includes *Munro's Annual Selection of twenty four country dances, waltzes, etc., for 1818. . . .*

One of the more prolific composers and arrangers of music for the flageolet was the Welshman John Parry (1776-1851), who settled in London as a teacher of the flageolet in 1807.[46] Though publishing in London with Goulding & Co. and with James Power, both of whom had agencies or partnerships in Dublin, much of his output had a direct Irish association. Parry arranged the music for Goulding & Co.'s annual publications of dances; the earliest of these in the National Library, Dublin, is dated on the titlepage, a fairly rare occurrence for the period: *Goulding & Cos. Collection of new and favorite country dances, reels and waltzes. Arranged for the piano forte & flute or patent flageolet, by John Parry. London, Goulding & Comy., 20 Soho Square, 7 Westmoreland St., Dublin. 1815.*[47] At the back of this volume there is a dated list of annual dance collections which provides dating evidence for certain topical titles occurring in other collections, including some of those noted above. These include in 1812: *Lord Wellington* and *Morgiana in Spain*; in 1813: *The Hero of Salamanca* and *Salamanca* (the Battle of Salamanca took place in 1812); in 1814: *Vittoria*[48] and *The Copenhagen Waltz;* and in this 1815 volume: *Wellington the Brave* and *Field Marshal Blucher.*

The 1819 edition of *Goulding & Cos. Collection of . . . Country Dances . . .* shares the same titlepage as the 1815 edition above, except for the details of publication which read: 'Goulding, D'Almaine, Potter & Co., 20 Soho Square and to be had at 7 Westmoreland Street, Dublin'.[49] As was noted above in the discussion of *O'Farrell's Companion*, the comment 'to be had at' must indicate a date after 1816/17 when the Dublin agency of Goulding & Co. (under its various names) was taken over by Isaac Willis & Co. at the same address. Dance titles which refer to the Napoleonic Wars have disappeared from the 1819 edition except possibly for *The Homberg Waltz*. The retrospective 'List of Dances' at the back includes for 1816: *Waterloo* and the *Duke of Wellington's New Waltz*; for 1817: *Wellington's Welcome Home*, *St. Helena*, and *The Cadiz Mortar*, with *The Waterloo Dance* being the only relevant title for 1818. This decline in popular dance titles within three or four years of the end of the Napoleonic Wars with the Battle of Waterloo in 1815 may serve as a guide to the general currency of such titles. A later edition of *Goulding & Co.'s Collection* . . . in the National Library, undated but with a watermark of 1817, can be dated more closely to 1821/2 by the inclusion of a dance *King George's Welcome to Ireland*.[50] King George IV visited Ireland in the summer of 1821. Other later editions of the same series, also printed by 'Goulding, D, Almaine, Potter & Co., 20 Soho Square and to be had at 7 Westmoreland Street, Dublin' are less easy to date closely, though one edition, which includes an arrangement of the *Hunters' Chorus* from Weber's *Der Freischütz* (1821) is dated 1826 on the titlepage.[51]

The Nightingale: a favorite military rondo . . . by John Marsh and dating from 1806/8 was noted above. This same melody provided the basis for one of a pair of more extensive works with bird titles arranged by John Parry specifically for the flageolet and printed by J. Power, 34 Strand, & W. Power, 4 Westmoreland Street, Dublin, providing a date between 1810 and 1820. These are amongst the few examples of true solo music for the instrument: *The Nightingale, a favorite military air arranged as a rondo for the piano forte, with an accompaniment for the flute or flageolet, by John Parry. Performed with the greatest applause at the Bath Concerts, by the celebrated Miss Randles & the author.*[52] Although indicating 'flute or flageolet' on the titlepage, the music itself is only marked for flageolet. It comprises 247 bars in 2/4 time with a flageolet part which is independant of rather than merely doublng the right hand of the piano. At the bottom of page four is the comment 'The author plays this Divertimento with an Octave Flageolet', while the fingering instruction 'D made open on the flageolet' is added in places where there are appeggiated semiquavers including d" (second line down) or repeated semiquavers b"-d".

The second bird piece is: *The Thrush, a rondo for the piano forte, with an accompaniment for the flute or flageolet, composed by John Parry. Teacher of the single and double flageolets. No. 2 . . . Published by J. Power, 34, Strand*

& W. Power, 4 Westmoreland Street, Dublin. Where may be had by the same author, The Nightingale arranged for the piano forte & flageolet or flute 3/-. A Sett of Divertimentos for Do. 5/-[.] Six Airs with vars. for the flageolet 2/- ... (four other titles are listed in which instrumentation is not specified).[53] Again, although the titlepage refers to 'flute or flageolet', the opening page of the music makes the first choice of flageolet clear with the comments: 'The flageolet part may be played (by a third hand) on the additional keys of a piano forte' and 'The flageolet part may be played on a flute or violin'. Similarily too, the flageolet part with many trills in imitation of birdsong is independant of the right hand of the piano, and the music relatively extensive, totalling 203 bars in 2/4 time.

Other music with flageolet by John Parry includes: *The Opera Hat, a favorite dance, composed & arranged as a familiar rondo, for the piano forte, also adapted for the flute or flageolet, by John Parry. Editor of the Welsh Melodies – London, printed by Goulding, D'Almaine, Potter & Co., 20, Soho Square, 124, New Bond Street, & 7, Westmoreland Street, Dublin.*[54] This can be dated fairly accurately to *c.*1811 by the combination of the two London addresses. Although the full rondo extends to 128 bars of 6/8 time, the dance melody itself is all that appears, separately, 'for the flute or flageolet'; also: *[The Voice of her Love] . . . with an accompaniment for the harp and pianoforte . . . London, Goulding, D'Almaine, Potter & Co., 20 Soho Square, and 7 Westmoreland Street, Dublin*[55] which has a part for 'flute or flageolet'. Dating here is between 1811 and 1816/17, when the Dublin agency closed.

Although not in the National Library of Ireland, an anonymous flageolet tutor printed in Dublin may be referred to here, listed by Warner:[56] *The Compleat Tutor for the English or French Flageolet containing every instruction relative to those instruments, which are elucidated in the most clear and simple manner by which anyone may learn to play with taste and judgment [sic] in a short time. To which is added a selection of the most approved airs, songs, duets etc. etc . . . Dublin. Published at W. Power's (4) Westmoreland St. & at J. Power's (34) Strand London.* Warner suggests a date of *c.*1810 on the basis of a watermark of that year. As has been noted above, the association of W. Power in Dublin with J. Power in London provides a possible dating between 1810 and 1820.

The remaining work with flageolet in the National Library dating from the 1810s is another song arrangement: *Patrick O'Dermot, the pride of Kildare, a favorite song sung with great applause in the opera of False Alarms . . . by Mrs Dickens, the music composed by Mr W.T. Parke . . . London, Goulding & Compy., 20 Soho Square and 7 Westmoreland Street, Dublin.*[57] A transposition of the melody (up a tone to D major) is included for 'flute or flageolet'. A dating of between 1811 and 1817/18 applies.

One of the more prominent Dublin music publishers of the 1820s was Edward

McCullagh, whose business was located at 1 Royal Arcade, College Green, between 1821 and 1830. Thereafter he moved to 22 Suffolk Street where, in 1831, he went into partnership with James McCullagh with a second premises at 108 Grafton Street between 1831 and 1851. From his address at Royal Arcade Edward McCullagh published enormous quantities of popular songs and other music including collections of national airs and dances, a number of which mention the flageolet. *A Collection of Irish Airs for the flute, violin or flageolet. Arranged as duetts or solos* . . . appeared in several volumes, sometimes with the additional description 'with new symphonies arranged as duetts or solos.'[58] These have illustrated titlepages showing two gentlemen playing flutes, with music on a circular table. Although closer dating within the period of McCullagh's address at Royal Arcade is uncertain, an earlier rather than a later date is suggested by the style of printing. Another comparable collection printed by McCullagh during the same period is *A Collection of the most famous quadrilles for the flute, violin or flageolet* [Books I-III(?)].[59]

A significant proportion of McCullagh's output consisted of single sheet arrangements of songs, often from popular operas and usually anonymous or unattributed. Sometimes these include a part for 'flute or flageolet', which may be transposed, consisting merely of the melody written out separately at the bottom of the page. Titles of this nature in the National Library, all with the address at 1 Royal Arcade indicating a date between 1821 and 1830, are as follows:[60]

– Away with melancholy [adaptation of Mozart's *Das klinget so herrlich* from *The Magic Flute*] NB. duet with parts for two flutes or two flageolets (Add. Mus. 10,676)
– *Black ey'd Susan* (Add. Mus. 1016)
– *The Boatie Rows* (Add. Mus. 11,954)
– *For Lack of Gold she left me, oh!*. (JM 2664)
– *How blest the Maid* [by Galuppi, from *Love in a Village*[61]] (JM 2808)
– *A Highland Lad my Love was born* (JM 5609)
– *My Heart was so free* (Add. Mus. 1169)
– *O had I been by fate decreed* [by Samuel Howard, from *Love in a Village*] (Add. Mus. 10,661)
– *O' we're a noddin' nid nid noddin'* (JM 5681)
– *Robin Adair* (JM 3273)
– *Rose Tree* (JM 3288)
– *Savourneen deelish* [beg. *'Oh! the torment was sad'*, from *The Surrender of Calais* (1791) by Samuel Arnold] (JM 3321)

Francis Panormo, son of the noted violin maker Vincenzo Panormo, was publishing music from an address at 5 Church Lane, Dublin, between 1823 and

1829. He produced *A Selection of . . . national airs, arranged with embellishments & variations also as duets for the German flute, violin, or flageolet . . .*[63] during this period.

This concludes the survey of music for the flageolet published in Ireland and held in the National Library. However, some additonal material, including both music and instruction books, may be added from other sources. A copy of *The Louvre Quadrilles* by Sir John Stevenson, published by I. Willis of 7 Westmoreland Street, Dublin,[64] includes a list of music printed by Willis. Willis operated from this address from 1816/17 (succeeding Goulding & Co.) until 1837, and a date for this publication in the latter part of this period is suggested by the style of printing and of the illustrated titlepage. The list includes the following: *A Small Pocket Edition of Quadrilles for the violin flute or flageolet. Bk.the First. Bk.the Second; Egan's Collection of Irish Melodies for one or two flutes or violins, to which is added instructions for the single and double flageolet;* and *Egan's Divertimento to 'Life let us cherish' & 'O Dolce' with an accompaniment for the single or double flageolet.* A similar publication to the last of these, if not the same under a different title (*The favorite airs of Life let us cherish, and Away with Melancholy, arranged with variations for a concert double flageolet or flute (ad libitum) and pianoforte*), also by Egan and published in Dublin, is listed in the British Library Catalogue of Printed Music.[65] This catalogue also lists a second work by Egan, which may be a different edition of the *Collections of Irish Melodies . . . to which is added instructions for the flageolet* noted above, and which is of particular interest in being an example of a full instuction book for the flageolet by an Irish author, printed in Dublin. The full title of the volume in the British Library[66] is as follows: *The Single and Double Flageolet Preceptor, to which is added a collection of airs, principally consisting of Irish melodies, with the Dublin cries composed, selected and arranged for the double flageolet or two single flageolets, likewise for two German flutes or two violins, dedicated to Mr Bainbridge, the inventor of the double and single patent flageolet, by F. Egan of Dublin. Dublin. Printed by I. Willis (late Goulding & Co.), 7, Westmoreland Street, who is constantly supplied with a great variety of pat[ent] flageolets, flutes, etc. etc.*

Despite the title's referring first to the instructions and secondly to the 'Collection of Airs', the contents follow the reverse order, corresponding with the title noted in the list of music published by Willis. The description of Willis as 'late Goulding & Co.' implies a date within the first few years of Willis's taking over the 7 Westmoreland Street premises in 1816/17. A date for this publication of *c.*1817/20 can thus be suggested. Sixteen pages are devoted to music which ranges from Irish melodies and dance tunes presented as simple duets, through more extended settings, mainly by Egan, with opening and concluding 'symphonies', to original works such as an opening *Divertiment* by

Egan. The style of duet writing is predominantly in parallel thirds and sixths, as befits the double flageolet.

The reputation of John Parry, a number of whose flageolet arrangments were noted above, as a leading flageolet teacher and player is reflected in a footnote to a d" sharp' in a Quick Step by Egan on page 5: 'Tho' Mr Parry has given the best gamut for the double flageolet,[67] he has not fingered this note properly. The way I recommend is to stop the three lower holes of the right hand, keeping up the back key'. The pages of music are followed by a 'Gamut for Bainbridge's single & double flageolet', giving the fingering for the full chromatic range from d" to g" two and a half octaves higher. There follows a 'scale for the double flageolet' showing how to finger thirds, with occasional sixths, from d" and f-sharp" up two octaves in G major and D major, plus the full ranges of each pipe when played separately with one hand on each pipe.

IRISH FLAGEOLET MAKERS

Three Dublin makers can be identified from instruments in the National Museum of Ireland and from other sources. The instruments in the museum are all on the Bainbridge model. A boxwood double flageolet is stamped 'Ellard 47 Sackville Street Dublin' together with the device of a unicorn's head.[68] This instrument has ivory mounts with ten keys, plus two wind-cutter keys. The overall length is 465mm. Andrew Ellard is recorded at this address between 1822 and 1838, having moved there from 27 [Lower] Sackville Street, where he had taken over the premises formerly occupied by J.B.Logier (see above) in 1818. During the period at 47 Lr.Sackville Street he did on occasion describe himself as a 'flageolet, and double and triple flute maker'.[69]

A boxwood triple flageolet by Ellard is also stamped with the same address and the device of the unicorn.[70] It is ivory mounted and, in addition to the two wind-cutter keys, there is one key on the head joint, seven on the left pipe, seven on the right, and four thumb keys plus a wind-cutter key on the third (drone) pipe. The overall length (ivory mouthpiece missing) is 490mm. A separate windcap only (with ivory mouthpiece) for a double flageolet, stamped 'Ellard Dublin' with a unicorn but without address, was acquired along with the above triple flageolet and is catalogued together with it. It would appear that this cap was used when it was desired to use the instrument as a double rather than as a triple flageolet.

The second Dublin flageolet maker represented is one of the Dollard family. John Dollard worked at 15 Essex Quay from 1822 to 1825, at 23 Essex Quay from 1826 to 1832, and at 28 Essex Quay from 1833 to 1835. He was joined at 23 Essex Quay in 1829 by Matthew Dollard, who also shared the address at 28 Essex Quay. A boxwood double flageolet stamped 'Dollard Dublin Patent'[71] has two silver keys on the left pipe, three on the right pipe, and a keyed soundhole on the head joint. There is a wind-cutter key for the right pipe but, although the wooden mounting was made, a wind-cutter key was never fitted to the right pipe. On the head joint beneath the maker's stamp an elliptical silver disc is inlaid with the initials 'JMMcD' with the crest of a dexter arm in armour couped holding a cross crosslet.

The third Dublin maker is the company of Wilkinson & Corcoran, whose name is stamped, together with the device of a unicorn's head, on the windcap (all that survives) of a triple flageolet.[72] The partnership of Wilkinson & Corcoran is recorded at 5 Essex Quay between 1836 and 1840.

CONCLUSION

The picture that emerges of the flageolet in Ireland in the early nineteenth century reflects its role and popularity in England and elsewhere. The repertoire is effectively confined to undemanding drawing-room music, mainly in the form of popular songs and of dance tunes and traditional melodies, a high proportion of which reflects the popularity of Irish music adapted for the drawing-room in the wake of the enormous success of Thomas Moore's *Irish Melodies* and similar collections. The relatively advanced technique called for in pieces such as John Parry's *The Nightingale* and *The Thrush* must represent the peak of the flageolet's limited technical demands. As was the case in England, a certain number of woodwind instrument makers in Ireland catered for the flageolet fashion by making instruments which display a considerable level of craftsmanship. The care put into manufacture and into the development of ways of avoiding problems of moisture from the player's breath through different designs of sponge chamber is evidence of the importance of the market for the flageolet

The limited dating evidence of surviving instruments and the music suggests that the initial novelty of the flageolet in the first decade of the nineteenth century developed into a peak of popularity around the 1820s and 1830s. However, it must be remembered that, even at the height of its popularity, the proportion of music published with reference to the flageolet represents only the smallest fraction of the music published at the time. This applies even for an acknowledged teacher and performer on the instrument such as John Parry in London, only a handful of whose numerous compositions and arrangements listed in the British Library Catalogue of Printed Music refer in their titles to the flageolet. In the words of Edgar Hunt: 'These musical toys had their day, but there were no lasting qualities to aid their survival . . . today they are only antique curiosities. Let them be a lesson to the inventors of novelty instruments'.[73]

NOTES

1. RISM/New Grove library siglum: Dn.
2. Progressive number 2693. Repr. Great Seal Patent Office, London, 1856.
3. See especially: Philip Bate, *The Flute* (2nd edn, London, 1975), 73.
4. An English flageolet by Proser of London, in the catalogue of the Galpin Society exhibition of *European Musical Instruments* in Edinburgh in 1968, is dated *c.*1790. However, the dates of Proser's output are not more closely known beyond the period 1777-95, the later date appearing on a bassoon (see: Langwill, *An Index of Wind Instrument Makers* (4th edn, Edinburgh, 1974)), so that this flageolet could date from later, as would seem probable.
5. Examples of rounded mouthpieces on recorders can be seen in a portrait dated 1769 by Nathaniel Hone the Elder, known as *The Piping Boy*, in which the artist's son is shown playing a recorder (National Gallery of Ireland) and on a tenor recorder by Thomas Stanesby (Junior), who died in 1754, sold at Sotheby's (London) on 30 March 1989.
6. See, for example, two instruments in the National Museum of Ireland: 1909:23 (unstamped) and 1911:306 (by William Bainbridge).
7. Edgar Hunt, *The Recorder and Its Music* (rev. edn, London, 1977), 100, refers to what could be an early appearance of the sponge-chamber to absorb moisture from the player's breath, a characteristic feature of the English flageolet, in a description by Burney of a person 'who plays on the common flute in a particular manner, blowing it thro' a sponge' (*Music and Manners in France and Italy*, 1770).
8. Thomas Warner, *An Annotated Bibliography of Woodwind Instruction Books 1600- 1830* (Detroit, 1967)
9. Warner (as n. 8), 47, 50. This date is approximate and could be anything up to three or four years later.
10. E.g. *The Bird Fancyer's Delight or Choice Observations, and Directions concerning ye teaching of all sorts of singing-birds, after ye flagelet & flute* . . . (Richard Meares, London, *c.* 1717). See Warner, 10. NB. In reproducing titles of publications in this article capitals have been retained for the short titles of works, but thereafter the often irregular use of capitals is not followed. Punctuation is also regularised where appropriate.
11. Warner (as n. 8), 63.
12. The French flageolet was sometimes made with a windcap and sponge-chamber to absorb moisture, as on English flageolets. Conversely, flageolets on the English model were made certainly in Germany and Austria in the 19th century. See for example Herbert Heyde, *Historische Musikinstrumente im Bachhaus Eisenach* (Eisenach 1976), 194, and Josef Zimmermann, *Von Zincken, Floten und Schalmeien. Katalog einer Sammlung historischer Holzblasinstrumente* ([Duren] 1967), 17.
13. Warner (as n. 8), 63f.
14. Hibernian Journal, 26/29 May 1780. Mr Ash appeared subsequently on a number of occasions playing duets and 'double concertos' in Dublin. I am grateful to Brian Boydell for this information.
15. The full subject list of patents referring to the flageolet is as follows: William Bainbridge, *Flageolet or English Flute (1803);* Thomas Scott, *Flageolet or English Flute* (1806); Henry Kauffmann, *Construction of the flageolet, or English flute* (1807); William Bainbridge, *Flageolet or English flute* (1807); Frederick Nolan: *Construction of flutes, flageolets, hautboys and other wind instruments* (1808); William Bainbridge, *English flute or flageolet* (1810); Ibid., *Double and single flageolet, or English flute* (1819). See B. Woodcroft, *Subject-Matter Index of Patents of Invention*, 1 (London, 1854). Note the

concentration of these patents within the period 1803 to 1810.

16. Progressive number: 2995. Repr: Great Seal Patent Office, London 1856.
17. Warner (as n. 8), 55.
18. Warner (as n. 8), 70.
19. Progressive number: 4399, dated 3 December 1819. Repr: Great Seal Patent Office, London 1857.
20. Progressive number: 3043 (*Certain Improvements on the Flageolet or English flute*). Repr: Great Seal Patent Office 1857. This patent also includes detailed improvements to the tuning and voicing of the higher notes and the tuning of the instrument as a whole.
21. See Anthony Baines, *European and American Musical Instruments* (London 1966), fig. 446.
22. Baines (as n. 21), fig. 449.
23. *Woodwind Instruments and their History* (corr. ed., London 1977), pp. 323/4.
24. Dn: Add. Mus. 12,218; JM. 342/343. NB: information on the dates and addresses of Dublin music publishers not otherwise acknowledged is drawn from an unpublished paper on 'The Music Trade in Ireland' by Brian Boydell.
25. See Bruce Corr, 'Thomas Simpson Cooke', *The New Grove* (London, 1980), vol. 4, 712-714.
26. The company was located at 117 New Bond Street, London, from *c*.1804 to 1808. See C. Humphries & W.C. Smith, *Music Publishing in the British Isles* (London rev. ed. 1970). In Dublin, where the company maintained an agency at 7 Westmoreland Street throughout the period 1803 to 1816 under various names, it was known as Goulding, Knevett & Co. (or simply Goulding & Co.) until 1806, when the name Goulding, Phipps, D'Almaine & Co. is used.
27. Dn: Add. Mus. 10,825.
28. Dn: Add. Mus. 805/6040/6815. It is worth noting that this is the only song amongst a large number by Mazzinghi in the National Library to specify the flageolet.
29. Dn: Add. Mus. 5650; JM. 4404/5. For John Marsh see *New Grove*.
30. Cited by Warner (as n. 8), 67. Not in Dn.
31. Dn: JM. 4657A; also JM. 4646 and Add. Mus.6516 (both imperfect). These two volumes were also published (later?) in London by George Ward, 90 Leman Street, Goodman's Fields with only slight changes, including the volume numbers being exchanged and a new title page with the description 'These airs may also be played on the flute, flageolet, violin or clarinet' (Dn: JM. 4655).
32. Dn: JM. 1444.
33. Dn: JM. 5330-5336; Add. Mus. 5629/30.
34. Arthur Wellesley became Viscount Wellington in 1809, Earl of and then Marquis of Wellington in 1812, and Duke of Wellington in 1814. In *The Annual Register, or a View of the History, Politics, and Literature* he is first referred to as Lord Wellington in the volume for 1810 (London, 1812).
35. The titles include: *Eighteen hundred and fifteen* and *New Post Office* [i.e. the General Post Office, Dublin, completed in 1814].
36. Dn: Add. Mus. 9005.
37. See *Dictionary of National Biography* (London, 1909).
38. Dn: JM. 5415.
39. Dn: Ir. 7844. a.2. (two copies, contents identical but different editions, bound together). Also: JM. 5428.
40. Dn: Ir. 7844. a.2. (vols.[1] and 3); JM. 5482. (vol.1).

41. Humphries & Smith (as n. 26).
42. Dn: Ir. 780941. d.2; JM. 5418.
43. See *Dictionnary of National Biography* (London, 1909).
44. Humphries & Smith (as n. 26).
45. Dn: Add. Mus. 9509.
46. See *New Grove*.
47. Dn: JM. 4576.
48. *A Grand March of Vittoria* is advertised on the titlepage of another publication with a printed date of 1814: *Up with the Orange . . .*, pub.Person, Robertson [London] (Dn: JM. 6059). The Battle of Vittoria took place in 1813.
49. Dn: JM. 4577.
50. Dn: JM. 4578; watermark information: National Library.
51. Dn: JM. 4579; JM. 4580 (1826 ed.); JM. 4581; JM. 4582. The 1826 edition, printed by Goulding, D'Almain, Potter & Co., contradicts Humphries & Smith (as n. 26) who state that Potter dropped out from Goulding & Co. *c*.1823, the firm thence becoming Goulding & D'Almaine.
52. Dn: JM. 4417.
53. Dn: Add. Mus. 12,639.
54. Dn: JM. 6046. *The Welsh Melodies* referred to in the title appeared between 1804 and 1848. See *New Grove*.
55. Dn: Add. Mus. 12,369 (defective).
56. See n. 55, 68.
57. Dn: JM. 1606.
58. Dn: JM. 5419 (vols. I and II pencilled on titlepage); JM. 5420 (vol. I only).
59. Dn: JM. 5840.
60. Rather than footnoting each short entry, the Dn. references here are given in each case after the title.
61. *Love in a Village*, a pastiche opera with music by Thomas Arne and sixteen other composers, had its first Dublin performance in 1763. See T.J. Walshe, *Opera in Dublin 1705- 1797* (Dublin, 1973), 109.
62. See note 61.
63. Dn: JM. 5483.
64. Dn: JM. 5659.
65. Lbm: h.250. a. (2).
66. Lbm: h.3212. c. (3). Not listed by Warner.
67. Warner (as n. 8), does not record any instruction books by John Parry, the existence of which is implied here. Note however the anonymous *Compleat Tutor for the English or French Flageolet . . .* cited above and printed by W.Power, 4 Westmoreland Street, Dublin, and J.Power, 34 Strand, London, sometime between 1810 and 1820. John Parry had some of his flageolet music published by Power during this same period.
68. Reg. no. 1900:123.
69. Brian Boydell (unpubl., see n. 24 above). Langwill (see n. 4) records a double flageolet by Ellard in the Royal Ontario Museum.
70. Reg. no. 226:1944.
71. Reg. no. 2:1955.
72. National Museum of Ireland: not catalogued.
73. *The Recorder and its Music* (rev. edn, London, 1977), 100.

Some Thoughts on Making Liturgical Reconstructions

NICK SANDON

During the last ten years a good deal of my research has involved the performance and study of medieval and renaissance church music, both plainchant and polyphony, in its original liturgical context. This has been some of the most interesting work that I have ever done, and I have learnt a great deal from it. I have been motivated by three especial convictions. The first is that, like any other scholar of the humanities, a musicologist should use his expertise in order to achieve a better understanding of human history, culture and society. The second is that an appreciation of the context in which any music of the past operated equips one to comprehend that music more fully. And the third is that early music can be be brought to life most sympathetically and enlighteningly when performed in a competent recreation of its original environment. There are reciprocal relationships between these principles: we can utilise contextual evidence to enhance our understanding of music; this will enable us to make more effective use of music itself as a type of evidence throwing light on a period; and knowledge of what was originally expected of music in performance can help us to give more convincing modern performances of it. The next few paragraphs amplify these ideas.

Whatever the level at which we study and practice it, music should surely be treated in a manner essentially similar to that in which we would treat any other humanities subject. The study of music is a means of discovery about wider issues, not an end in itself. Like history, or a language and its literature, or philosophy (to mention only three subjects central to the humanities), music offers us a body of evidence which, when investigated in appropriate ways, is able to enhance our understanding of our predecessors and their worlds, which may in turn help us attain a better understanding of ourselves and our world. Even if we have to accept that nothing in the past is completely knowable, all of us who work in an historical discipline must surely believe that we can achieve enough understanding and enlightenment to make our efforts worthwhile. What motivates me as a student of history is the desire imaginatively to recreate my predecessors and their world and participate in it. My prime interest is not in historical documents (using that word in its widest sense) themselves, but in what those documents may be able to tell me about the people who created them. If there were no possibility of creating a reasonably faithful and complete image of the past, there would be no point to my work. I would not deny that there are considerable problems impeding the creation of this image. These problems are, however, not simply a function of the passage of time; other kinds of remoteness are also involved.

Music does not exist and never has existed in a vacuum, and it does not create itself; the musicologist has a responsibility to recognise that the works which he studies are not arbitrary phenomena whose genesis and nature do not require explanation. Any musical work is an artefact, like a building, a treaty, a sculpture, an account roll, the debris of human settlement, or any other document of human activity. Music confronts us with products of the human intellect, created at particular times, in particular circumstances, in response to particular needs, and informed by characteristics peculiar to one individual. Even if we happened to believe that there reside in music certain innate principles (or conventions so long-established that they appear to us to be innate principles), we would have to concede that these principles have been given expression and allowed to operate in endlessly varied ways in accordance with the aesthetic values and stylistic conventions of different times and places. This being so, the nature of the musical object cannot be comprehended without a grasp of the factors which called it into being and conditioned it. Many of these factors, for instance the intellectual climate of a period, are obviously of the impalpable kind that cannot be recreated in a concrete sense; but others, such as the actual order of events into which an artefact fitted and the physical conditions in which it was presented and perceived, often can be recreated, and such a recreation may be very informative about the work itself. Such considerations apply particularly to medieval and renaissance church music, which fulfilled definite functions within a mature, complex and extremely highly organised system. They arguably apply equally well to other kinds of early music, for the concepts of convention, ritual and ceremonial influenced the minds of medieval and renaissance men in very many aspects of their lives. The logical extension of my argument, namely that we should try to perform any and every kind of early music in an appropriately reconstructed context, strikes me as being entirely acceptable.

I will mention only a few of many instances in which a knowledge of liturgical background has enhanced my appreciation of a musical composition. First, in the 'Benedictus' of Nicholas Ludford's Mass *Lapidaverunt Stephanum*, the plainchant cantus firmus is stated continually and very audibly in a three-part texture: an extremely unusual procedure. One might think that this was no more than caprice on Ludford's part until one reads the Gospel for the day and notices that it ends with these very words, 'Benedictus qui venit in nomine domini'; it then becomes clear that Ludford noticed the cross-reference between the Mass text and the words of the martyr and chose to underline it by making Stephen, embodied in the cantus firmus, present while these words are sung. Secondly, in his setting of the penitential antiphon *Emendemus in melius*, Cristobal Morales uses as a regularly recurring cantus firmus a stark melodic phrase sung to the words 'Memento homo quia pulvis es et in pulverem reverteris' ('Remember, man, that thou art dust, and to dust thou shalt return'). Only when one realises that *Emendemus* was sung by the choir during the imposition of ashes on Ash Wednesday, and that the priest intoned 'Memento homo . . .' as he imposed the ashes upon each penitent, does the point of the association become clear. Thirdly, some of the polyphonic Credo settings in the Old Hall manuscript begin at 'Factorem caeli et terrae' rather than at the usual 'Patrem omnipotentem'; no plausible reason for this suggests itself until one discovers that in some Benedictine institutions the celebrant intoned 'Credo in unum deum', the rulers continued 'Patrem omnipotentem' and the choir came in only at 'Factorem caeli'. This observation does not prove that these settings came from a Benedictine foundation, but it provides a practical explanation of an otherwise baffling peculiarity, and it suggests a line of investigation that might usefully be pursued in other circumstances.

The third conviction, namely that much early church music works very unsatisfactorily within the confines of a modern concert, stems from my practical experience, and it has led to my involvement in making what are often called 'liturgical reconstructions'. A liturgical reconstruction is simply a recreation and re-enactment of the rite and ceremonial of a particular period and locality; it will usually involve plainchant, and it may involve polyphony as well, but I can imagine that such reconstructions could be useful to students of liturgy who had no musical interest at all. Perhaps I should emphasise that a musicologist may choose to involve himself in reconstructing defunct liturgies irrespective of his own religious convictions or lack of them; his reason may simply be that this activity enables him to discover more about the music that is his main interest. Nevertheless, many people including myself have found that this work can be spiritually extremely rewarding. What begins as no more than an academic exercise can quite unexpectedly take on great intensity and significance, because the participants' artistic and spiritual instincts and their intellects are being allowed to cross-fertilise each other, just as those who originally designed the liturgy intended them to do. It is also noteworthy how much interest the performance of liturgical reconstructions has aroused among the general public. Some of the reconstructions broadcast in recent years by BBC Radio Three, such as *The Octave of the Nativity* (Christmas 1984, rebroadcast Christmas 1987) and *Trinity Sunday at Worcester Cathedral* (May 1988) have elicited an unprecedentedly large and positive response from a remarkably diverse audience. Clearly, many Christians continue to regret the discarding of traditions built up over so many centuries, and find current modes of worship meretricious, shallow and trivial. For such people, attendance at or participation in the enactment of an ancient liturgy can be a profoundly fulfilling experience, which is perhaps why some ecclesiastical authorities are suspicious of and hostile towards such activities.

Many people interested in early music will probably have shared my disappointment and frustration at the inadequacy of the conventional concert as a suitable occasion for its performance. This inadequacy is revealed especially clearly in the performance of cyclic Masses; the movements of a Mass by, say, Josquin or Fayrfax can sound direly monotonous if heard immediately after one another. One can try to reduce the monotony by interspersing non-related items such as motets or secular vocal music or instrumental pieces among the Mass movements, but this has considerable disadvantages. It may, for example, create sensations of incongruity and triviality, and at the very least it can hardly avoid reducing the stature and impact of the Mass movements themselves. But if one intermingles these same Mass movements with appropriate plainchant items, they will take on an altogether different character, thrown into relief against their surroundings and revealing inter-relationships working across a larger time-span. In recreating as completely as possible the conditions which a composer had in mind, we give his music the best possible chance of making whatever effects he intended. Some of these effects are very simple but nevertheless extremely powerful. The impact of polyphony breaking in upon a lengthy passage of plainchant preparation can be quite shattering, for instance when the luxuriant Sanctus of Machaut's *Messe de Nostre Dame* follows the chanted Preface. The effect of polyphony bringing a service to a ringing conclusion, for example when a *Deo gratias* substitute such as the motet *Post missarum sollemnia* in the Old Hall manuscript is sung after the plainchant *Ite missa est* at the end of Mass, can also be very powerful. Interestingly, the musical similarities between Mass movements which can sound so irritatingly predictable when the movements are heard in close succession, can seem entirely appropriate and helpful when other non-related items intervene.

Polyphonic Mass movements are not the only kind of early church music which can benefit from a careful re-creation of the original performance context. Renaissance motets (here I use the word 'motet' in the widest possible sense to mean any polyphonic setting of a sacred Latin text not being part of the Ordinary of the Mass) often respond well to such treatment. A few years ago it was fashionable to assert, and it is sometimes still asserted, that during the Renaissance composers took less and less account of liturgical circumstances and requirements in their production of sacred polyphony; the proliferation of new texts, an apparently widespread failure to observe liturgical forms, and the increasing prominence of secular patronage were and are commonly cited in support of this assertion. One consequence of this was that many responsible and thoughtful performers had no serious qualms about performing motets in concerts of sacred music; this, it was felt, merely reproduced the original intention. Recent research suggests, however, that such views were overstated; work on local liturgical and institutional customs, and close musical analysis itself, have revealed hitherto unsuspected liturgical functions in the music of composers such as Josquin and Compère. As a result, composers such as Isaac and Palestrina, whose work shows a strong liturgical basis, no longer seem as untypical of their period as some commentators have implied. Motets with a liturgical function, be they responsories such as Gombert's energetic setting of *Surge Petre* for the feast of St Peter's Chains or Sheppard's sinewy *Reges Tharsis* for the Epiphany, or Communions such as Senfl's *Exiit sermo* for the feast of St John the Evangelist, or any other liturgical form, arguably reveal their full stature and significance only when heard in their intended liturgical context.

It is possible that the disruptive influence of the late-medieval votive antiphon upon liturgical polyphony has also been over-estimated. Although such antiphons functioned within a devotional context and thus strictly speaking were non-liturgical, by the mid-fifteenth century their usage had apparently become so frequent and formally conventional that it is more appropriate to regard them as an addition to the established liturgy. Performing, say, one of the Eton choirbook antiphons in association with the versicle, response and prayer which it was intended to accompany, emphasises the meaning and intention of the antiphon text and enhances the musical effect of its setting.

I do not, of course, mean to argue that every renaissance motet has a definite liturgical context waiting to be discovered. There are numerous motets which fit convincingly into no known liturgical environment. Some of these may indeed have been composed as recital pieces for the delectation of a discriminating patron; there is evidence that the 'sacred concert' was a fairly familiar concept by 1500. Other motets have texts and sometimes other features (such as an unusual cantus firmus treated in a striking way) implying that they were intended for a particular and special occasion. Several funerary motets, such as Isaac's *Quis dabit capiti meo aquam* and (probably) Josquin's *Absalon fili mi* fall into this category, and some other motets seem to have a precise political significance. But the very topicality of such works should surely stimulate the scholar's curiosity about the circumstances and format of the original performance, and prompt him to attempt to locate or reconstruct the surrounding material.

Plainchant itself benefits particularly from performance in a liturgical context. This may be thought so self-evident as to be hardly worth stating, but that aesthetically repellent contrivance the 'concert of plainchant' is still all too common. The musical and literary characteristics of a plainchant item are conditioned by its position and function within a service and by the intended method of performance so heavily that removal to a non-liturgical environment will at best distort and at worst completely efface the item's character. Several considerations are important here. Association with the appropriate activity (or absence of activity) throws light on the character of a chant: for example, hearing an Introit accompanying the ceremonial at the beginning of Mass, or a Communion during the ablutions, reveals to the listener qualities of functional and artistic fitness in the chant that would be hidden in a concert performance. Similarly, hearing a Gradual or a responsory at the intended moment after a scriptural reading or homily enables the listener to appreciate more fully the chant's musical qualities because the reasons for them now become plain. Another reason for performing plainchant in the correct context is that very often successive items were intended to have a cumulative effect, or to interrelate with each other in other ways. For example, the chant items in a service or sequence of services on a particular day may play an exegetical role in quoting, requoting, amplifying and developing scriptural texts relevant to the day; even a cursory reading of the items for virtually any festival will demonstrate this. Performing any one of these items out of context will deprive it of much of its significance. Such textual considerations are of very great importance, although the cynic might ask how many listeners actually pay any attention to the words of music from any period. There may also be important musical interrelationships; for example, the psalm antiphons in an Office service may form a complete or partial modal cycle, proceeding along the line from Dorian to Hypomixolydian, and the contrasts of modality will enhance the impact of each individual chant.

Some plainchant items depend so heavily upon their liturgical context for their effect that they are virtually unperformable outside it. Sequences, for example, sound convincing only when heard at the end of the carefully controlled raising of the emotional and musical temperature that begins with the Gradual, continues with the Alleluia and culminates with the Sequence itself; also, the strenuously literary character of a Sequence, indeed its very wordiness, make their point fully only when juxtaposed with the textual economy and melismatic style of the Gradual and (even more) the Alleluia. Plainchant has generally suffered from under-exposure during the modern early music revival because the liturgical developments and ecclesiastical politics of the last thirty years have impeded its performance. It has thus been difficult to explore and perform even the previously familiar chant repertory, and it has been nearly impossible to resuscitate more recondite types of chant at all. I am thinking particularly of the huge family of plainchant called 'tropes'. Tropes, which are textual and musical additions to existing chant items designed to introduce and comment on the parent item, were one of the highest literary and musical and indeed intellectual achievements of the Romanesque period, and they have a great deal to tell us about the creative concepts of the time; but their existence is known only to a few specialists and they are practically never performed, because they are so indissolubly linked to a particular liturgical environment.

Anybody intending to make a liturgical reconstruction has to take a wide range of decisions which will affect the nature of the reconstruction on different levels; many of these decisions interconnect and influence each other. The most fundamental decision of all concerns the reason or reasons behind the enterprise. If the intention is to explore a particular liturgy by bringing it to life, many subsidiary elements of choice will be decided automatically. For example, the scholar will probably choose to make his reconstruction as realistic as he can by including both the rite (the items to be performed) and the ceremonial (the method of their performance) and by locating the reconstruction with the greatest possible precision in terms of time and place. At the other extreme, if the intention is to provide an appropriate and sympathetic context for what would otherwise have to be treated as concert items, one will be tempted to keep things as simple as possible, for instance by performing a polyphonic Mass in conjunction with a plainchant Ordinary, or a polyphonic psalm along with its antiphon. Yet even this elementary situation involves some important matters of principle. Is one, for example, going to attempt even rudimentary authenticity by using plainchant sources from the same rite, date and locality as the polyphony? Is the polyphony to be performed actually sufficiently homogeneous to allow even this degree of fidelity? Such matters may seem so elementary as to be unworthy of comment, but I believe that they do need to be considered. I can think of some recent performances advertised as 'liturgical reconstructions' which were nothing of the kind: polyphonic items from several different centuries and localities were sung in association with 'restored early-medieval' plainchant from the *Liber usualis* in the context of a modern (that is, pre-Vatican II) version of the Tridentine rite. Whatever other virtues such mongrel enterprises may have (and I would concede that they may be appropriate in certain situations), they cannot realistically be called liturgical reconstructions.

My own experience is that the more complete, accurate and faithful a reconstruction is, the more aesthetically rewarding and intellectually illuminating it is likely to be (I am, of course, assuming that the performers are acceptably competent). I assume as a prerequisite for making even the simplest kind of reconstruction that the music involved (whether plainchant or polyphony) will be chronologically and geographically homogeneous. The absolute minimum in a liturgical reconstruction should probably be the inclusion of all the main material that would actually have been sung, not chanted or spoken: the Ordinary and the sung Proper of Mass, for example. In the case of an Office service, however, it would be inappropriate and misleading to sing the psalm antiphons without the chanted psalms themselves, and so one naturally progresses to the next stage, in which the chanted items are added. One may then decide to go another step further by including such other items as were performed in a publically audible manner. The main constituents in this category are the recited readings and prayers: the Collect, Lesson, Epistle, Gospel and Postcommunion of Mass and the readings and prayers of the various Office services. Some musical items benefit greatly from association with the readings which they follow; for example, Sheppard's and Tallis's polyphonic responsories are clearly designed to match in scale and intellectual stamina the Lessons which precede them. One may then feel that the formal exchanges between participants, such as the versicle and response 'Dominus vobiscum: et cum spiritu tuo', are so intimately linked to the following item (usually a prayer or reading) that they need to be included too. Similar considerations may recommend the inclusion of the Preface before the Sanctus and the Pax before the Agnus dei. The next step will be to add the audibly chanted conclusions of prayers the main body of whose texts are said privately, such as the Secret, Canon and Embolism of Mass; these audible terminations are certainly of major practical importance in that they coordinate the activity of the leader of the service and the other participants. Having gone this far, one may well be tempted to include all of the material spoken during a service, whether it be audible or inaudible, because only by doing this can one arrive at realistic timings for the various constituents within the service; such timings are important if one wishes to assess accurately how the course of a service is paced, and how the musical elements contribute to and are affected by the pacing. Now the final stage, in which one attempts to recreate all the ceremonial as well, is almost inevitable, because many of the elements already brought into the reconstruction will have brought ceremonial activity with them. One often finds that it is the ceremonial that creates the greatest practical difficulties, because singers either are totally unused to performing ceremonial actions, or (even worse) come from a certain kind of religious background where they learnt ceremonial habits which they find hard to break. There are, nevertheless, many advantages in striving for the most complete fidelity, not least because the sheer mental and physical strain of carrying through such a performance can intensify and enhance the impact of the experience.

Making a liturgical reconstruction involves the use of a variety of documents. Ideally one would like to have a complete set of liturgical books from the selected place and time: an Ordinal for information about the rite, a Consuetudinary or Customary for the ceremonial, a Missal and a Gradual for the texts and the plainchant of the Mass, a Breviary and an Antiphonal for the Office, and a Processional for the pre-Mass, post-Vespers and other processions. For special services such as baptism, burial, the reconciliation of penitents or the enclosure of a leper one will also need a Manual, and for ceremonies conducted by a bishop a Pontifical will be necessary. For early medieval services, which often contained a sizeable amount of material later discarded, one will also need a Troper and perhaps also a Sequentiary. To locate all of this material, if indeed it still exists, one will need to know where the main liturgical collections are, how they are organised and how (if at all) they are catalogued. The older standard bibliographical guides such as Frere's *Bibliotheca musico-liturgica*, Ker's lists of medieval Latin manuscripts in British libraries, Leroquais's catalogues of liturgical manuscripts in French public libraries and van Dijk's hand-list of liturgical manuscripts in the Bodleian Library are still indispensable, but they need to be supplemented by reference to more recent works (the bibliography to the article 'Plainchant' in *The New Grove* is admirably complete up to the late 1970s). One will also find oneself making a great deal of use of *Patrologia Latina* (and perhaps also *Patrologia Graeca*), the publications of the Henry Bradshaw Society and the Alcuin Club, as well as individual works by liturgiologists, such as Chevalier's editions of the rites of Bayeux and Rheims and Wordsworth's studies of the Salisbury rite. This by no means exhausts the opportunities for reading; archival studies, the work of art historians and the discoveries of archaeologists can all be directly relevant, and in some cases they may suggest solutions to problems insoluble by other means (for instance when a particular ecclesiastical building has completely disappeared).

The degrees of completeness and fidelity which can be achieved vary enormously. Many of the rites of the later Middle Ages and Renaissance are very fully documented, but this is by no means true for many earlier medieval liturgies. It is, for example, impossible fully to recreate any of the Gallican or Celtic liturgy because sources for the plainchant simply do not exist. In the case of the Mozarabic rite some reconstruction is possible but still has to be tentative because the plainchant is notated in a melodically equivocal manner. Sometimes the opposite problem is encountered; for instance, the plainchant of the Milanese rite survives in unambiguous notation but detailed information about the ceremonial is hard to come by except for the twelfth century. One encounters some melancholy ironies, such as the survival of very detailed information about liturgical conduct in institutions of which little or no physical trace now remains, as in the case of St Mary's Abbey, York. Conversely, almost nothing is known of the liturgy and plainchant of some great medieval foundations whose buildings substantially survive, as in the case of Rochester Cathedral. The situation concerning Worcester Cathedral and its rite adds another twist, in that we have the building and a uniquely complete set of plainchant sources, but possess virtually no other information about the liturgy. Such problems can sometimes be partly circumvented by recourse to contemporary documents from similar institutions, but the results of such improvisation cannot claim to be totally authentic. Attempts to evade the issue by claiming, for example, that all Benedictine houses followed the same liturgy, or that the Use of Salisbury was everywhere observed in an identical fashion, take insufficient account of the considerable degree of local variation that medieval and renaissance liturgies almost always permitted. Furthermore, the further back in time that one goes, the more difficult it is to make good such deficiencies even by these inadequate means, because the requisite documents become more and more scarce.

Once the necessary information has been located, one has to make good use of it. Almost always the material will be in medieval Latin, and reading this can be problematic, not so much on account of its accidence and syntax (which are looser than classical Latin and more reflective of contemporary vernacular usage) but because of the rather specialised vocabulary. I have in mind the many technical terms used to denote parts of a building, items of ceremonial equipment, types of movement and gesture, modes of performance, and so on. Many of these terms are unknown in classical Latin, and some of them do not even appear in modern dictionaries of medieval Latin. Fortunately modern editors of medieval service books generally provide glossaries of words occurring in the text, but these glossaries themselves are not always totally reliable. Problems concerning terminology range from the general to the particular. On the broad scale, one has to decide whether a writer had the intention and ability to use technical terms with precision, and whether he was being consistent. A thoroughly critical understanding of terminology is very important; words that one might be tempted to treat as synonymous can turn out to have significantly different meanings. For example, in books of Salisbury Use the verbs 'intonare' and 'incipere' are frequently encountered, and it is easy to assume that they both mean 'to begin'. But they actually have distinct meanings, and the distinction is liturgically important. 'Incipere' means to sing the first few notes of a chant in order to set the pitch, while 'intonare' means to sing the first half of a psalm or canticle verse up to the *metrum* or mid-verse cadence. In such a case correct interpretation of an apparently innocuous word is essential for a liturgically correct performance.

Sometimes one encounters terms whose full significance can only be guessed at. For example, the medieval Milanese rite refers to singers performing 'in modo coronae', that is, 'in the manner (or shape) of a crown'. It does not take much ingenuity to work out that since a medieval crown usually took the form of a circlet, and because many churches had a wheel-shaped candelabrum called a 'corona' in front of the altar (there is a splendid example in Charlemagne's chapel at Aachen), this phrase refers to a choir standing in a circle. But a great deal is still left unanswered: did the singers stand in a complete or partial circle; where in the church did they stand; how were the different grades of singer arranged in the circle; which way did they face; did they hold books, sing from a lectern or sing from memory? Another type of problematic situation, namely the occurrence of an apparently unequivocal description so bizarre as to be hard to believe, can also be demonstrated from the Milanese rite. Beroldus, a twelfth-century official of Milan cathedral who wrote an apparently expert, clear and precise description of the rite as it existed in his own day, describes a method of performing the Alleluia of Mass which seems to involve singing the very lengthy Alleluia itself no less than four times before the verse. This is unlike any other known method of performing the Alleluia, and it is not practised by those who in our own day claim to perform the Milanese rite authentically. But Beroldus gives the impression of having known what he was talking about, and his words appear unambiguous, so if one were reconstructing a twelfth-century Milanese Mass one should probably trust him and follow his description.

When interpreting a description or a set of instructions concerning a liturgical event one also has constantly to visualise and preferably try out in practice the consequences of what the words seem to mean; only thus is one likely to detect quite simple errors, for instance when a writer says 'this' instead of 'that' or 'left' instead of 'right'. Sometimes one encounters real or apparent inconsistencies, in which case one has to decide whether there really is an inconsistency and, if so, how to resolve it. In the books of the Salisbury rite, for example, there is frequent disagreement about the manner of censing the choir during Mass, about the way in which the Gospel books are carried back from the pulpitum after the Gospel reading, and also about the conduct of the ablutions after the communion. Sometimes a discrepancy will turn out to be real, in which case it may reflect a change in custom that occurred between the dates at which two conflicting descriptions were devised. In other cases there may in reality be no discrepancy at all, merely a scribal miscopying or misunderstanding of his exemplar. The copyists of liturgical books tended to work as literally as they could (indeed, they were instructed to do so), so once an error had crept into a text it was likely to be perpetuated and disseminated, acquiring a spurious authority through its multiplication. I suspect that a minor peculiarity of the Salisbury rite may have begun in this manner: namely, the melodic formula to which the versicle and response 'Dominus vobiscum: et cum spiritu tuo' is sung. In many Western rites the versicle was sung to the notes A-C-C-BC-CB-B, the response to the notes A-C-C-B-B-C-C, but the standard Salisbury version has the first of these formulae for both the versicle and the response; a scribe's momentary carelessness in copying could easily have caused such an error, if it really is an error.

One of the most common problems encountered in working with liturgical books is that while they sometimes go into almost insane detail about matters which seem to us quite peripheral, such as how heavy candles and tapers should be and how a bishop should hold his crozier, they tend to be uncommunicative about matters which were obvious to those concerned at the time but are far from obvious to us nowadays. The books will, for instance, almost always tell us when the elements and vessels are brought in during Mass, but simply go on to say that they should be put 'in the usual place'. Similarly, the Salisbury books prescribe that on a double feast the officiating deacon and subdeacon should both carry 'texts' (we have to discover by other means what 'texts' are) in the procession to the altar at the beginning of Mass; later in the service they are clearly assumed not to be holding them any more, but we are not told when they set them down or where they put them. A further example: one always tends to assume that hymns, sequences and some other items were habitually performed *alternatim*, but it is very exceptional to find a medieval liturgical source that actually specifies this. It is also rare to find detailed information about the use of bells, but casual references indicate that bells were prominent in many services. One quite often suffers from a similar lack of information concerning the more purely musical aspects of a service. If one is lucky one may come across a pointed Epistle-book or Gospel-book (that is, one with symbols above the text showing how the recitation should be inflected), but the inflection of Collects, Lessons and other recited items usually has to be worked out either by experiment or by reference to a contemporary treatise on pointing. On a more basic level, one is seldom told how to relate the pitch of one chant item to that of another (except for the useful advice that plainchant should be sung neither too high nor too low); editors who do not test their reconstructions in performance may fail to realise that this problem exists at all.

Many of the issues involved in liturgical reconstruction are points of detail, but it is important to keep in mind some more general points. We have to remember that liturgy has never been static; it has always been developing; it is important to keep this in mind to correct the comfortable assumption that liturgical documents provide permanently and universally valid answers. We should also ask ourselves how likely it is that the written-down liturgical instructions were always faithfully observed. The provisions of the Salisbury rite, for example, are impressively detailed and water-tight, yet some fifteenth-century critics imply that in Salisbury Cathedral itself at that time the rite was no longer fully understood or observed. The attempt to achieve liturgical fidelity may also involve us in artistic compromise or even crises of conscience. For example, it will mean performing seventeenth-century sacred polyphony in company with the heavily bowdlerised chant of the period; it may entail singing chant at an unaccustomed speed or in an unfamiliar style; it may require the continual (and to us perhaps cacophanous) ringing of bells throughout the singing of a Sequence; it it likely to prompt a protracted and ultimately unsuccessful search for fully authentic vestments and equipment; and it can involve quite complex 'choreography' which we may find distracting. To some people the aesthetic results of such procedures will be as repellent as playing Mozart's keyboard music on a fortepiano, but if true understanding is our aim we must resist the influence of our own assumptions and taste.

Claude Goudimel's Contribution to the Musical Supplement of Pierre de Ronsard's *Amours* (1552)

MÁIRE EGAN-BUFFET

The main facts surrounding Goudimel's involvement with the musical supplement to Pierre de Ronsard's *Amours* (1552) are well known and well documented.[1] François Lesure suggests that the poet and the composer came together in the artistic circle which formed around the wealthy patron Jean de Brinon.[2] He also explains how Goudimel, corrector and subsequently musical adviser in the publishing house of Nicolas Du Chemin, was ideally placed to assume responsibility for the preparation of the musical supplement and to collaborate with the literary editors Veuve et Fils De La Porte.[3]

Critical assessments of the musico-poetic success of the supplement have tended to be unfavourable. Julien Tiersot questions the merits of a venture which recommends that a substantial number of verses having similar rhyme schemes and metric structures should be sung to the same music. He concludes that, from a musical point of view, the initiative was a failure and rightly points out that it was not destined to be repeated.[4] D.P. Walker agrees with Tiersot's assessment. He gives as one of the reasons for this, the fact that Ronsard did not appreciate that the type of music composed by his contemporaries would prevent the metre, or the rhythm of the text, or even the meaning of the words from being clearly heard.[5] In a more recent study, Brian Jeffery maintains that the extent of Ronsard's involvement with the preparation of the musical supplement was minimal. He concludes: 'Rather than a significant neo-classical achievement, this musical supplement is more modestly a collection of nine good settings of nine poems by Ronsard'[6].

Closer examination of Goudimel's rôle in the preparation of the supplement allows us to view the enterprise more positively and from a slightly different perspective. Goudimel, and the publishing firm of Du Chemin for whom he worked, stood to gain obvious advantages by encouraging Ronsard's declared interest in musical settings for his verses and by helping the poet laureat of France to realise his Humanist objectives. Goudimel's rôle was two-fold: to assume responsibility for editing the music of the supplement and to compose four of the ten pieces it contained:[7]

Errant par les champs de la grace (ode)
En qui respandit le ciel (épode)
Quand j'apperçoy ton beau chef jaunissant
Qui renforcera ma voix.

His obectives would have been to secure for the printing house the greater prestige and consequent commissions that would undoubtedly accrue from a successful outcome and an advancement of his own standing in the French capital as musical adviser and composer.

The printing of a musical supplement to a literary edition posed a new problem for the firm of Du Chemin: instead of presenting the *chansons* in the customary two-volume format, one for *Superius* and *Tenor*, the other for *Contratenor* and *Bassus*, all four parts had to appear in a single-volume format that could be attached to the literary edition. Goudimel prepared for this carefully. On 5 July 1552, he first printed an anthology of *chansons*, the *Dixiesme Livre*[8] in both a one-volume and a two-volume format. Less than three months later, on 30 September 1552, the one-volume supplement appeared as an appendix to the literary edition.[9] The one-volume anthology, then, was clearly intended as a rehearsal for the compilation of the music for the literary edition. It is perhaps no coincidence that this volume features the first musical setting of a poem by Ronsard to appear in print. The composer was Marc Antoine Muret, a prominent literary figure and associate of Ronsard who not only composed one of the musical settings in the supplement but also provided a commentary for the re-edition of the *Amours* in 1553.[10]

From a music publisher's point of view, the new venture was thus successfully completed, since the music for each *chanson* had been set out so that the four parts could be read simultaneously from the opened book: *Superius* and *Tenor* on the *verso* side of one page facing the *Contratenor* and *Bassus* parts on the *recto* side of the next page. Care had also been taken to make page turns coincide for each part. Ronsard and his contemporaries would have seen that music publishers were willing and able to meet poets' requirements and would thus have been encouraged to seek further collaboration with composers.

Complying with Ronsard's requirements for music appropriate to his verses proved a much more difficult task and it is in this respect that Goudimel and his fellow musicians are accused of failure. Ronsard's principal aim, and that of the artistic circle surrounding him, was to raise the status of the French language and to imbue it with a new richness, beauty, grandeur and prestige. It was for this reason that Ronsard sought to capture the elevated tone of the Horatian and Pindaric odes in his verses:

[. . .] ne voiant en nos Poëtes François chose qui fust suffisante d'imiter, j'allai voir les étrangers, et me rendi familier d'Horace, contrefaisant sa naïve douceur, [. . .] et osai, le premier des nostres, enrichir ma langue de ce nom, Ode, [. . .].[11]

Telles inventions encores te ferai-je veoir dans mes autres livres, où tu pourras (si les Muses me favorisent comme j'espère) contempler de plus près les saintes conceptions de Pindare [. . .].[12]

Ronsard's pindaric *Ode à Michel de l'Hospital, Errant par les champs de la grace*, for example, is manifestly grandiose and complex. In his sonnets, more directly in imitation of Bembo and Petrarch than of Horace, he expresses his sentiments of love for Cassandra with a refinement, nobility and delicacy which elevate the tone of this poetry far above that of the simple *dixains* and *huitains* of his great predecessor and compatriot Clément Marot who died in 1543. Ronsard wanted music that would enhance and reflect both the form and the content of his verses after the manner of the Ancients:

[. . .] et ferai encores revenir (si je puis) l'usage de la lire aujourd'hui resuscitée en Italie, laquelle lire seule doit et peut animer les vers, et leur donner le juste poix de leur gravité.[13]

Il est certain que telle Ode est imparfaite, pour n'estre mesurée, ne propre à la lire, ainsi que l'Ode le requiert.[14]

Goudimel's music for the *Ode à Michel de l'Hospital* (*Errant par les champs de la grace* (ode) *En qui respandit le ciel* (épode)) is both complex and contrapuntal in style.[15] Ronsard could only have approved of his way of contributing musically to the elevated tone and esoteric language of this Pindaric ode. He clearly appreciated the nature of Ronsard's verses since much of this music is directly inspired by the text. When setting the sixth line of the *ode*,

D'une laborieuse main

he reflects the idea of arduous labour by letting the three lower voices descend into the lower limits of their range under a sustained *Superius* line (Example 1):

EXAMPLE 1: Goudimel *Errant par les champs de la grace*, meas. 22-4

Further on, the Pindaric metaphor in line eight 'Trois fois torce d'un ply
Thébain' is musically pointed by three successive entries (the second being in
parallel thirds between the *Bassus* and *Superius*) (Example 2).[16]

EXAMPLE 2: Goudimel *Errant par les champs de la grace*, meas. 28-30

Finally, the descending melodic line which spans the entire plagal octave of the
principal mode (transposed hypoionian) is first presented in the *Superius*
(measure 20) and then taken up in imitation by the other voices in the final
measure to express the meaning of the concluding lines of the ode's first strophe:

'Qui ça bas ramena des cieulx
Les filles qu'enfanta Mémoire.' (lines 11-12).

It is hardly coincidental that, in the final phrase of the music allotted to the
twelfth and last line of the text, the *Superius*, *Contratenor* and *Bassus* are each
accorded a single note for each of its nine syllables, the intention being, no
doubt, to draw the singers' attention to the nine daughters of the Muse (Example
3):[17]

EXAMPLE 3: Goudimel *Errant par les champs de la grace*, meas. 45-8

The music for the epode *En qui respandit le ciel* is no less text-inspired. In
contrast to the rather sombre conclusion of the ode, it opens with each voice
singing in the upper range of its total ambitus for this *chanson*.[18]

Given that the *Ode à Michel de l'Hospital* is not only text-inspired but also
stylistically very different from Goudimel's *chansons parisiennes* published
before 1552, it would seem obvious that a lofty, complex musical style was

deliberately chosen as being appropriate to the elevated tone of Ronsard's Pindaric verses.[19]

Goudimel's music for the first strophe of Ronsard's *Hymne triomphal sur le trepas de Marguerite de Valois, Qui renforcera ma voix*,[20] is equally elevated in tone, complex and through-composed in its construction and clearly text-inspired. A high tessitura is consistently maintained to accompany references to the heavens and, in addition, in the final line, a descending three-note figure repeated in close imitation admirably conveys the poet's desire to send his verses soaring unbridled on their journey heaven-wards (Example 4):

'Ores il fault que le frein
Qui ja par le ciel me guide
Peu serviteur de la bride
Fende l'air d'un plus grand train.' (lines 9-12)

EXAMPLE 4: Goudimel *Errant par les champs de la grace*, meas. 38-43

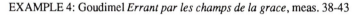

Though appropriately simpler in style, Goudimel's music for Ronsard's sonnet *Quand j'apperçoy ton beau chef jaunissant*[21] is a model of elevated dignity, almost hymn-like melodic beauty and classical restraint which perfectly captures the spirit of Ronsard's verses. Its essentially homophonic style radiates a warm sonority and allows the chief melodic interest to be placed in the *Superius*. Discreet imitative entries and graceful melismatic approaches to the cadences sustain the contrapuntal interest of the four-part writing. The structural divisions of the sonnet into two quatrains and two tercets are respected in the musical design and although the music of the initial quatrain and tercet is repeated for the second quatrain and tercet, the rhythmic flow of the melodic lines seems to respond naturally and effortlessly to the prosody of each line of the text.[22]

Goudimel's four musical settings for the *Amours* have thus been shown to respond admirably to the Humanist ideal of musico-poetic union in imitation of the poet-musicians of Classical Antiquity. The problem arises when one attempts to follow the recommendations given by Ambroise De La Porte in his *Advertissement au Lecteur* that precedes the music of the supplement.[23] In it he states that the greater part of Ronsard's poems in the *Amours* may be sung to the music contained in the supplement. Thus, four of the six sonnet settings are followed by a list of further sonnets which may be sung to the same music. The allocation of the sonnets to the different musical settings is determined solely on their having identical rhyme schemes to the poems set to music. P. Laumonier lists the four rhyme schemes as shown below, he matches them with four of the musical settings and points out that the two remaining sonnet settings (*Las je me plain* by Muret and *Bien qu'à grand tort* by Certon) belong to group I and group II respectively:[24]

Qui vouldra voyr	Janequin I – 2(fmmf), m^2 m^2 f^2 m^3 m^3 f^2
Nature ornant	Janequin II – 2(mffm), f^2 f^2 m^2 f^3 f^3 m^2
J'espere et crains	Certon III – 2(fmmf), m^2 m^2 f^2 m^3 f^2 m^3
Quand j'apperçoy	Goudimel IV – 2(mffm), f^2 f^2 m^2 f^3 m^2 f^3

Ambroise De La Porte also states in the final page of the supplement that each strophe of the hymn to Marguerite de Valois *Qui renforcera ma voix* may be sung to Goudimel's music for the first strophe (the rhyme scheme being identical in each), that, similarly, all strophes and antistrophes of the Pindaric *Ode à Michel de l'Hospital* may be sung to Goudimel's music for the first strophe *Errant par les champs de la grace* (ode), and all the epodes may be sung to the music of the first epode *En qui respandit le ciel.*[25]

It has been pointed out that Goudimel's complex musical settings of the initial sections of Ronsard's *Ode* and *Hymne* could not withstand a full musical performance of each poem involving 40 consecutive hearings of the music of the hymn, 48 and 24 renderings of the music of the strophe and epode respectively.[26] Referring to the different musical conventions in the sixteenth century which often prefaced poems or sacred hymns with a musical timbre associated with a secular song bearing no relationship to the new text, one author attempts to defend the recommendation that one sonnet setting may indeed be adapted to several others, even though their content and sentiments are totally different.[27] Closer examination of Goudimel's music in the following paragraphs should disprove the relevance of this argument.

It has generally been assumed that since Goudimel was responsible for the preparation of the music of the supplement, he was also at least partly responsible for selecting the poems to be set to music. However, there is no direct evidence for this. Laumonier has demonstrated that the sonnets were chosen on technical grounds to illustrate four rhyme schemes in which alternating masculine and feminine rhymes are observed between the last line of the quatrain and the first line of the sestet.[28] Although the *Ode* (strophe, antistrophe and epode) and *Hymne*[29] were submitted for a musical setting primarily because of Ronsard's desire to imitate the poets of Classical Antiquity who advocated a musical accompaniment for these two poetic genres, regularly alternating masculine and feminine rhymes are also evidenced in these poems. It is clear from the *Amours* that, in 1552, Ronsard sought to promote alternating masculine and feminine endings and strophic regularity as the norm in lyrical poetry destined to receive musical interpretation. It was not until 1565, however, 13 years later, that Ronsard, in his *Abbregé de l'Art Poetique*[30] set out the rules governing the metrical construction of poetry destined to be set to music, by which time musical settings of his poems evinced a very different style from that found in the *Amours*.[31] The composers would therefore have supplied the music for the poems in 1552 being aware of the general Humanist desire for musico-poetic union but without any clear ideas as to the poet's intentions with regard to technical matters. Moreover, the musical treatment of the masculine and feminine endings, whether alternating or not, posed no specific difficulties for the composer in 1552, who never fails to differentiate them in his music.[32]

A fact that is often overlooked in discussions concerning the merits of the supplement is that the statement concerning the manifold repetition of the music in the supplement to new texts came from neither Goudimel nor Ronsard but from Ambroise De La Porte. It is he who stipulates that many of the poems of the *Amours* can be sung to the music in the supplement. Again, it is he who points out the experimental nature of the enterprise, promising to publish further editions of a similar nature should the demand arise.[33] Finally, since the recommendations concerning the musical interpretaion of Ronsard's *Ode* and *Hymne* obviously constitute the final section of the *Advertissement au Lecteur*,[34] it must have again been De La Porte and not Goudimel who not only explains how all the strophes of the *Ode* and *Hymne* are to be accommodated to Goudimel's music, but also establishes the lists of sonnets in accordance with their rhyme schemes. I suggest, therefore, that in 1552, Ronsard clearly favoured musical accompaniment for his verses on the grounds that this would help to raise the tone of the poetry, come close to the much-publicized Humanist ideal of musico-poetic union and follow in the steps of the poets of Classical Antiquity whom he sought to emulate. I suggest that the *Amours* represents one of his first attempts to put his theories concerning strophic regularity and regularly alternating masculine and feminine endings into practice. It was not until much later, after renewed contacts with musicians, having sufficiently understood how musico-poetic union could be achieved in this regard, that he set out practical recommendations to achieve this in his *Abbregé* of 1565. Finally, I suggest that it was the literary editors, not those responsible for the music in the supplement who decided (perhaps as an afterthought and certainly without consultation with the composers),[35] that most of the poems in the *Amours* could be sung to the music in the supplement.

It could be argued that Ambroise De La Porte could have established the lists of sonnets to be sung to the same music and advised the reader with regard to the performance of the Pindaric ode and hymn to Marguerite de Valois, *after consultation with Goudimel*, the musician responsible for the music in the supplement. Internal analysis of Goudimel's music does not support this theory. When we try to apply his music to alternative sonnets or strophes, musical problems inevitably arise where the *internal* structure of a poetic line or the syntax of a group of lines within a strophe differs from that found in the texts set by Goudimel.

In his setting of the sonnet, *Quand j'apperçoy ton beau chef jaunissant*,[36] Goudimel marks the customary caesura after the fourth syllable in line twelve by a cadence followed by a rest in three out of the four parts, and by initiating a new imitative phrase in the *Tenor* (Example 5):

'Doncques (mon tout) / si dignement je n'use'
  1   2   3   4   5 6 7 8   9 10

EXAMPLE 5: Goudimel *Quand j'apperçoy ton beau chef jaunissant*, meas. 44-9

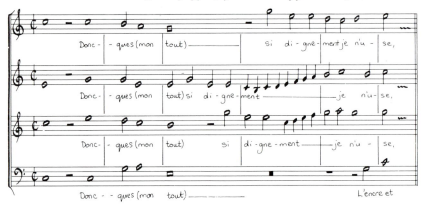

In the corresponding twelfth line of one of the sonnets listed by Ambroise De La Porte *Le pensement qui me fait devenir*, the caesura after the fourth syllable is followed by a silent 'e' which should be elided with the vowel that begins the fifth syllable:[37]

'Reçoy ma vi-/e   o déesse et languide'
  1 2   3   4   5 67   8   9   10

Goudimel's music does not allow for this new type of caesura since the silent 'e' following the fourth syllable cannot be elided on account of the rests. Nor would it be musically desirable to suggest that the singers modify the melodic lines so that the silent 'e' be sung. The following illustration (Example 6)

EXAMPLE 6: Goudimel *Quand j'apperçoy ton beau chef jaunissant*, meas. 44-9, adapted to the text of *Le pensement qui me fait devenir*.

is a possibility but not an ideal one since it diminishes the textual clarity of the successive entries marking the opening of the second part of the line. It also introduces an extra (twelfth) syllable into the poetic line which, in other *chansons*, Goudimel is at pains to avoid.[38] Similar examples can be found in Goudimel's *Ode à Michel de l'Hospital*[39] where the introduction of a rest in a melodic line composed for the first strophe *Errant par les champs de la grace* renders the music totally unsuited to subsequent verses. Any modifications of the text distribution or of the note values, introduced in order to remedy the difficulty, inevitably destroy the essentially syllabic nature of Goudimel's setting. If, for example, following A. De La Porte's recommendation, the eighth line of the first antistrophe

'La double voûte de son front
  1 2   3 4 5 6 7   8
        (1st antistrophe, line 8)

were to be sung to Goudimel's music for the corresponding line in the first strophe,

'Trois fois torce d'un ply Thébain
  1   2   3 4 5   6   7 8
(1st strophe, line 8)

the final three syllables and not four would have to be set to the four notes after the rest so as not to have a new phrase commencing in the middle of the word *voûte*.[40] Likewise, the music of the first epode (*En qui respandit le ciel*) in the Ode does not always suit that of the following epodes. Goudimel clearly composed its final phrase specifically to match the concluding heptasyllabic line,

'Le soing des Dieux et des hommes.'
(1st epode, line 10)

since the first half of the phrase is formed around the first four syllables preceding the conjunction 'et' while in the second half, the last four syllables are isolated in an extended cadential formula.[41] The music for this line is clearly quite unsuited to the corresponding last line in the sixth epode,

'De ces neuf Musiciennes'
(*Ode à Michel de l'Hospital*, 6th epode, line 10)

since here the beginning of the cadential formula coincides with the second syllable of the word 'Musiciennes'. A possible solution in the *Tenor*, for example, might be to modify the note values in order to incorporate the entire word 'Musiciennes' in the cadential phrase (Example 7).

EXAMPLE 7: Goudimel *En qui respandit le ciel*: (a) *Tenor*, meas. 29-33;,
(b) adapted to the text of the sixth *épode*

In the first of the forty strophes of Ronsard's *Hymne triomphal sur le trepas de Marguerite de Valois, Qui renforcera ma voix*,[42] the division of the strophe into three distinct quatrains, each with its own rhyme scheme (AbAb CCdd EffE (alternate rhymes, rhyming couplets, aaba rhyme scheme, respectively)) is respected in the syntax:

Qui renforcera ma voix	A
Et qui fera que je vole	b
Jusqu'au ciel à ceste fois	A
Sur l'aesle de ma parolle?	b
Or mieulx que devant il fault	C
Avoir l'estomac plus chault	C
De l'ardeur qui ja m'enflamme	d
Le coeur d'une plus grand' flamme.	d
Ores il fault que le frein	E
Qui ja par le ciel me guide	f
Peu serviteur de la bride	f
Fende l'air d'un plus grand train.	E

Goudimel reflects this division by marking the conclusion of each quatrain with a perfect cadence. Since Ronsard's syntactical divisions do not consistently correspond to the metrical division in all of the ensuing strophes, were Goudimel's music to be sung to these, it would actually hinder rather than contribute to the intellegibility of the text. The eighteenth and twenty-fourth strophes clearly illustrate how totally inappropriate the perfect cadences would be at the conclusion of the enjambed lines four and eight:

'L'Humilité s'attacha
Contre la Gloire mondaine
Et sa lance luy cacha
Droit en ceste part où l'aine

Se joint aveque le flanc;
Le Peché, de crainte blanc,
N'attendit la Repentance,
Ains évitant sa puissance
Vint où Grace l'enserra
Dedans sa troupe hardie,
Et, d'une lance brandie
Jusques au coeur l'enferra.

(18th strophe)

Jésus Christ à ceste fois
Esbranlant dans sa main nuë
Le grand fardeau de la Crois
Perçoit l'autre d'une nuë
A l'escart, pour voir çà bas

> La fin de ces deux combas.
> Ayant ferme souvenance
> D'une fatale ordonnance
> Que l'Ame au Ciel monteroit
> Par une nouvelle porte,
> Dont la main saintement forte
> Sa chair propre donteroit.'

(24th strophe)

We have already seen how well Goudimel's music expresses the imagery in the concluding line of the first strophe of the *Hymne*.[43] However, Goudimel isolates its first three syllables, *Fende l' air*, by repeating a descending melodic figure followed by a rest and thus renders this music quite unsuitable for the concluding line of many of the following strophes: the break either makes a nonsense of the first three syllables heard in isolation from the following four:

'L'ame, le/ fer et le sang.'	(16th strophe)
'Jusques au/ coeur l'enferra.'	(18th strophe)
'Que mort le/ desarçonna.'	(19th strophe)
'Prenant sa/ verge en son poing.'	(27th strophe)

or, worse still, it falls in the middle of a word:

'Se fist mais/tresse du pris'	(4th strophe)
'Pour mieux for/cer les plus forts'	(5th strophe)
'Là l'Espé/rance et la Foy;'	(13th strophe)
'Seule au com/bat main à main.'	(20th strophe)

While it is true that modifications can be made to accommodate these changes in the poetic design of successive strophes, we have shown that they are not always entirely satisfactory. Moreover, we do not consider that Goudimel would have expected the performer to effect these modifications. We note that when, in his sonnet setting (*Quand j' apperçoy ton beau chef jaunissant*), Goudimel uses repeated music for the two tercets even though each has a different rhyme scheme (ccD eDe), he is careful to re-write the music over the second tercet so that he can include his simple but highly effective modifications to accommodate the masculine ending that replaces the feminine ending and *vice versa*. In the quatrains, on the other hand, where the text requires no such modifications, Goudimel is content to print the music once only over the text of the two quatrains.[44] That Goudimel was a perfectionist and so remained all his life is clear from a letter he wrote two years before he died (in August 1572) to his friend, the poet and scholar Paul Schede Melissus, in November 1570:

Mitto ad te secundam tui epigrammatis concentibus Musicis pro temporis brevitate ornatam, quam pro tua humanitate eo animo quo tibi offero excipias. Nam si fuisset mihi otium diuturnum politius atque ornatius tibi reddidissem, me habuisse tantillum spatii summo dolore afficior. Scias autem me hesternam diem total contrivisse atque consumsisse in illa concinnenda. Sed ut es mortalium, praesertim in eo quod fit celerius errare; tamen si quid mendarum in illa reperias, tuarum est partium emendare. Mali enim meam ignorantiam prodere, quam tanto viro deesse, quidquid autem ab amico proficisci par sit, à me expectato [. . .].[45]

One cannot imagine that a composer so anxious to perfect his own art and to respect the wishes of the author of the poetic text could consent to have his music modified at will by performers in order to accommodate a text for which it was never intended in the first place.

Goudimel's first strophic *chansons* to poems by Ronsard were published in 1562, ten years after the *Amours* (*Celuy qui n' ayme est malheureux, Du jour que je feuz amoureux, Il me semble que la journée* and *Tu me fais mourir de me dire*).[46] In these, the music is consistently more homophonic in style than in his previous *chanson* settings and all attempts to render musically the images depicted in the text have been abandoned in favour of a more unified setting consistent with the overall mood and tone of the poem. Each line of the text is clearly articulated in an independent musical phrase entirely devoid of rests. As in his earlier *chansons*, alternating masculine and feminine rhymes are reflected in the music, but here we see emerging for the first time two repeated minim chords being used to articulate a feminine ending. The most arresting feature of this strophic music is, however, its use of distinctive rhythmic patterns which are *not* governed by the prosody of the text. This type of *chanson* received the designation *Chanson en forme d' air*.

Goudimel's strophic *chansons* did not appear in an appendix to a literary edition but in the musical anthologies of Adrian Le Roy and Robert Ballard. In these editions, we find that the number of repetitions to which the strophic music may be subjected has been restricted. Thus, the fourth and final strophe of *Il me semble que la journée* does not appear alongside the second and third strophes beneath Goudimel's setting of the first one.[47] Similarly, only the second and third strophes of *Il me semble que la journée* appear beneath the music, the remaining four strophes having been omitted.[48] The number of strophes printed cannot be put down solely to the printer's desire to restrict the text to the page containing the music. For Goudimel's strophic setting of Ronsard's *Ode à Pierre Paschal, Tu me fais mourir de me dire*, care has been taken to present all five strophes on the one page beneath the music that accompanies the first strophe.[49] Goudimel was, no doubt, aware that the sense of the text required that all six strophes should be sung. For this *chanson*, he deliberately wrote the simplest and most unobtrusive musical setting of all, one whose catchy, distinctive rhythm would bear sustained repetition.

It is evident therefore that for his strophic *chansons* of 1562, Goudimel adopts a style and tone that differs considerably from that observed in his musical settings for the *Amours* composed ten years earlier. In these later pieces, Goudimel is responding with equal sensitivity to Ronsard's texts for these are no longer inspired by the complexities of the Pindaric odes but by the lighter, simpler and more direct verses of Anacreon. The new poetic content evokes from Goudimel simple, strophic settings which are most appropriate to the immediacy of Ronsard's language and sentiments.

It was not until 1565, three years after the publication of Goudimel's first strophic settings of his poems, that Ronsard published in his *Abbregé de l'Art Poétique François* clear guidelines for strophic poems destined for a musical accompaniment.[50] The relevance of each recommendation to Goudimel's settings of 1562 is so readily apparent that one is led to suggest that they were formulated after renewed collaboration between Goudimel and Ronsard while the composer was writing these *chansons*. By this time, Ronsard would have been aware of Goudimel's considerable musical reputation and prestige among his fellow French Humanists.[51] He had risen to become partner to Nicolas Du Chemin prior to his departure from the publishing house in 1555 and he was rapidly acquiring notoriety for his musical settings of the Psalter whose publishers included Adrian le Roy and Robert Ballard since 1556.[52] It was not until after 1562 that other composers (with the possible exception of Pierre Clereau) became seriously interested in Ronsard's poetry,[53] whereas nine of the fifteen Ronsard poems set by Goudimel appeared before 1562. Unfortunately, Goudimel's links with Ronsard were inevitably severed in 1562 when, with the outbreak of the first War of Religion, the Huguenots and Ronsard began to engage openly in hostilities.[54] Placed in the broader perspective of Goudimel's *total* involvement with Ronsard's verses, we can now see that the fruits of Goudimel's initial collaboration with the poet in 1552 were not limited to a single edition. The appearance of several subsequent editions attests to the growth in mutual understanding between the two artists.

The true significance of the musical supplement to the *Amours* has been generally misunderstood because of the failure to recognize that the ultimate responsibility for the misleading presentation of its contents to the public as strophic music lies with the literary editors Ambroise and Veuve Marie De La Porte and not with Goudimel or Ronsard.[55] It must therefore be considered a positive outcome of the venture that this aspect of the experiment in musico-poetic union was never repeated: all subsequent settings of Ronsard's poetry appeared in musical editions with the result that the music, remaining in the control of the musicians, was thus free of misunderstandings.

From a publishers point of view, the *Amours* with its supplement was not a failure since it was re-edited the following year (1553) this time with a commentary by Marc-Antoine Muret.[56] If it were, as Tiersot maintains,[57] a musical failure, this did not deter Ronsard from continuing to strive for musico-poetic union in his strophic verses by applying once again to the chief musical participants in the 1552 venture. It was his willingness to adopt the simpler style of Anacreon in his poetry that allowed Goudimel and other composers such as Nicolas de la Grotte and Pierre Clereau to compose music appropriate to a strophic text.[58] Rather than being viewed negatively, the 1552 experiment should be seen as a major initial step towards the Humanist ideal of musico-poetic union. What was achieved was proof that music could indeed express the content of a poetic text and capture its spirit and tone. What was also gained, by default, was the realization that the musician would never be subservient to the poet and his literary editors. Musicians and music publishers were provided with proof of the dangers inherent in allowing the music to be taken over by the editors of a literary publication and in having the music relegated to the inferior position of an appendix. Once the principle of musico-poetic union had been admitted and welcomed by poets, musicians were then in a position to insist that their music should remain in the control of music publishers. This is, in effect, what subsequently transpired. By a happy coincidence, in 1553, scarcely a year after the first edition of the *Amours*, A. Le Roy and R. Ballard, who were destined to publish the greatest number of Ronsard settings, inherited from P. Attaingnant the prestigious position of Royal Printers of music.[59]

In the light of this examination, Goudimel's rôle in the preparation of the music for the *Amours* emerges as being much more positive than hitherto believed. The actual music for the *Supplement* is impeccably presented. Blame for misunderstandings that may have arisen concerning its possible strophic interpretation must be attributed not to the composers nor to Goudimel in his capacity as musical adviser, but to the literary editor Ambroise De La Porte who penned the *Advertissement au Lecteur*. Internal analysis has shown that each of the four Goudimel settings was deliberately composed with the musical expression of one strophe or of one sonnet only in mind and they all serve as ample proof that Goudimel would never willingly have agreed to De La Porte's recommendations. Any idea that relations between Goudimel and Ronsard may have been strained as a result of this misunderstanding must be discounted in view of the evidence which points to Goudimel's continued interest in Ronsard's poetry and of the success of his strophic settings published in 1562. These *chansons* were successfully published in a musical edition and the number of strophic repetitions was sensitively controlled by its editor. Ronsard clearly approved of these settings for they provide perfect illustrations for his fellow poets of his recommendations concerning the union of music and poetry in his *Abbregé de l'Art Poétique François* published three years later. These chansons also constitute some of the first examples of the highly successful *chanson en forme d'air*, itself a forerunner of the *Air de Cour*. One regrets that the political climate in France and the intensification of the Wars of Religion in the 1560s put an end to such a fruitful musico-poetic union between two great artists who were thereafter fated to remain on opposite sides of the religious and political divide.

NOTES

1. *Les Amours de P. de Ronsard [. . .] Ensemble le cinquiesme livre de ses Odes [. . .] A Paris, chez la veuve Maurice de la Porte [Supplément musical,* Paris (N. Du Chemin)] 1552. See F. Lesure and G. Thibault, 'Bibliographie des Editions musicales publiées par Nicolas Du Chemin 1549-1576', in *Annales Musicologiques* 1 (Paris, 1953), no. 28. Hereafter *DCh.* Modern edition of text with facsimile reproduction of the music in: *Pierre de Ronsard, Oeuvres complètes, édition critique par Paul Laumonier. Revue et complétée par I. Silver et R. Lebègue* (Paris, 1903-67), vol. 4, Hereafter *Ronsard-L.*

2. F. Lesure, 'La chanson française au XVIᵉ siècle', *Histoire de la Musique, 1, Des Origines à Jean-Sébastien Bach,* Roland-Manuel (Paris, 1960), 1058.

3. See *DCh* (as n. 1), 274-5.

4. J. Tiersot, 'Ronsard et la musique de son temps', *S.I.M.G.,* (Leipzig, 1902-03), pp. 70-140. Hereafter: *Tiersot-R.*

5. See D.P. Walker, 'Le chant orphique de Marsile Ficin,' *Musique et Poésie du XVIᵉ siècle,* (Paris, 1953), 27.

6. See Brian Jeffery, 'The idea of music in Ronsard's poetry', *Ronsard the Poet,* ed. Terence C. Cave (London, 1973), 209-39. Hereafter, *Jeffery, The idea of music.* Jeffery counts as one the separate settings Goudimel composed for the ode and epode of Ronsard's Pindaric ode.

7. The other six *chansons* are: *J'espère et crains, me tais et supplie, Bien qu'à grand tort il te plaist d'allumer* (both by P. Certon); *Las je me plain(s) de mille et mille et mille* (M.A. Muret); *Qui vouldra voir comme un dieu me surmonte, Nature ornant la dame qui devoit, Petite Nymphe folastre* (all by Cl. Janequin). See *DCh* (as n. 1), no. 28.

8. *Dixiesme Livre contenant XXVI chansons [. . .] en un volume* (Paris, 1552); *DCh,* no. 27. *Dixiesme Livre contenant XXVI chansons [. . .] en deux volumes* (Paris, 1552); *DCh,* no. 27 *bis.* The *Dixiesme Livre* was subsequently re-edited two years later in the two-volume format. See *DCh* (as n. 1), no. 38.

9. This is the date given by the printer at the end of the supplement: 'Achevé d'imprimer le trentiéme jour de Septembre, Mil cinq centz cinquante deux'. See *Ronsard-L* (as n. 1), vol. 4, 250.

10. See *Les Amours de P. de Ronsard [. . .] Nouvellement augmentées par luy, et commentées par Marc Antoine de Muret* (Paris, 1553). *DCh* (as n. 1), no. 27 *bis.* See above, n. 7.

11. *Préface Au Lecteur Les Quatre premiers Livres des Odes* (1550). See P. de Ronsard, *Ronsard Oeuvres Complètes. Avant-Propos, Notes, Glossaire par Gustave Cohen,* (Paris, 1958), vol. 2, p. 971. Hereafter: *Ronsard-C.*

12. *Ronsard-C* (as n. 11), 973-4.

13. *Ronsard-C* (as n. 11), 974.

14. *Ronsard-C* (as n. 11), 972.

15. Goudimel's setting is published in *Goudimel (Claude), Oeuvres complètes publiées par H. Gagnebin, R. Häusler et E. Lawry sous la direction de L.A. Dittmer et P. Pidoux*. See Volume 13 of this series: *Chansons (Profanes et Spirituelles). Transcriptions de P. Pidoux et M. Egan. Notes Critiques de Pierre Pidoux* (New York, Basle, 1974), *chanson* no. 20, 80-5. Hereafter: *Goudimel vol. 13.*

16. The number three refers to the Pindaric triad *strophe- antistrophe-épode*. See *Ronsard-L* (as n. 1), vol. 3, 119, note 4.

17. The silent syllable of the feminine ending is disregarded when reckoning the length of a line in French poetry. Since, however, it is no longer silent in a musical setting, an octosyllabic line with a feminine ending is heard as a nine-syllable line.

18. See *Goudimel vol. 13* (as n. 15), 83-5.

19. It has been pointed out that sixteen simple, predominantly homophonic chansons, all on strophic texts printed in full by P. Certon (one of the four composers of the supplement) were published in 1552 (see *RISM*, series C, 1709). Had Ronsard expressly wished this musical style for his strophic hymn and ode, it could therefore readily have been provided. See J. Whang, *From Voix de Ville to Air de Cour: the Strophic chanson c. 1545-75*, (Ph.D. dissertation, University of North Carolina at Chapel Hill, 1981), 8.

20. See *Goudimel vol. 13* (as n. 15), 205-7 and *Ronsard-C*, vol. 1, 593-604.

21. See *Goudimel vol. 13* (as n. 15), 194-8.

22. Only the opening measures of the reprise of the tercet are modified (see *Goudimel vol. 13*, 196-7, meas. 30-2 and 44-6). There are also minor alterations in text distribution (see the discussion below). The music of the two tercets is nonetheless *not* through-composed as stated in Gustave Reese, *Music in the Renaissance* (New York, 1954, revised edition, 1959), 387 and in *Tiersot-R* (as n. 4), 110.

23. 'Ayant recouvré le Livre des Amours du Seigneur P. de Ronsard, & le cinquiesme de ses Odes, avec aultres siens opuscules: Et puis après entendu que pour ton plaistir & entier contentement il a daigné prendre la peine de les mesurer sur la lyre (ce que nous n'avions encores apperceu avoir esté faict de tous ceux qui se sont exercités en tel genre d'escrire), suyvant son entreprise avec le vouloir que j'ay de luy satisfaire, & pour l'amour de toy Lecteur: J'ay faict imprimer, & mettre à la fin de ce present livre, la Musique, sus laquelle tu pourras chanter une bonne partie du contenu en iceluy: te promectant à l'advenir de continuer ceste maniere de faire (en ce qui s'imprimera de la composition dudict Ronsard) si je congnoy qu'elle te soit aggreable.' *Ronsard-L* (as n. 1), vol. 4, 189.

24. See *Ronsard-L* (as n. 1), vol. 4, XVII.

25. 'Au reste saches, Lecteur, que tous les Strophes & Antistrophes de l'Ode à Monsieur de l'Hospital se chantent sus la Musique du premier Strophe *Errant par les champs*. Et les Epodes de l'Ode mesmes sus la Musique du premier Epode *En qui respandit le ciel.*' *Ronsard-L* (as n. 1), vol. 4, 250.

26. *Tiersot-R* (as n. 4), 73-97.

27. Fernand Desonay, *Ronsard poète de l'amour, Livre Premier Cassandre* (Brussels, 1965), 137-97.

28. See *Ronsard-L* (as n. 1), XVII-XVIII and note 24 above. Laumonier points out that the only sonnets to have been rejected are those in which this alternating scheme is disregarded.

29. Ode: aBaBcDcDeFFe (strophe and antistrophe); AbbACCdEEd (épode);
Hymne: AbAbCCddEffE.

30. See *Ronsard-C* (as n. 11), vol. 2, 997.

31. See the discussion below, 193-4.

32. See the discussion below, 193.

33. See note 23 above.
34. See note 25 above.
35. Laumonier has pointed to the many errors and omissions in the lists and correctly adds a further sonnet (*Puisqu'aujourd'huy*) to the three named after Goudimel's *Quand j'apperçoy* on the grounds that it has the same rhyme scheme. See *Ronsard-L* (as n. 1), vol. 4, XVII, note 2 and 250, note 1.
36. See *Goudimel vol. 13* (as n. 15), 194-8.
37. This is known as 'la coupe féminine réformée'. See H. Chamard, 'Versification', *Dictionnaire des Lettres françaises (Le Seizième Siècle)*, (Paris, 1951), 689.
38. Comparison with Goudimel's setting of *Tant de beaulté n'a elle pas* (see *Goudimel vol. 13, chanson* no. 64, 240-3) and that of Pierre Symon (*RISM-I*, ser.1, 1549(22); modern transcription in M. Egan-Buffet, *Les Chansons de Claude Goudimel* (doctoral dissertation, Université de Paris-IV- Sorbonne, 1985, 3, 884-8) shows that, confronted with an octosyllabic line (line 5)
    'Elle est doulce / elle est [toute] humaine'
    1   2   3   4   5   6   7 8
    containing a silent syllable (*doulce*) at the caesura demanded by the meaning, Goudimel goes so far as to suppress the adverb *toute* in order to reflect both the caesura and the meaning of the text without unduly extending the octosyllabic line.
39. See *Goudimel vol. 13* (as n. 15), 80-5. For the complete text, see *Ronsard-C* (as n. 11), vol. 1, 386-406.
40. See Example 2 above.
41. This line has a feminine ending. It is thus interpreted musically by sounding the extra silent syllable. See note 17 above.
42. See *Goudimel vol. 13* (as n. 15), 205-07. For the complete text, see *Ronsard-C*, vol. 1, 593-604.
43. See the discussion on this point above, 185. See also Example 4 above.
44. See *Goudimel vol. 13* (as n. 15), 194-8 and the facsimile reproduction of the supplement in *Ronsard-L*, vol. 4, 212-17.
45. I am sending you the second part of your epigram which I have set to music as well as time permitted. Accept it with the same goodwill with which it is offered. It distressed me greatly that I had so little time, for had I had more, I would have returned it to you more polished and ornate. I would have you know that I spent all of yesterday polishing it. However, to err is human especially when pressed for time. If you find any errors, you are welcome to correct them for I should rather display my ignorance than to achieve less than perfection for one such as you [. . .].
    See *Melissi Schediasmatum Reliquiae Privilegio Caesureo authori concesso Lutetiae Parisorum. Apud Arnoldum Sittarum sub scuto Coloniensi, monte divi Hilarii [. ..]* 1575, vol. 2, fol. 84. (Paris, B.N., yc 1065). Full text of letter reproduced in *Cl. Goudimel, Oeuvres Complètes [. . .] Vol 14, Opera Dubia. Transcription et Notes Critiques de Pierre Pidoux Avec une notice d'une nouvelle source de Máire Egan* (Henryville, Ottawa, Basle, 1983), xvii.
46. See *Goudimel vol. 13* (as n. 15), ch. 11, 46-7; ch. 19, 78-80; ch. 23, 90-1; ch. 65, 243-4.
47. See *Unziesme Livre de chansons nouvellement composé en musique à 4, & 5 parties* (Paris, A. Le Roy et R. Ballard, 1562), fol. 15. See F. Lesure and G. Thibault, *Bibliographie des éditions d'Adrian Le Roy et Robert Ballard (1551-1593)* (Paris, 1955), no. 79. Hereafter: *LRB*.
48. See *LRB* (as n. 47), fol. 16.
49. See *LRB* (as n. 47), fol. 14; *Goudimel vol. 13*, 243-4; *Ronsard-C*, vol. 1, 573.

50. See *Ronsard-C* (as n. 11), vol. 2, 995-9.

51. Louis Des Masures refers to him in one of his poems as a friend of the renowned Humanist teacher Pierre Ramus (1515-1572). See *Ad Claudium filium adolescentem in: LVDOVICI MASVRII [. . .] Poemata. Secundo edita ab authore ipso recognita & nouis aucta. Basileae, Thomas Guarinus, 1574*. London (BL 11409 e 26) fol. 90ʳ, line 113.

52. See F. Lesure, 'Claude Goudimel, etudiant, correcteur et éditeur parisien', *Musica Disciplina*, 11, (1948), 225- 30. Reprinted in F. Lesure, *Musique et Musiciens français du XVIe siècle*, Geneva, Minkoff, 1976, 229-37.

53. Only nineteen publications featuring *chansons* to Ronsard's texts appeared before 1562. See G. Thibault and L. Perceau, *Bibliographie des Poésies de P. de Ronsard mises en Musique au seizième Siècle* (Paris, 1941).

54. See J. Pineaux, *La Polémique Protestante contre Ronsard* (Paris, 1973).

55. This point has already been raised by Brian Jeffery. See Jeffery, *The Idea of Music* (as n. 6), 212.

56. See note 10 above.

57. See the discussion on this point at the outset of this paper.

58. See *LRB* (as n. 47), no. 116 and no. 132.

59. See *LRB* (as n. 47), 12.

Adam Drese's 1648 Funeral Music and the Invention of the Slide Trumpet

PETER DOWNEY

A dam Drese (*c*.1620-1701), the most important member of a family of Thuringian musicians, is remembered today as the composer of a handful of well-known Lutheran chorales and as the Gamba-playing Kapellmeister at Arnstadt under whom served a number of members of the Bach family. However, this student of Marco Scacchi and follower of Heinrich Schütz was the composer of a wide variety of music, ranging from instrumental dance movements to festive cantatas and German operas, who had served in the same capacity at Weimar (1648-62) and Jena (1663-78) before moving to Arnstadt during the early 1680s.[1] It is unfortunate, then, that assessment of his importance as a composer and influence as a teacher is difficult due to the loss of most of his musical output, including a treatise on music. Despite this, one of the surviving works is of particular interest and merits organological investigation in view of claims made for it by Drese himself.

The *Trauer- vnd Begräbnüs-Lied* was composed in 1648 for the funeral of the Swedish military Governor of Erfurt. Caspar Ermes, a Livonian nobleman who had governed that city since 1640, was also the commander of a regiment of foot and a squadron of horse in the Swedish-led Army of the Confederation which had opposed the Imperial forces for most of the Thirty Years' War (1618-48). He passed away peacefully in Erfurt on 12 May 1648 and was buried there 'with appropriate Christian ceremony' on 2 July. In view of the strong political connections between Sweden and its inveterate allies the dukes of Saxe-Weimar, Duke Wilhelm IV not only had his newly-appointed Kapellmeister Adam Drese compose the above-mentioned work but also had the same music performed 'by some members of the same princely chapel of Weimar'.[2] The composition was printed by the Erfurt firm of Friederich Melchior Dedekind and two copies survive to this day.[3]

The customary account of the circumstances leading to the composition of the music is found on the title-page (see plate I), followed by an announcement that the music was itself 'set as the result of *invention* having given advantage

Traur- vnd Begräbnüs-Lied
Auff
Den tödtlichen jedoch seeligen Hintritt
Deß
Hoch-Wohl-Edelgebohrnen / Gestren-
gen vnd Groß-Mannvhesten Herrn
Caspar Ermes /
Auff Kockenberg in Lieffland
Erbsassen /
Königlicher Majestät vnd Cron Schwe-
den / wie auch deren Hoch-Löblichen Confœderirten Haupt-
Armee hochverdienten Obristen über ein Regiment zu Fueß /
vnd Esquadron zu Pferd:
Wie auch wohllölichen Achtjährigen Gouverneu-
ren der Stadt vnd Burg Erffurt in Düringen /
Welcher selbiges Orths
Den 12. Maji Anno 1648. im HERRN seelig verstorben / vnd
darauff den 2. Julij mit Christlichen vnd hochansehnlichen
Ceremonien zur Erden bestattet worden /
Welches
Nach vorgegebener Invention
Zur Music vnd Trombetten gerichtet
Von
Adam Dresen / der Weimar: Music Capell-Dire-
ctore, vnd von etlichen Persohnen auß gedachter Weim.
Fürstl. Capell musiciret worden.

PLATE I

Text:

Wie seelig sind die Todten/ die in dem HERREN sterben / von nun an;
Ja der Geist spricht daß sie ruhen von jhrer Arbeit/ vnd jhre Wer=
cke folgen jhnen nach.

Hier liegt der Edle tapffer Held / welcher
durch sein so Ritterliches Kämpffen/
den Thron der Ehren rühmlich erstie=
gen / vnd muß gleichwohl dem letzten
Lebens=Feinde so früh zu theile wer=
den.

Der seelig Verstorbene:

Zu früh scheint es zwar zu seyn/ jhr allerlieb=
sten Kinder/daß Ich so bald von euch
muß scheiden: Aber klagt doch nicht
zu sehr / wer seelig stirbt / der stirbet
nicht zu früh; Jetzt küß ich euch zu
letzt vnd befehle euch dem lieben
Gott / der wird euch wohl behüten/
vnd an jenem Tage mir mit Frewden
wieder geben.

Der Hinterlassenen Kinder schmertzliche Klage:

Ach! Gott das macht die
Sünde/daß wir Ewrer/
O allerliebster Herz
Vater in dieser Frembd=
de so bald beraubet wer=
den.

So schlaffet denn nun gantz mit Frieden / vnd helffe Gott auff daß jhr si=
cher wohnet biß an den Jüngsten Tag/ da jhr werdet hören die frö=
liche Stimme: Ey du frommer vnd getrewer Knecht/ du bist über
Wenigem getrew gewesen / Ich wil dich über viel setzen/gehe ein zu
deines HERREN Frewden.

PLATE II

to *music* and to the *trumpet*'.[4] There is no additional information or clarification, either on the title-page or on any Praetorius-style 'Ordinantz oder *Admonitio Generalis*',[5] to be found that might explain and elaborate on the twofold claim. Such classic understatement only serves to encourage the reader to investigate the music itself, the sole repository of evidence that may be examined to satisfy a desire for truth whetted by intrigue and enigma. (The same may well have been the intention of the composer and printer.)

The first 'invention' employed by Drese is a compositional '*Invention* Zur *Music*' which may be explained fully through textual and musical analysis. The funeral music, as Drese's work will be called, is composed in six separate sections. Biblical texts are found in the first and last sections only; the former sets the Lutheran funeral sentence 'Wie seelig sind die Toten' (*Revelations* xiv:3), made famous by Brahms in his 'Ein deutsches Requiem', while the latter quotes from the parable of the faithful servant 'Ei, du frommer und getreuer Knecht' (*Matthew* xxiv:47 and *Luke* xii:44). Between these two is found a remarkable and worldly drama in three scenes, a strange and unusual occurrence in an ostensibly sacred composition. The six-part vocal choir divides into two unequal groups during this drama, the one for the four lower voices and the other for two sopranos.

The first scene is set at the graveside. Adult mourners are represented by the low voices, who question the deceased's untimely demise at a dignified *piano* dynamic marking. The sopranos interject on two occasions with heart-rending cries of anguish marked to be sung *forte*. The latter represent 'the sad lament of the surviving children' according to a printed rubric,[6] and indeed their agitated outbursts contrast with the calmer imitative lines of the softer low voices (plate II). That same contrast is further enhanced with the simultaneous presentation of different texts by the two groups of singers (Example 1). Scene two continues along similar lines, with further loud and increasingly fragmented soprano outbursts on the same text as before. The low voices continue to sing softly, now taking on the rôle of the 'blessed deceased', according to another rubric.[7] They address the lamenting children (that is, the sopranos) with words of comfort and reassurance before bidding a tender farewell. The final scene marks a return to the graveside. The soprano outbursts have subsided and the low voices, once more representing mourners, quietly urge the deceased to rest in peace until the Last Day. As they then go on to describe the joyful voice that will be heard on that day by the 'holy and faithful servant' Caspar Ermes, the low voices are rejoined by the sopranos in a rousing passage – a cascade of paired-voice imitative entries marked *forte* in each part. The final section, with its appropriate New Testament text, then follows, sustaining and reinforcing the optimism that has just been expressed.

This polytextual drama and its layered musical realisation well illustrate one important aspect of Drese's musical personality: a compulsive, even obsessive,

EXAMPLE 1

penchant for dramatic situations, in this case a näively realistic portrayal of an actual funeral. Drese was probably responsible for the text also, for it is known that he composed an opera on the theme of Adam and Eve and caused a scandal with a sacred comedy on the Resurrection.[8] In essence, a funeral drama of this type is not unprecedented at this time, for among the works by Schütz is found Drese's model. The final motet of the master's *Musicalische Exequien* of 1636 is set for two choirs.[9] One, singing now loudly, now softly, presents the Nunc dimittis (*Luke* ii:28-32). It alternates and overlaps with a smaller group, consisting of two soprano 'seraphim' and one baritone 'beata anima', which sings softly and in the distance the different text 'Seelig sind die Toten' that is also found in Drese's own funeral music. Schütz refers to this particular use of *cori spezzati* as his own invention in an accompanying ordinance,[10] and it is this same musical invention that Drese employs in his 1648 funeral music, although the latter handles that technique without the nobility and profundity of the former composer's more mature setting.

The second 'invention', or the '*Invention* Zur . . . *Trombetten*', may also be identified by examining the music once more. However, there is one major problem: there are no trumpet parts to be found anywhere in the print, even though a number were originally employed, for a printed instruction at the *Clausula finalis* indicates that a trumpet ensemble plays there.[11] Have all of these trumpet parts, and only these parts, somehow become detached from the rest and then lost? A study of the surviving copies of the print indicates that this is an unlikely coincidence. The two are identical in all respects and appear to be complete.[12] They both consist of a cover, which supplies the place and year of printing and the printer's name only, and seven consecutively lettered bifolia: Basso Continuo (bifolium a), Tenore Primo (b), Canto Primo (c), Tenore Secundo (d), Canto Secundo (e), Alto (f), and Basso (g). The title-page occupies the first recto of the Basso Continuo and rubricated texts are printed on the final versos of both soprano parts, the voice parts with the least music. All of these parts contain rests and the indication *Tr:* each time the trumpets enter. This applies equally to the Basso Continuo, which would normally supply a continuous bass line and accompaniment even in passages during which only trumpets are heard (plate III).[13] Finally, all the voices rest for the same length when the trumpets play and, as a result, the piece is performable in a satisfactory manner by voices alone, omitting or respecting those rests according to the musical context.[14] It would appear that Drese very deliberately stopped publication of the trumpet parts, realising the significance of the 'invention' he was announcing. This is not without precedent either, for there are numerous instances of trumpets being specified without one note of their music being supplied – from Praetorius's pioneering *Epithalamium* of 1614[15] to the extreme example of Schütz's *Weihnachts-Historie* of 1664, in which not only trumpet parts but also everything else bar recitatives were withheld from publication.[16]

In view of the formidable lack of hard evidence, any further search for the trumpet 'invention' might appear futile, but the opposite is, in fact, the case. The mention of a trumpet ensemble *Intrada* at the end of the funeral music is of great importance. At this very time the standard five-part court trumpet ensemble – ranging from the high *Clarino*, through the *Quinta*, *Alto e Basso* and *Volgano*, to the low *Basso* according to the portion of the instrument's range that was employed in each trumpet part[17] – was in the process of expanding to a six- part ensemble with the addition of a second *Clarino*, this taking place in Italian, Austrian, Hungarian, German, and in other North European court ensembles.[18] Timpani were, of course, added to the number when they were available at individual courts. The Weimar court records, which might be expected to help decide which ensemble Drese had in mind, are unfortunately extremely fragmentary. All that is certain is that, while there were five trumpeters at the court in 1638,[19] the total had increased to six trumpeters and one timpanist by 1658.[20] There is also evidence, dated 1652, which indicates that the Weimar court trumpet ensemble was modelled after that at the electoral court in Dresden,[21] and a printed ensemble sonata composed by the Dresden head trumpeter, Johann Arnold, also dating from 1652, calls for the older

PLATE III

five-part ensemble.[22] Therefore, on balance, it is reasonable to assume that Drese employed an ensemble of five trumpets, with the possible addition of timpani.

The trumpet ensemble is used only in the biblical first and last sections, an appropriate use for instruments that can boast a singular sacred origin.[23] On each occasion the voices sing at the dynamic *forte* to match their timbre. When the trumpets enter all of the printed parts have the rests qualified by the indication *Tr:*, as was mentioned above. The context of each of these rests is instructive. While elsewhere the voices are involved in imitative textures, at each of these places they combine in homophonic declamation of a short phrase of text which is then treated sequentially, a rest separating each sequential entry. The individual rests have different durations and these, when combined with the syllabic content of each phrase of text, help establish and reconstruct what the trumpets might have played on 2 July 1648. On the simplest level it is found that they merely echo the preceding chord, or even the cadence just sung; that echo may be at the unison or at the interval of a minor third lower, depending on the chord(s) just sung or on the chord which follows the vocal rest on each occasion.[24] On a slightly more complex level the trumpets echo entire phrases that have just been sung and antiphonal canon results, with or without overlapping of the two choirs. On a more sophisticated level still the trumpet imitation is sequential and the antiphony is at the fourth, resulting in circle of fifths progressions. There are only two single instances of the choirs combining and here the I-V-I cadence in C minor is distinguished from the surrounding music as it comes at the end of a major passage in the composition, has a considerably slower harmonic rhythm than the other music, and contains vocal part writing that has been reduced in a dramatic manner to present the simplest type of chord writing imaginable.

All of these uses of the trumpet choir may be noticed in Example 2, which presents the conclusion of the first section of the composition (bars 22-8). Considering only the surviving printed parts, this passage consists of a three-bar phrase which is repeated, with a little modification, at the interval of a fourth, after which the last cadence is repeated in augmentation with some voice exchange. The trumpet parts, which have been reconstructed in the manner of early seventeenth century court trumpet ensemble music, contribute to and also embellish the sequential progressions already outlined by the voices, adding antiphony that includes some overlap. The E-flat chord reached by the voices in bar 23 is answered by the trumpets with a sequential echo in the home tonality of C minor in preparation for the cadential progression to G minor that ensues. The trumpets then echo that cadence, finishing on G major to effect a smooth transition with the next entry of the voices. Further sequential antiphony is again followed by a trumpet echo, this time at the unison, before the voices cadence in C minor, which the trumpets again echo. Finally, as the harmonic rhythm

EXAMPLE 2

slows down markedly, the two choirs unite in another C minor cadence.

This passage is typical of all of those that include trumpets in the funeral music. They are employed in short-winded phrases that generally include just one change of chord, only I-V-I progressions in C minor being excepted. It may be argued that simple unison echos could often be substituted for the reconstructions in example 2, and elsewhere in the work; however, a number of other factors including trumpet ensemble style and practical limitations to be explained later must also be taken into consideration.[25] Perhaps the most striking, and even most alarming, feature of the funeral music is its C minor tonality which permeates and governs the entire composition, even in the joyous final section. At this point the voices sing in a lively and homophonic triple-time passage. The addition of the trumpet choir results in overlapping canonic antiphony at the unison, driving the music to the final cadence that climaxes with a C major triad. This, the first use of the major mode on C in the entire work, heralds the above-mentioned *Intrada* and also establishes the pitch of the trumpets as C, the standard trumpet pitch of the seventeenth century.[26] However, as is well illustrated by Example 2, these are no ordinary trumpets restricted to a natural harmonic series based on the fundamental C for, with the exception of that *Intrada*, their music is characterised by continual employment of non-natural harmonics in passages ruled by C minor. Clearly any attempt to substitute only natural harmonics (see Example 3) in the reconstructions results in a meaningless tangle of disjoint and unrelated juxtapositions of modalities and in the creation of a chaos of polytonalities. Nor can they be pitched on another fundamental, for this is precluded by the C major *Intrada* as well as the C minor orientation of the funeral music itself. The latter requires natural harmonics to be lowered by up to one tone in trumpet-accompanied passages. This is the second 'invention' mentioned by Drese: the employment of either a playing technique or some mechanical device on a natural trumpet to enable a trumpeter to perform in flat key tonalities, contrasting sharply with the normal C major restrictions of the natural harmonics.

EXAMPLE 3

If the 'invention' was a playing technique, then it involved forcing the instrument to produce notes missing from its normal range by altering the pitches of existing harmonics. Such a technique, called 'lipping', was available to the seventeenth century trumpeter and was employed to correct out-of-tune natural harmonics, to supply short duration semitone lowerings of a few of the same, and even to feign other pitches as well. Although a number of natural harmonics are indeed out-of-tune with regard to equal temperament when played on natural trumpets with eighteenth-century exponential bells, the situation is much less clear both with regard to other temperament systems and also to seventeenth century instruments with their conical bell flares.[27] Surviving trumpet music shows that, until around 1620, only harmonics 7 and 14 were considered troublesome and were totally avoided as a result.[28] At the same time harmonic 8 was being lipped down to supply its auxiliary b' so useful for *groppi* at cadences.[29] By 1626 it was recognised that harmonic 11 – which is a little sharp – could supply either f" or f"-sharp, the latter allowing excursions to the dominant,[30] while within another three years harmonic 14 was being freely lipped up to a true b"-flat, opening up the subdominant area.[31] Further experimentation led to harmonic 9 supplying its own lower auxiliary c"-sharp and harmonic 13 being raised to a good a" – the harmonic is naturally very flat – or lowered to give g"-sharp (later also treated as a"-flat).[32] To complete the chromatic top octave harmonic 10 was made to supply e"-flat (later also d"-sharp), this being achieved during the 1660s.[33] The same decade saw harmonic 7 accepted as b'-flat and also supplying its own lower auxiliary a'.[34]

Feigned notes were apparently first employed by the Tuscan virtuoso trumpeter Girolamo Fantini (*c.*1602-?), who pointed out that 'they are imperfect if sustained, but are acceptable if they pass by rapidly' in his *Modo per imparare a sonare di Tromba* of 1638.[35] Thus, in addition to harmonic 4 being lowered for another auxiliary b, he made harmonics 4, 5, and 6 supply their upper auxiliaries d', f', and a' respectively. These feigned notes enjoyed some popularity for a short while,[36] despite objections that they sounded 'confused and disordered',[37] before a new conservatism forced a return to the purity of a natural harmonic series enlivened only by the f'/f"-sharp split and the lower auxiliary b', with just a few exceptions.[38] Before that retreat took place, however, composers such as the *Thomaskantor* Sebastian Knüpfer (1633-76) could expect good trumpeters to play passages like Example 4, although the sound was more veiled and less resonant than usual.[39] But such trumpeters were unfortunately few and far between.[40]

Lipping may appear to solve the problems posed by Drese's composition as it does supply many additional notes. Yet three salient features preclude such an inference, attractive as it may be. Firstly, the majority of the notes concerned

EXAMPLE 4

lie in the top octave and result from an attempt to complete a chromatic range there, while the less popular remainder tried to produce a diatonic scale in the triadic octave. Secondly, lipped notes must be preceded and followed by neighbouring natural harmonics, almost exclusively by stepwise motion. Finally, they are always of short duration and last for semiquaver or quaver values at moderate tempi in general. On these three counts lipping must be rejected as a solution and attention must then be focussed on the other possibility.

What pitch-altering mechanical devices were available to the Baroque trumpeter to enable the production of notes both within and outside of the natural harmonic series at whim? Up to and including the age of Praetorius and Mersenne only two pitch-changing devices are mentioned in musical literature: the mute, which muffled the sound and also raised the entire natural harmonic series by one tone, and the crook, which lowered the series by one tone to a perfect fourth. In both cases only natural harmonics result.[41] Mersenne, to be sure, also muses over the possibility of employing a trombone slide mechanism on the trumpet, but this is mere speculation.[42] Yet, in 1802, Koch could report that

> people have endeavoured in various ways to obtain on this instrument [ie the natural trumpet] the advantage given to the French Horn by the so-called [hand-]stopping – to produce the notes b'-flat, f', f"-sharp, a" etc, purely according to equal temperament , and also to sound f', f'-sharp, and a' – some with a special single slide, some others with the addition of keys, and even with a special mouthpiece. None of these attempts has been successful as of yet.[43]

Hand-stopping, which had been used on the French Horn since 1750 at the latest, was attempted on the trumpet around 1774 but entailed remodelling the instrument in a half-moon shape.[44] The 'special mouthpiece', about which nothing further is known, also dates from the second half of the eighteenth century.[45] Both permitted natural harmonics to be lowered by only one semi-tone. More successful was the placing of small finger-holes strategically along the tubing of the instrument, which began around 1752,[46] and then covering these with keys, which took place during the 1790s. This 'keyed trumpet' was, in its final form, completely chromatic over the top two octaves of the range and its agility is attested to by the concertos written for it by Haydn and Hummel, for example.[47] None of these could have been used in 1648, however, but there is one important connection: each of these types of trumpet was described as an *Inventionstrompete* in contemporary German literature,[48] a term that very closely ressembles the *'Invention* Zur . . . *Trombetten'* used by Drese (plate I).

The same term figures in an Imperial Mandate of 1736, thus predating the above instruments. In this legal document townplayers are forbidden not only the use of the natural trumpet but also horns and *Inventionstrompeten* played in the manner of a natural trumpet, with a few specific exceptions.[49] While the restrictions on their use of a natural trumpet had been in force since 1623, and of horns played in trumpet style since 1711 (the latter replacing similarly played trombones, prohibited since 1650), the inclusion of the *Inventionstrompete* is new.[50] And this particular instrument is the other type mentioned by Koch, that 'with a special single slide', the 'slide trumpet'.

The slide mechanism was a long, extendable mouthpiece pipe that was fitted within the first length of tubing of the trumpet. While the slide was kept stationary, the instrument was itself moved along the slide, allowing the natural harmonics to be lowered in pitch. This type of *Inventionstrompete* was also called the *Zugtrompete*, but is best-known under the Italianate title *Tromba da Tirarsi* due to its employment by Bach. His predecessor as *Thomaskantor*, Johann Kuhnau (1660-1722), not only left a cantata requiring an *Oboe ov. Tromba da tirarsi*[51] but also described the instrument as 'constructed according to the recent invention (*Invention*) so that it [ie the trumpet] may be moved in a manner similar to the trombone' in 1700.[52] He also added that the instrument was totally unknown in Italy.[53] Both Leipzig composers required lowerings of up to one tone from the instrument. Further clarification and confirmation of the restricted area of use of the instrument is found in a statement, dated 1698, by Johann Christoph Weigel:

> . . . one can obtain all the tones and semitones in both diatonic and chromatic music on the trombone as it is constructed with a double slide, which the trumpet lacks. However, quite a few years ago some of these were made with a single slide, but they were set aside for they did not produce the desired effect. . . .[54]

At least they were abandoned by court trumpeters, for townplayers in some parts of Germany came to use them for the performance of chorales etc, as the example of Leipzig shows.[55]

A number of years before Weigel the Nuremberg composer Georg Kaspar Wecker (1632-95) included two slide trumpets in his cantata *Allein Gott in der Höh sei Ehr*.[56] Although both trumpet parts bear only the simple indication *Tromba*, each includes lowerings of the harmonic series of up to one tone. Earlier still, in 1658, an inventory of music and instruments kept in the Wenzelskirche in Naumburg and played by the townplayers there includes the following entry:

> . . .four [natural] trumpets with mouthpieces.
> Two slide trumpets with mouthpieces, quite new. . . .[57]

The same instruments were also mentioned in another inventory, dated 1728, and they survive to this day.[58] Both slide trumpets were made in 1651 by Hans Veit of Naumburg. One still has its extendable single slide, a modern replica of the original that was lost during WorldWar II but that had already been studied and photographed by researchers.[59] Natural harmonics may be lowered by up to a minor third with this slide. The resultant range for a trumpet in C is given in Example 5, the black semibreves indicating notes produced using the slide. In addition, the slide could be used to correct the out-of-tune natural harmonics. Every note in this extended range, whether a natural harmonic or not, may be sustained, has the same resonance and tone quality as those around it, and may be played in isolation or by leap from any other note in the range. Thus all of the criteria required for the successful performance of the trumpet parts to Drese's funeral music are to be met in the slide trumpet.

The particular *Inventionstrompete* called the slide trumpet does have some defects, as Weigel noted. The most obvious of these is to be found in Example 5. There are a number of gaps in the bass clef part of the range which, of course,

EXAMPLE 5

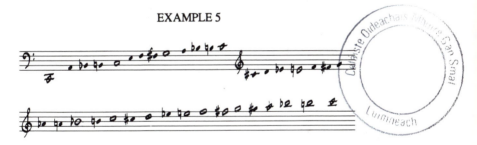

restrict the use of the instrument in the *Volgano* and *Basso* parts, even though the top two octaves are fully chromatic. Additionally, as it is the instrument itself that is moved along the slide and not *vice versa* as is the case with the trombone, it is more difficult to make such movements with any speed hence the later use of the slide trumpet for the performance of chorales. Both of these defects are reflected in Drese's funeral music, the former in reconstruction and the latter in the contexts of the trumpet entries. Whatever music the trumpeters played on their slide trumpets in 1648, they generally played no more than two chords in any one entry, C minor cadences apart. As a result, most of the trumpet phrases require only one change of slide position, the small remainder requiring two. As for the reconstructed music, the implications of the incomplete scale in the bass clef register have dictated the use of echo, sequential antiphony and canon at the unison. Thus, for example, when in bar 23 the voices sang an E-flat chord the trumpets had to reply with a C minor triad due to the absence of e-flat in the range. Moreover, they have to play a first inversion of the D major chord in the next bar for the very same reason (see Example 2). In short, Drese was well-acquainted with the capabilities and limitations of the new instrument and took them into account when setting his funeral music. In fact, it is because of his diligence that the lacunae found in the printed parts can be reconstructed with such a degree of certainty.

The slide trumpet, then, is the second 'invention' announced in Drese's funeral music of 1648. There are no earlier references to the instrument before that date, despite the all-embracing works by Praetorius, Mersenne and Fantini, and the year 1648 fits in with the evidence presented by later writers, such as Weigel and Kuhnau, and also by the surviving instruments.[60] That invention was made, and the later use of it is found, in a small geographical area centred on the Nuremberg-Leipzig axis. In addition, the inventors of the instrument were the court trumpeters at Weimar, who were trying to improve on the range that had just been made available to a very limited extent by lipping. The available evidence, written, musical, and organological, adds up to the one conclusion: the slide trumpet was an invention of the Baroque. As a result, the *Trauer-vnd-Begräbnüs-Lied* of 1648 by Adam Drese marks the *fons et origo* of the first chromatic trumpet of the Baroque, the slide trumpet.[61]

NOTES

1. See under 'Drese' in *Die Musik in Geschichte und Gegenwart* (Kassel, 1949-) and *The New Grove Dictionary of Music and Musicians* (London, 1980).
2. All of this information is to be found on the printed title-page: see plate I.
3. The copies are found in Berlin, Deutsche Staatsbibliothek, and Gotha, Forschungs-bibliothek.
4. 'Welches Nach vorgegebener *Invention* Zur *Music* vnd *Trombetten* gerichtet': see plate I.
5. Just such an ordinance is to be found in the *Polyhymnia Caduceatrix et Panegyrica* (Wolfenbüttel, 1619) by Praetorius, for example; modern edition *Werke* XVII.
6. 'Der Hinterlassenen Kinder schmertzliche Klage': see plate II.
7. 'Der seelig Verstorbene': see plate II.
8. Composed in 1676 and 1677 respectively.
9. Printed in Dresden in 1636 (SWV 279-81); modern edition *Sämtliche Werke* IV.
10. Schütz (as n. 9), 8: 'Mit welcher *invention* oder *Choro Secundo* der *Autor* die Freude der abgeleibten Sehligen Seelen im Himmel . . . in etwas einführen vnd andeuten wollen.'
11. The printed parts have either *Tr:*, *Intrada*, or *Tr: Intrada* printed at the *Clausula finalis*, a typical Late Renaissance/early Baroque practice in works with trumpet participation.
12. See n. 3.
13. For example, in *Missa Veni sponsa Christi* by Christoph Straus (*c.*1575-1631), the fifteenth Mass-setting in his *Missae* (Vienna, 1631).
14. The rests need be retained only in the final section in triple- time.
15. Wolfenbüttel, 1614; modern edition in *Werke* XXI.
16. SWV 435; modern edition in *Sämtliche Werke* I.

17. Various local variant names were also used, mainly similar to those given – the terminology used by Monteverdi in the *Toccata* to *l'Orfeo* (Venice, 1609). The only significantly different names were *Principal*, for *Quinta*, and *Grob*, for *Basso*.

18. France and England are excluded from all of these developments, for the two fostered a different style.

19. Adolf Aber, *Die Pflege der Musik unter den Wettinern und wettinischen Ernestinern* (Leipzig, 1921), 162.

20. Aber (as n. 19), 132.

21. Aber (as n. 19), 144.

22. Published in Dresden in 1652.

23. See in Numbers 10:1 on its origin, for example.

24. The limitations of the instrument must also be considered; see later.

25. That style is central to my PhD thesis 'The Trumpet and its Rôle in Music of the Renaissance and Early Baroque' (The Queen's University of Belfast, 1983).

26. The use of other pitches began to appear only during the second half of the seventeenth century.

27. Changes in construction are discussed in Willi Worthmüller, 'Die Nürnberger Trompeten– und Posaunenmacher des 17. und 18. Jahrhunderts', *Mitteilungen des Vereins für Geschichte der Stadt Nürnberg*, XLV(1954) and XLVI(1955).

28. Mersenne discussed this avoidance in *Harmonie Universelle* (Paris, 1636) III, 251-2.

29. First met in *Tutta l'Arte della Trombetta*, 1614, by Cesare Bendinelli; facsimile edition Kassel, 1975, folio 54ᵛ.

30. In 'Nun ist das Heil' by Schein, included in the collection *Opella Nova, Ander Theil* (Leipzig, 1626).

31. In 'Buccinate/Jubilate Deo' by Schütz, found in *Symphoniae Sacrae* (Venice, 1629), (SWV 275-6); modern edition in *Sämtliche Werke* XIV. The motets are in the F major mode but include a trumpet in C which is employed with great freedom and virtuosity.

32. Both are found in Fantini's *Modo per imparare a sonare di Tromba* (Frankfurt, 1638), on pages 77 and 81 respectively; facsimile edition Nashville, 1972.

33. In the *Sonata Tribus Quadrantibus* of Pavel Josef Vejvanovsky, dated 2 July 1667; modern edition in *Musica Antiqua Bohemica* XLVIII.

34. In *Sonata XII* of the *Sacro-profanus Concentus Musicus* (Nuremberg, 1662) of Johann Heinrich Schmelzer; modern edition in *Denkmäler der Tonkunst in Österreich* CXI/CXII.

35. Fantini (as n. 32), 6: 'che voler fermauisi sono imperfette, ma perche passano presto possono seruire.'

36. In his sonata of 1652 (see footnote 22), Johann Arnold calls for quaver a' and b' notes between g' and c". In 1687 Nicola Matteis makes much use of lower auxiliaries in the triadic octave in a *Concerto di Trombe* for three trumpets printed in a reissue of *Ayres for the Violin* (London).

37. Marin Mersenne, *Harmonicorum Libri* (Paris, 1635), 109: 'spurios, confusos'.

38. Among the exceptions are the trumpet parts in Bach's cantatas, especially those for solo trumpet; on his affective use of lipped notes see in Andreas Brischle, 'Zum Gebrauch der Trompete bei J.S. Bach', *Archiv für Musikwissenschaft* XLIV, 306-12.

39. In *Ach Herr, strafe mich nicht* (Psalm 6); modern edition in *Denkmäler deutscher Tonkunst* LVIII/LIX.

40. According to Weigel in *Abbildung der gemein-nützlichen Haupt-Stände* (Regensburg, 1698), 235.

41. Discussed by Praetorius respectively in *Polyhymnia Caduceatrix*, 4, and in *Puericinium*

(Wolfenbüttel, 1621), before piece number III.

42. Mersenne, *Harmonicorum*, 109.

43. In his *Musikalisches Lexikon* (Offenbach, 1802), col 1606: 'Man hat sich verschiedentlich bemühet, diesem Instrumente theils durch einen besondern Zug, theils auch durch angebrachte Klappen, und durch besondere Mundstücke eben den Vortheil zu verschaffen, den das Horn durch das sogenannte Stopfen gewonnen hat, nemlich, dass man dadurch die Töne b', f'', fis'', a'' u.s.w. nach dem temperirten Tonsysteme vollig rein angeben, und ausserdem noch die Töne f', fis' und a' intoniren könne; allem bis jetzt hat sich noch kein damit gemachter Versuch mit Vortheil behaupten können'.

44. E.L. Gerber, *Neues-Lexikon der Tonkünstler* (Leipzig, 1812-14), cols 597-8.

45. E.L. Gerber, *Historischen-Biographisches Lexikon der Tonkünstler* (Leipzig, 1790-2), col 936.

46. According to J.E. Altenburg, *Versuch einer Anleitung zur heroisch-musikalischen Trompeter– und Paukerkunst* (Halle, 1795), 112.

47. Concertos in E-flat (Hob VIIc 1), from 1796, and in E, from 1803, respectively. Both were composed for the Viennese virtuoso Anton Weidinger.

48. In, for example, Gerber, *Neues-Lexikon*, cols 597 and 571. Altenburg, *Versuch*, also uses the term on page 12, but incorrectly. Here he confuses the half-moon stopping trumpet with a simple coiled trumpet, showing that he was quite far removed from late eighteenth century developments – he does not even mention the keyed trumpet.

49. Printed in Dresden in 1736. Facsimile in D. Altenburg, *Untersuchungen zur Geschichte der Trompete im Zeitalter der Clarinblaskunst* (Regensburg, 1973) II, 121-31.

50. The Imperial Privileges and Mandates are discussed by J.E. Altenburg in his *Versuch*, 31-9; facsimiles of the most important of these are found in D. Altenburg, *Untersuchungen* II.

51. In the cantata *Gott der Vater, Jesus Christus, der Heilge Geist, wohn uns bey* listed in *Denkmäler deutscher Tonkunst* LVIII/LIX, xlvi.

52. In his *Der Musicalische Quack-Salber* (Dresden, 1700), 82-3: 'noch ietziger *Invention* eingerichtet ist/ dass sie sich nach Art der *Trombonen* ziehen lässet'.

53. Kuhnau (as n. 52). On the English Slide Trumpet see footnote 61.

54. Weigel, *Abbildung*, 235: '. . . doch kan man in beeden generibus alle Tonos und Semitonia auf der Posaune anstossen/ weil sie mit zweyen Zügen versehen/ deren aber die Trompete ermangelt/ wiewohl man vor sehr vielen Jahren auch einige mit einem Zug verfertiget/ weil sie aber den verhofften Effect nicht gethan/ wieder abgeschafft worden . . .'.

55. J.E. Altenburg, *Versuch*, mentioned the slide trumpet rather vaguely on page 12. His contempt for the instrument is revealed in a letter he wrote in 1767, which is printed in *Monatshefte für Musikgeschichte* XXIV, 159-60. Although working as a church organist, he had trained as a court trumpeter and would naturally have scorned the use of trumpets by townplayers, enemies of the court trumpeters.

56. Modern edition in *Denkmäler der Tonkunst in Bayern* IX, 46-68.

57. Arno Werner, 'Die alte Musikbibliothek und die Instrumentensammlung an St. Wenzel in Naumburg a.d.S.', *Archiv für Musikwissenschaft*, VIII, 415: '. . . Vier Trompeten mit Mundstücken. Zwey Zugtrompeten mit Mundstücken, ganz neu . . .'.

58. See n. 57., 415; the trumpets are preserved in the Musikinstrumentenmuseum in Berlin.

59. Among these are Sachs, Galpin and Carse. A photograph may be found in D. Altenburg, *Untersuchungen*, III, plate 42.

60. For a refutation of the use of a slide trumpet during the Renaissance, approached from a different angle, see my article 'The Renaissance Slide Trumpet – Fact or Fiction?', *Early Music* XII, 26-33.

61. The English slide trumpet, or 'Flatt trumpet', with its characteristic double slide dates from around 1690 and may be viewed as an attempt to improve on the German model. Interestingly, the former instrument was developed under the influence of the Bohemian-born composter, Gottfried Finger (*c.* 1660-1730), then a member of 'the King's Musick', who must have encountered the latter version of his journey from Olomouc to London.

Scales and Intervals: Theory and Practice

HORMOZ FARHAT

For nearly three centuries, European art music has been created on the basis of the tempered tuning system which theoretically divides the octave into 12 equidistant semitones. The scales used prior to the adoption of this tuning system, at best, only approximated equidistant relationships; in practice considerable variations were obtained.

The establishment of equal temperament was necessitated by the ever greater complexity of polyphonic compositions in the high Renaissance and in the baroque eras. In the early Middle Ages and before, European music was largely monophonic, and, in its secular traditions, remained so until the fourteenth century. It was in the realm of sacred music that the elementary polyphony of parallel organum (perfect intervals of fourth fifth and octave) was developed from the ninth century onwards. By the late medieval period, from its humble beginnings, polyphony progressed to a high level of refinement utilising all consonant and, in one way or another, all dissonant intervals in richly textured four-part compositions.

From the Renaissance to the present the main thrust of development in European art music has been in its polyphonic and harmonic enrichment. The complexity of the harmonic system, requiring multi-layered sound structures, frequent modulations, pitch alterations, and the simultaneous application of diverse musical instruments in orchestras, in time, necessitated a system of fixed relationships between all tones. Existing minor variations have had to be sacrificed in favour of uniformity, without which the full potentials of harmony could not be realised. The outcome of this uniformity is the tempered tuning which affixes B-sharp as equal to C and C-sharp as equal to D-flat, etc. In fact, this is a distortion of the natural phenomenon of sound generation and the harmonic series. The tempered tuning and the division of the octave into 12 equidistant semitones, which we take for granted as the right foundations for musical composition, are in reality artificial creations not sustained by any other musical culture.

In non-western civilisations musical developments have moved in different directions. Some have cultivated modal diversity and melodic subtlety (e.g.

Indian, Persian, Turkish), some have emphasised rhythmic complexity (e.g. African, Indian, Turkish), and yet others have developed magnificent orchestral sonorities (e.g. Javanese, Balinese, Japanese and Korean). In no musical tradition, however, have polyphony and harmony come to dominate musical developments in the way that they have in west-European art music.

It is true that the orchestral music of Japan, such as the Gagaku ensemble, and the gamelan music of Java and Bali employ a kind of rudimentary polyphony. This, however, is generally a skeletal and static harmonic background arising out of the limitations of some of the musicial instruments and the structural stratification of the music. It is in no way comparable to the systematic and dynamic use of harmony in western music.

A type of polyphony is also practised in the vocal folk music of certain regions of the Balkan peninsula, notably in Serbia, Macedonia and Bulgaria. Singing in parallel seconds is a feature of this music in addition to the use of a drone which is common to instrumental folk music in many parts of the world. Again, these are examples of limited and static polyphony not to be compared with the elaborate harmonic principles which govern western art music.

Equal temperament is therefore a unique development necessitated by the growth of a singularly rich polyphonic practice which stands as the highest achievement of western art music. Other traditions have remained, by-and-large, aloof from polyphony and, as such, have had no need to adopt a system of equal temperament.

Since the Renaissance, western Europe has gradually moved to a position of economical and political ascendancy over the rest of the world. In modern times, the rapid technological and industrial progress of the west has confirmed this dominating position to the point that much of the world eagerly emulates all things western. Western music has found varying degrees of acceptance beyond its own cultural context.

In the Middle East, for example, western musical influence became apparent early in the nineteenth century. The Ottoman Empire was a neighbour and a foe of the European powers and held much of eastern Europe under her suzerainty. Accordingly, the inroads of western music were felt earliest in Turkey and in her Arab dominions of the eastern Mediterranean. North Africa was largely influenced, due to geographic proximity, by France. Persia, more remote and isolated, was exposed to western inroads somewhat later, in the second half of the nineteenth century.

A consequence of western musical influences was the gradual prevalence of the notion that there is something inherently good in equal temperaments and in the systematic use of harmony. To native musicians who had come in contact with western music, the fact that their music did not seem to support such a system was seen as an indication of retarded musical development. Their monophonic musical tradition was regarded as a degrading proof of inferiority.

For well over a century, Middle Eastern musicologists of various nationalities have endeavoured to put forward theories of scales and intervals which would make possible the use of harmony in their native music. A 24 quarter-tone scale was proposed in the nineteenth century by the Syrian musician Mikhail Maschaqa, as the 'basic scale' of Arabian music. In the same way that the 12 semitones of the chromatic scale embody all pitches used in western music, this 24 quarter-tone scale is supposed to represent all pitches used in the entirety of Arabian modes. Furthermore, this was conceived as a tempered quarter-tone scale presumably allowing for the adoption of a system of harmony related to the harmony in use in western music.

In Persia, similar aspirations led Ali Naqi Vaziri to espouse, in the early twentieth century, the same 24 quarter-tone scale as the 'basic scale' for Persian music. He promoted his theory with numerous harmoniased compositions of his own which utilised the quarter-tone scale.

The blind acceptance of such theories has been so prevalent that nearly all practising musicians in both the Arab world and in Persia firmly believe that their music is founded on the quarter-tone scale. That the realities of their music do not agree with such a scale does not stand in the way. They think in quarter-tones even if they don't actually produce them. Even worse, the intervals are adjusted so as to allow approximate three-quarter intervals.[1] Western musical notation has been accepted with added symbols to express the quarter-tone intervals. In the Arab World the following symbols are used.

ǂ	to raise a pitch by a quarter-tone
♯	to raise a pitch by two quarter-tones
♯♯	to raise a pitch by three quarter-tones
♭	to lower a pitch by a quarter-tone
♭	to lower a pitch by two quarter-tones
|♭	to lower a pitch by three quarter-tones

In Persia a different set of symbols is in use:[2]

♯	(sori) half-sharp
♯	(diese) sharp
ρ	(koron) half-flat
♭	(bemol) flat

The promoters of the quarter-tone concept were not deterred by the lack of historic evidence for its support. The Moslem scholars in the medieval period had established a musical science of great sophistication founded on the knowledge gleaned from the writings of ancient Greeks. Scores of treatises were produced by Persian, Arabian and Turkish savants between the ninth and the fifteenth centuries, many of which survive in major libraries around the world.

Diverse theories of scales, intervals, modes, rhythms and tuning systems were given; but none suggests the quarter-tone as having had any function in model structures.

According to all known theories, the tetrachord was the basic unit in all modes. By the thirteenth century, a wide range of possibilities existed for the division of the tetrachord into its component parts. For example, in the major tetrachord of, say, C-D-E-F, the whole-tone C-D could be divided into seven, and the whole-tone D-E in five different ways, depending on what theoretic principle was followed. In other words, seven possibilities of the lowered D and five of the lowered E were known. To what extent these microtonal variations of D-flat and E-flat were known and practised by the performing musicians is a matter of conjecture.

The most enduring theory of the division of the octave was proposed by Safiaddin Ormavi (d. 1294), the founder of the Systematist School, who set out to create a synthesis out of the confusion of theories on intervals and scales. According to Safiaddin, the octave is divided into two conjunct tetrachords plus a whole-tone. Each tetrachord is composed of two whole-tones and one semitone. Each whole-tone, in turn, is divisible in two Pythagorian limmas (ratio or 256:243, or 90.2 cents) and one comma (ratio of 531441:52488, or 23.46 cents). In total, the scale of Safiaddin divides the octave into 17 tones as follows:

	Limma	90 cents
	Limma	90 cents
	Comma	24 cents
Tetrachord I	Limma	90 cents
	Limma	90 cents
	Comma	24 cents
	Limma	90 cents
	Limma	90 cents
	Limma	90 cents
	Comma	24 cents
Tetrachord II	Limma	90 cents
	Limma	90 cents
	Comma	24 cents
	Limma	90 cents
	Limma	90 cents
Whole-tone	Limma	90 cents
	Comma	24 cents

This is indeed a logical and systematic scale, although it must be understood that the comma was only used as an incremental interval, never employed independently. The question, however, remains as to the capability of medieval instruments or the human voice to reproduce such neatly measured intervals with accuracy.

The same question holds true when we consider the scales suggested by the forerunners of the Moslem scholars, the ancient Greeks. How seriously are we take, for example, the theories of Aristoxenus of Tarentum? In his enharmonic and chromatic tetrachords he gives us intervals (pyknon) of 1/4, 1/3 and 3/8 of a tone. Other theoretricians, such as Achytas and Ptolemy, have proposed even more exacting intervals. How relevant were these theories to actual musical practices of the time? How were these intervals to be produced on instruments which, by today's standards, were primitive and probably incapable of maintaining reliable fixed pitches? How, moreover, was the human voice to manage these subtle intervals with any degree of consistency and accuracy? It is in terms of such questions that we must conclude that the theoreticians were playing their own games and that their scientific resolutions were not necessarily corroborated by musical practice.

It is important to keep in view the fact that writers on musical theory, ancient Greeks and medieval Moslems alike, were primarily scientists, not practicing professional musicians. They were mathematicians, physicists, astronomers and philosophers. Music obviously can be studied as a science, but, as an object of scientific enquiry, it tends to lose touch with its reality which is emotional expression through sound and, as such, not subject to rigid laws and principles.

Some of the more recent studies by Middle Eastern scholars reject the use of quarter-tone and suggest scales and intervals of greater precision. In Turkey, a theory espoused by Suphi Ezgi and H.S. Arel suggests the pythagorian comma (23.46 cents) as the smallest incremental unit. Their system, resting on Safiaddin's theoretical foundations, recognises two semitones, three whole-tones and three augmented tones as follows:

Semitones	Limma	90 cents	(equated with 4 commas)
	Limma + Comma	114 cents	(equated with 5 commas)
	2 Limmas	180 cents	(equated with 8 commas)
Whole-tones	2 Limma + Comma	204 cents	(equated with 9 commas)
	2 Limmas + 2 Commas	228 cents	(equated with 10 commas)
	3 Limmas	270 cents	(equated with 12 commas)
Augmented Tones	3 Limmas + Comma	294 cents	(equated with 13 commas)
	3 Limmas + 2 Commas	318 cents	(equated with 14 commas)

In the Ezgi-Arel system the western notation is yet again supplemented with different symbols to express the number of commas with which a pitch is raised or lowered, as shown below:

        ♯   to raise a pitch by one comma

        ♯   to raise a pitch by four commas

♯	to raise a pitch by five commas
↓	to lower a pitch by one comma
♭	to lower a pitch by four commas
♭	to lower a pitch by five commas

The division of the octave in this system also gives 24 tones, but of uneven size. Each mean whole-tone (204 cents) can yield four tones: 90, 114, 180 and 204 cents. The semitone can be either 90 or 114 cents. Accordingly, with five whole-tones and two semi- tones in the octave, a total of 24 tones can be had. Other Turkish musicologists, however, have suggested more complicated divisions of the octave; Gültekin Oransay has given an octave of 29 and Ekrem Karadeniz has proposed an octave divided into 41 tones.

In Persia, during the 1940s, Mehdi Barkeshli, having enlarged on the 17-tone scale of Safiaddin, proposed a 22-tone scale as the basis of Persian modes. His scale gives the same four divisions for the whole tone (90, 114, 180 and 204 cents) as does the scale of Suphi-Arel, but he gives only one version of the semitone (90 cents).

These are all absorbing theories and have not been set forth thoughtlessly. In fact, in each case, considerable research and measurement of intervals have been cited in support of the conclusions reached. On the other hand, such theories are often as easy to disprove as to prove. The fact is that pitch instability in the musical traditions of the Middle East is so extensive as to make possible all manner of conclusions.

With regard to the intervals of Persian music, the present writer has concluded that no logical, stable or historically consistent system is maintained. Most intervals are very flexible and any notion of an octave division as 'the scale' of Persian music is entirely misleading. This conclusion was reached through measurement of intervals with the use of stroboconn and melograph, and analysis of many hours of recorded music as performed by numerous musicians. It was found that the semitone is generally close to 90 cents, but can be as small as 80 cents. The whole-tone is comparatively stable and is close to 204 cents. There are two very pliable intervals between the semitone and the whole-tone; one of these varies between 125 and 145 and the other can be anywhere between 150 and 170 cents. I have called these two flexible intervals the small and the large neutral tones. There is also an interval larger than the whole-tone, but smaller than the western augmented tone, varying between 260 and 280 cents. This interval, called a plus-tone, has a comparatively limited application in Persian modes.

The fact that the intervals in Persian music, or in other traditions, are not stable troubles neither the performer nor his audience; it only bothers the theoretician. It is the theoretician who feels compelled to bring order out of chaos, and to present beautiful and well-articulated abstract models.

Let us consider some of the other major musical traditions of the east. Indian music, sometimes thought to employ quarter-tones, is theoretically based on an octave containing 22 microtones (srutis). These microtones are not equal in size, however, and are not featured by themselves in any raga; larger intervals may be raised or lowered by one or more srutis. Indian musicians have fortunately never been self-conscious about their own music and have not attempted to justify Indian music on western terms.

There is no question of microtones in the music of the Far Eastern civilisations as all musics there are based on pentatonic and, to a lessser extent, heptatonic scales. One would expect to find very rigid scale patterns in musical cultures where most musical instruments have fixed pitches as is the case with the gamelans of Indonesia and the Pi Phat of Thailand. By far the majority of instruments in these ensembles are idiophones of wooden or metalic substance which are struck and produce unvarying tones. It would be very reasonable for this type of music to have developed very precise scales and intervals. The reality is however very different. Although the instruments within each gamelan or Pi Phat ensemble are in tune with one another, it is highly unusual to find two sets of instruments, from two different orchestras, which are tuned to exactly the same pitches. Yet, broadly speaking, different scales are maintained and their separate identities are not in doubt.

A further investigation of other musical cultures, for example, the African, the native American, or most folk musics in Europe, for that matter, will confirm that precision and consistency in scales, intervals and tuning systems are both relative and non-essential. This reality does not hinder but enhances the expressive potentials of the music. Scales and intervals that are moulded (within given traditional norms) to the taste of the performer, who is often also the composer, give a more personal and human dimension to the music which heightens its expressive qualities.

Another equally significant conclusion reached through the study of diverse musical traditions is the fact of the absence of microtones, quarter-tones, or any intervals appreciably smaller than the semi-tone (90 cents), from direct application in all modal systems. Such intervals, where found at all, function as increments with which larger intervals may be raised or lowered. It is not unreasonable to suggest that intervals significantly lower than the semitone are too difficult to reproduce with the human voice, the foremost musical instrument in all cultures, and therefore that they have not come to play an independent part in indigenous musics.

Ironically, it is in western composition that the quarter-tone has been brought into some use in the twentieth century. Composers such as Alois Haba, Julien Carillo, Ivan Vishnogradsky, Pierre Boulez and Krysztof Penderecky have written compositions employing quarter-tones. Smaller microtones have also been used in modern compositions, notably in the works of Harry Partch. It can be asserted with some validity, however, that the use of microtones by western composers has caused great difficulties in performance and has failed to stimulate broad interest to encourage widespread application.

To return to western art music, it must be admitted that here, since the Renaissance, the disparity between theory and practice has been significantly reduced. Rules of contrapuntal and harmonic techniques have been indeed extracted from the creative practice of the great masters. Yet it would be very wrong to assume that these rules have been observed to the letter. The obvious fact is that no self-respecting composer has been a slavish follower of the 'rules'.

As to the pervasive equal temperament, it has reigned supreme in the case of instruments with built-in pitches, such as piano, organ, xylophone, etc. In a symphony orchestra, with a large number and types of instruments used, adherence to a uniform tuning obviously becomes obligatory. It is not altogether certain, however, that a very exact tempered tuning is always maintained. The subtle difference that a sensitive ear can detect in the intonation between the piano and orchestra, as in a piano concerto with a lengthy orchestral exposition, demonstrates this point.

How widely singers can deviate from any precise tuning system is all too well known. The erratic singing style of many of the most revered singers further indicates that faithful observance of the tempered tuning is neither feasible nor desirable. Particularly in solo music, not only singers, but also string and wind players exhibit considerable freedom from the rigidity of equal temperament.

A genuine understanding of any musical tradition can clearly be best reached through the study of the music on its own terms, and not on predetermined notions as to what it ought to be. Rules and theories can be valid only if they are extracted from the life of any given music which is its practice. If the practice displays irregularities or contradictions in the theory, then it is the theory which is at fault; the music cannot be adjusted in order to validate it. Music is not the possession of the few who endeavour to explain it, it belongs to those who make it out and perform it and to all who live with it and enjoy it. It is they who determine the right or wrong of their music, be it in accordance with that which the theoreticians have expounded or not.

NOTES

1. The quarter itself has no application; it is rather the interval between the semitone and the whole-tone which gives rise to such pervasive theoretical debate.
2. A pitch raised by three quarters is recorded as equal to the pitch a whole-tone higher if lowered by a quarter. Similarly, a pitch lowered by three quarters is equal to the lower tone raised by a quarter. Accordingly, no symbols to express raising or lowering by three quarter-tones are employed.

Purcell's *Laudate Ceciliam*

AN ESSAY IN STYLISTIC EXPERIMENTATION

MARTIN ADAMS

Purcell is known to have written two works in honour of St. Cecilia during 1683, when he was twenty-three or twenty-four years old.[1] One, his setting of Christopher Fishburn's *Welcome to all the pleasures* (Z.339), has become quite well known and is historically significant for being the first of an occasionally distinguished lineage of Cecilian odes, the best of which are Purcell's 1692 setting of Brady's *Hail, bright Cecilia* (Z.328) and Handel's 1739 re-setting of Dryden's *From harmony, from heav' nly harmony*, originally set in 1687, by Draghi.

If the nature of the Cecilian odes written between 1683 and Purcell's death in 1695 is anything to go by, the celebrations of 22 November were seen as a venue in which composers might attempt to display their skill, not only by outdoing their predecessors in imagination and in technical resourcefulness, but also by adaping *á la mode* foreign styles to native purposes.

Such aspirations were not confined to these odes, for which the celebrations have become most famous. After 1683, and possibly before, other specially composed music was performed.[2] Purcell's *Te Deum and Jubilate* (Z.232) was part of the 1694 celebrations, and its popularity, which lasted well into the next century, was founded partly on its brashly Italianate idiom.[3]

It seems likely that *Laudate Ceciliam* (Z.329) is an earlier example of stylistic experimentation, for in many respects there is nothing like it in Purcell's output, and this from a composer who, especially when he was young, was much given to producing groupings of specific types of piece over a fairly short period – the fantasies and the sonatas are perhaps the most obvious examples. Given the work's text – a hymn of praise to St Cecilia – one might expect it to be closely related to Purcell's sacred music, perhaps to the verse anthems with strings, or to the two Latin motets composed not long before it. Two other plausible generic connections might be to the odes or to the chamber cantatas such as *Hark, how the wild musicians sing* (Z.542).

At first sight it is these last two connections which seem the more promising. Like the above cantata, *Laudate Ceciliam* is scored for two violins and continuo, with vocal forces of three soloists; also, it was composed during the period 1682-84, when Purcell wrote most of the cantatas.[4] Such connections are also suggested by its being in the same autograph volume, Royal Music 20.h.8., as most of the odes and all of the chamber cantatas. Here it comes immediately after the court ode *Fly, bold rebellion* (Z.324), probably composed for September 1683, and before a number of chamber cantatas; these in turn precede the ode for September 1684, *From those serene and rapturous joys* (Z.326). This all fits with a date of late 1683 for *Laudate Ceciliam*.[5]

But on closer examination, resemblances to any ode or cantata are limited, a point apparent in the work's overall structure (see Example 1). Prior to the first Cecilian ode *Welcome to all the pleasures* (Z.339), Purcell had composed at least six for the court; these develop further the methods used by Blow in particular, in court odes of the late 1670s. Blow in his turn seems to have developed his ideas out of the methods of Henry Cooke, who wrote the earliest Restoration odes.[6]

These composers met the challenge of setting a long text and reflecting the magnificence of the occasion by intensifying certain structural principles of the verse anthem. Typically they ordered a succession of solos and ensembles to create one or more sequences of movements, each sequence culminating in a large ensemble item. The imagination and flexibility with which Blow applied this principle appealed greatly to Purcell, for there are a number of instances of the pupil's odes being closely based on those of his teacher. Indeed, while *Welcome to all the pleasures* exhibits a number of features not found in the court ode, it is basically an imaginative adaptation of these same structural principles.

Not so *Laudate Ceciliam*, the unusual structure of which has attracted attention, especially that of Ernest Walker, who comments in particular on the amount of sectional repetition. He regards this as 'hardly paralleled elsewhere in the English music of the period, whether by Purcell himself or by any other composer'.[7] Although no specific evidence is offered in support of his claim, and many of Blow's and Purcell's verse anthems with strings include much sectional repetition, there is no doubt that this application is highly unusual (see Example 1).

Particularly striking are the two restatements of the opening 'Laudate Ceciliam' section. Whether or not these were prompted by the original text is not clear. There is no known source for the text other than this piece, and the text extraction given in the Purcell Society Edition omits the two later statements of 'Laudate Ceciliam'. However, it seems quite likely that both were in the original form of the text, for such repetitions of a central thought are common in Latin choruses and hymns, especially those glorifying someone.[8] Both musical repetitions are identical to the original, and by methods which will be referred to in detail later, each is prepared for in the preceding music. So the effect is of progression which keeps returning to the central musical and poetic matter.

EXAMPLE 1

A	Symphony			bb. 1-42
B	Trio	'Laudate Ceciliam'	atb	43-68
C	Recit. & ritornello	'Modulemini'	atb	69-91
D	Solo	'Quia preceptum	b	92-107
B	Trio	'Laudate Ceciliam'	atb	108-133
A	Symphony			134-174
E	Recit.	'Dicite Virgini'	at	175-191
F	Trio	'Adeste Celites'	atb	192-205
G	Recit.	'Nobiscum matryri'	atb	206-221
B	Trio	'Laudate Ceciliam'	atb	222-247

Laudate Ceciliam in voce et Organo.
Modulemini psalmum novum, in insigni
   die solemnitatis ejus.
Quia preceptum est in Ecclesia
   sanctorum tu lex in
   tabernaculis Justorum.
Laudate Ceciliam in voce et Organo.
Dicite Virgini, Canite Martyri, qual
   excelsum est nomen tuum, O beate
   Cecilia, tu gloria Domus Dei,
   tu letitia que sponsam Christo paris,
   respice nos.
Adeste Celites, plaudite
   psalite nobiscum, Virgini
   pangite melos.
Nobiscum Martyri alternate Laudes,
   Citheras vestras jungire voces, Citheras
   nostris sociate contibus.
Laudate Ceciliam in voce et Organo.

Praise Cecilia with voice and organ.
Sing out a new psalm on the glorious
   occasion of her feastday
Because it is prescribed in the assembly of
   the Saints you are the law in the
   tabernacles of the Just.
Praise Cecilia with voice and organ.
Sing to the Virgin, sing to the Martyr, how
   exalted is your name, O blessed Cecilia,
   you are glory of God's house, you, who
   joyfully produce a bride for Christ, look
   with regard on us.
Attend, inhabitants of heaven, applaud and
   play with us, compose a song to the
   Virgin.
Sing praises in alternation with us to the
   Martyr, join your voices with the harp,
   link the harp to our songs.
Praise Cecilia with voice and organ.

As far as the chamber cantatas are concerned, there is even less connection with *Laudate Ceciliam*, for although they use methods comparable to the odes, there is practically no sectional repetition.

To a large extent these differences are accounted for by the odes and cantatas having to set much longer texts. For such works, repetition of instrumental sections can be a punctuative device, and can help articulate a musical structure complementary to textual structure and meaning. Repetition of vocal sections is more hazardous. Not only do few ode texts call for it, but it risks making the piece inappropriately long.

This brings us readily to considering the verse anthems, for these usually set texts of a length comparable to that of *Laudate Ceciliam*. As with the odes, we find that Cooke, Humphrey and Blow, plus Matthew Locke, who seems to have been less active in ode composition, were all interested in repeating instrumental sections in anthems. One of the most successful instances is Blow's *The Lord is my Shepherd*, which dates from no later than 1679.[9] This includes restatements of portions of the second part of the opening symphony, on whch the first vocal section is based; Blow calls each restatement 'ritornella'. Also, there are close motivic relationships between each section, so the statements sound as the most open manifestation of a general underlying unity.

Repetitions of vocal sections are less common. Humphrey's *O Lord my God* uses a method Purcell was to follow. The two widely separated statements of 'But be not thou far from me', the second followed by a choral repetition to end the anthem, reinforce the central point of the text.

Interesting as these two examples are, it must be admitted that in the work of these composers there are many cases in which the repetition, especially of instrumental sections, sounds forced, because it does not articulate an inherent structure.

Purcell's verse anthems too can be patchy in these and other respects, but some of the better ones take these methods much further. Two well-integrated examples are *It is a good thing to give thanks* (Z.18) and *My beloved spake* (Z.28). In the former, which may date from around the period of *Laudate Ceciliam*, repetitions of two vocal sections are symmetrically disposed across the piece to reinforce the central theme of Psalm 92 – the goodness and rightness of giving thanks to God. The latter piece is much earlier, certainly not later than 1679 and quite possibly earlier than 1677.[10] Its repetition of part of the opening vocal section towards the end of the anthem is motivically integrated with the surrounding material; the repetition is called for by the text, and it is interesting to see that its beginning is overlapped into the preceding section in a way comparable to the first repetition of 'Laudate Ceciliam'.

These two anthems, many others, and *Laudate Ceciliam*, also repeat the second section or all of the opening symphony. This too was a frequent device with Humphrey and Blow, and also appeared in the former's 1672 ode *When from his throne*. In most cases it is used to separate distinct sections of the text: in Humphrey's *O Lord my God* it separates the psalmist's plea to God from the next verse of his complaint – 'For many dogs are come about me'; in Purcell's *It is a good thing to give thanks* (Z.18) a repeat of the triple-time section of the symphony separates the first four verses of Psalm 92, which proclaim the goodness of giving thanks, show ways of doing it and give reasons for doing it, from the bass exclamation 'O Lord, how glorious are thy works'.

The first repetition of 'Laudate Ceciliam' concludes the first two lines of text, and creates a musical unit of them. The repetition of the symphony separates this from the exhortation 'Dicite, Virgini, Canite Martyri', and the work concludes with a further repetition of the central poetic theme – 'Laudate Ceciliam'. The crucial structural feature is that given this context the symphony repetition offers not completion, but a new beginning; this makes the impact of the following expressive duet all the more telling.

There is a further important connection with the verse anthem. Unlike any ode by Purcell, but like some earlier ones such as Humphrey's *When from his throne* of 1672, the symphony to *Laudate Ceciliam* is of the type commonly used in the verse anthem, including those of Purcell, Humphrey and Blow. In this, a slow first section featuring dotted rhythms might be repeated, and is followed by a binary form, top-line-dominated section, in a dance-like triple time. As with a number of verse anthems written before 1686, but unlike any ode, the first section of this symphony ends with a full close in the tonic.

So the disposition and functional relationships of sections in this piece owe more to the verse anthem than to any other English antecedent: yet once we get beyond the symphony the work does not sound remotely like a verse anthem. Walker suggests that Purcell might have had a specific model in mind, a hypothesis which is both plausible and tantalizing; certainly it goes a long way towards explaining the work's peculiarities. However, the seach for such a model is anything but straightforward.

Purcell's title is 'A Latine Song made upon St Cecilia, whose day is commerated Yearly by al Musitians made in the year 1683.' The designation 'song' offers no guidance as to a possible model, for at that time English composers commonly used it for almost any secular, non-operatic text setting, including solo songs, duets with instruments, and full-blown odes for chorus and orchestra. More helpful for our understanding is Purcell's mention of 'Latine', for the available evidence suggests that for Purcell and many of his contemporaries, setting a Latin text went hand in hand with adopting a distinctive musical style.

Prior to 1683 Purcell had completed at least two large settings in Latin, both using texts from the Psalms. *Jehova, quam multi sunt hostes mei* (Z.135) and *Beati omnes qui timent Dominum* (Z.131) were copied into his autograph manuscript B.L. Add. MS. 30930 almost certainly in or soon after 1680. There are also a few bars of *Domine, non est exaltum* (Z.102), which is known in no other source. Significantly, these pieces do not appear in the Fitzwilliam MS 88 autograph, or in any other autograph source of early sacred music. Instead Purcell chose to put them in the manuscript containing the sacred part-songs, the fantasias, sonatas and other domestic music.

This and their distinctive style set them apart from the main body of Purcell's sacred music. Moreover, while both completed pieces are avowedly polyphonic and economical with their material, neither shows the obsessive contrapuntal concentration on a limited amount of material so characteristic of most of the other music in the autograph manuscript, and even of much of Purcell's English-language church music. Rather, the recitatives and the choruses probably owe something to the expressive, declamatory style of much early- and mid-seventeenth-century Italian sacred music. Carissimi's and Cavalli's motets are perhaps the most famous examples, and the former in particular are well represented in English manuscript sources of the 1670s and 1680s.

If these pieces make a nod in the direction of Italy, then *Laudate Ceciliam* takes an elaborate bow. There seems little doubt that in this piece Purcell was out to demonstrate his ability to write in the same style as those esteemed foreign composers for whom Latin settings were a mainstay; he also wished to impress his older English contemporaries, a number of whom, and of his predecessors, had shown an interest in Italianate Latin settings. In 1674 John Playford had published the second book of *Cantica Sacra* which included Latin and English settings for two voices and organ continuo; the contributors included Richard Deering, Christopher Gibbons, Benjamin Rogers and Matthew Locke. This was a follow up to a similar volume devoted to the music of Deering alone which, according to Playford's preface, had met with some success. Interestingly, the surviving fragment of Purcell's *Domine, non est exaltum,* is a two-part setting close in style to some of Locke's Latin settings, including those in this volume. While it is therefore quite likely that Purcell's perception of Latin style was affected by the works of English composers, there is no question but that the inspiration for all this music, and the origin of *Laudate Ceciliam's* distinctive vocal style, lay in the work of Italian composers.

EXAMPLE 2

Bars 1-11 of the first vocal section are reproduced in Example 2, including Purcell's distinctive notation.[11] Several features distinguish them from Purcell's English settings of this period. In particular, the odes and anthems hardly ever use sequential motivic repetitions as a primary means of expansion. The dotted rhythms and the several melodic ways of filling out thirds are the most obvious repetitions.

This can be compared with Purcell's typical English practice of around 1683 and before, exemplified in the setting of 'Praise him in the sound of the Trumpet' from *O praise God in his holiness* (Z.42). Here the roulade is formed of various kinds of irregular repetition (Example 3). It is significant that in the anthems the most frequent exceptions to this are settings of 'Alleliua', which of necessity require repetition, and which use one of the few untranslated words. Example 4 demonstrates how close is the Italian connection with such sections. Characteristically, both Purcell examples are ground basses.

EXAMPLE 3

Returning to *Laudate Ceciliam*, two more examples of Carissimi will demonstrate the link with the stylistic practice Purcell adopted. Unlike Purcell's English language settings, small motifs transposed to different harmonic and pitch levels are a primary means of expansion (Example 5).

All the vocal sections show similar stylistic links. The first recitative, 'Modulemini psalmum novum' (Example 6), like the first recitative from Purcell's motet *Jehovah, quam multi sunt hostes* (Z.135.2), is closely based on the recitative style of Carissimi and his contemporaries. One piece which Purcell almost certainly would have encountered is Carissimi's *Lucifer coelestis olim hierarchiae princeps*, for bass voice and continuo, which is particularly well represented in manuscript sources of the period. The degree of variance between these, plus the work's publication in the second book of Playford's *Harmonia Sacra* (1693), in a very corrupt version for soprano, all suggest that it was well known and much admired. Its first few bars are here reproduced as found in the generally reliable B.L. Add. MS 33234 (Example 7).

In this style, passages designed to reflect the text's rhythm, often using repeated notes to create extended upbeat patterns, are contrasted with passages of melisma based on motivic repetition, and with passages which stretch the

EXAMPLE 4

EXAMPLE 5

and

EXAMPLE 6

rhythm of speech to give impetus to a following melisma. So, in bars 2-3 of the Carissimi (Example 7) and bars 1-2 of the Purcell (Example 6), the musical rhythm reflects faithfully that of the text, and subtly uses pitch movement to paint in detail, as in the gradual ascent to 'praeclarissimus'. In bars 6-7 of the Carissimi the slowing of vocal rhythm, while just text accentuation is preserved, gives the following melisma great impetus. In the Purcell, the D on 'die' is tied so that it leads into the next bar and towards the melisma.

EXAMPLE 7

This section of the Purcell expands by giving every voice a turn at the main idea, each on a different harmonic and pitch level, and by then bringing in all three in progressively closer imitation, culminating in extended melismata for all three voices. To cap this the instruments play a short 'ritornello' derived from these melismata, their only contribution other than in the symphony. This vocal technique is similar to that of many of Purcell's own verse anthems, the opening verse of *It is a good thing to give thanks* (Z.18) and 'Therefore will I offer' from *The lord is my light* (Z.55.6) for example. But it is also common in his English contemporaries and forebears, and in earlier seventeenth-century Italian music, including that of Monteverdi.

The second recitative section, 'Dicite virgini', is replete with expressive devices associated with early- and mid-seventeenth-century Italian music. The carefully controlled chromaticism, the repetition of expressive words set to suggestive ideas, and the relationship between all this and a more slowly moving yet regular harmonic progression, are evident in Carissimi's setting of *Anima mea*. This piece also is well represented in contemporary English manuscripts and was sufficiently well known to be quoted by Roger North in 'Of composition in general', being referred to as 'that admirable song of Sigr. Charissime'.[12] (Example 8)

EXAMPLE 8

The sumptuous parallel thirds of the second recitative in the Purcell are a clear instance of him borrowing a device associated with certain types of sacred music, but originating primarily with Italian opera. There, parallel thirds could be used to represent the unanimity of lovers, as in the duet commonly associated with the end of Monteverdi's *L'Incoronatzione di Poppea*; or the imagery could be sublimated into a sacred context. It is no coincidence that it is common in Marian motets; for Mary substitute Cecilia.

While the repetitions of the opening vocal section in *Laudate Ceciliam* owe something to the methods of the verse anthem, the extent to which they dominate the work seems unique in English music of the period, but it is not unusual in Italian music, especially in secular cantatas. Carissimi's serenata for two sopranos, bass and continuo, *Sciota havean*, commonly known as *I naviganti*, was popular in England at that time; it includes several repetitions of complete sections.[13] In B.L. Add. MS 33234, which has already supplied a number of quoted examples, an anonymous setting of *Lontani del core* shows many of the stylistic characteristics associated with the triple-time sections of *Laudate Ceciliam*; but more significantly its opening section is repeated in the middle and at the end. As with the Purcell, the purpose is to reinforce the text's central thought. (Example 9)

EXAMPLE 9

Any study of external influences must take account of the distinctive notation in the triple-time sections, which is unique in Purcell's autographs (see Example 2). More than any other features of the work it suggests that in composing this piece Purcell was trying to make a point to his musical colleagues, and in the case of the notation at least it seems to have been a rather esoteric one. The unusual nature of the practice is underlined by the only other source for this piece, Royal College of Music MS. 518, which seems to be derived from the autograph yet does not preserve the notational style.

Purcell was using a relic of notational colouration, a practice which stretched back several hundred years, and which was occasionally used in the eighteenth century. I have not traced any examples of this specific type of colouration in sources which can be linked firmly to mid- or late-seventeenth-century England, but it was not rare on the continent, where it survived into the eighteenth-century: an example from François Couperin is illustrated in the *New Grove* article on notation, which claims that the practice was usually adopted in triple time and when the time unit was the semibreve rather than the minim. Certainly that fits with Purcell's usage.

However, another type of colouration contemporary with Purcell is fairly common in late-seventeenth-century sources. I have found no examples in English music of the period, but many in Italian. Carissimi's *I naviganti*, which has already been referred to, survives in B.L. Add. MS 31473, an exceedingly fine late-seventeenth-century copy almost certainly produced by a professional Italian copyist.[14] This uses black semibreves to indicate hemiola rhythm; and thus it was transcribed by Roger North when he quoted this evidently popular piece.[15] Other examples of this type of colouration are in Stradella's oratorio *San Giovanni Battista* (1675), as written out by the same copyist in B.L. Add. MS 45882, and in the incomplete parts for Cesti's *Filie Jerusalem* surviving in B.L. Add. MS 31480.

The point about Purcell's usage is that while it might be consistent with continental practice, it is not his usual way of indicating triple time. As in a number of early pieces, such as the verse anthem *Bow down thine ear* (Z.11), he here uses time signatures of $3^{\mathbb{C}}_{1}$ and $\frac{\mathbb{C}}{3}$, but normally this was regarded as sufficient, with notation conforming to standard late-seventeenth or early-eighteenth-century practice. So this was a matter of pleasing the eye, of reinforcing the continental connection in a somewhat *recherché* way which would have been understood by the performers.

So who were the performers, and where would the piece have received its first performance? It has been suggested that it was written for the Catholic Chapel of Charles II's wife, Catherine of Braganza.[16] This is possible, for on the continent in particular, liturgical commemoration of St Cecilia stretched back well into the previous century.[17] But there is another possibility at least as strong.

The Music School at Oxford seems to have played a particularly prominent role in fostering an interest in Latin settings of the kind discussed. The connections of Christopher Gibbons and Matthew Locke with the school are well documented, and many of the latter's Latin settings seem to have been composed for the delectation of his colleagues there.[18] Charles Morgan of Magdalen College was the compiler of B.L. Add. MS 33234, from which are taken many of the Latin settings quoted above; and he inscribed the date 16 September 1682 into the front of the volume. Finally we might consider that Purcell's brother Daniel became organist of Magdalen College in 1687. This appointment might have owed nothing to Henry's then rapidly rising reputation; but it does increase slightly the possibility of a family connection with Oxford.

Cecilian celebrations at Oxford might well have begun at around the same time as those in London,[19] and it seems quite likely that *Laudate Ceciliam* was composed for just such a musical gathering, be it at Oxford, at London, or elsewhere; or it could have been intended for the kind of meeting which Locke and Gibbons used to attend. While the occasion was not necessarily a private one, there is no question of the piece being conceived for a musical public in the way in which the court odes and even *Welcome to all the pleasures* (Z.339) were – too much of it is designed to appeal to those with inside knowledge, and it makes few of the grand, straightforward gestures characteristic of those odes.

Despite the strengths of these stylistic connections, the piece includes a particularly interesting stylistic anomaly. An Italian origin for the vocal style seems fairly certain; but the origin of symphonies such as this one has been the subject of a heated scholarly debate.[20] While the evidence clearly favours a French connection – see Lully's overture to the prologue of *L'Amour Malade* of 1657, for example – there is no doubt that the vast majority of such pieces Purcell would have known were by Humphrey, Blow and other English composers. This stylistic diversity is an enriching element in a piece integrated on a level much deeper than the surface differences presented by that diversity.

The integration is largely dependent on the relationships between sections, and on the constant reworkings of certain seminal melodic and harmonic progressions. The most directly related reworkings are in the triple-time sections. However, their basis is set out in the opening symphony. (Example 10)

EXAMPLE 10

In a texture animated by lively, independent part writing, and by a diversely ornamented upper line, melodic phrasing is articulated by ascending leaps after an elaborated descent, more or less by step. In the first phrase the descent *a* gets under way with the stressed F of bar 2, the first stepwise descent after the initial G-E-G oscillations *b*, which are used in conjunction with the I-IV-I harmonic progression, to affirm the tonic area. This first descent skims over E and, reaching C treated as the third of vi, turns back up to D, the prominence of which is articulated by its being enclosed within this ascent and a brief descending line from F (*c*). The phrase desribes a harmonic progression from I, through vi to a half close (*d*).

The second descent, beginning in bar 5, also ends with a close onto the dominant, made much stronger than the previous one by the opening sub-dominant inflection, and by the subsequent raising of F to F-sharp in bar 7 (*e*). A basically diatonic progression is elaborated by the minor mode inflections of bars 6 & 7. The close in bar 8 ends with the third uppermost. So do all local dominant-tonic progressions (to vi in bar 3, IV in bar 5 and V in bar 8), except for that in bar 4, the only one which involves ascending fundamental movement.

The opening of the triple-time section reworks a number of the above features, most obviously the descent from G to D via C (*a* in Example 11), and the move in the bass from C to G with a strong A en route (*b*).

EXAMPLE 11

The vocal entry (bars 43-44) reworks motifs of this triple-time section (cf. bars 18-20 & 43; the 4-3 of bars 16 & 45), and in its broad octave sweep up and down paraphrases the melodic movements described by both sections of the symphony. Also derived from the symphony is the scalic descent from C to G in the bass, with a prominent A en route (cf. *d* of Example 10 & *b* of Example 11). This vocal section features a number of already established harmonic relationships: so in bars 51 and 52, V is approached via subdominant-related inflections and vi is prominently relation to I, this time during the return from V to I. Moreover, in this section all closes except the last, emphasise the third of their final harmony (bars 46, 50, 54 & 60).

In the second triple-time vocal section the bass describes a similar progress from C to G, including a prominant A (bars 92- 85, Example 12), and then inflects this dominant to the minor mode.

EXAMPLE 12

The third triple-time section reworks motivic ideas related to the first, notably the dotted rhythm and the appoggiatura figures (cf. *a* and *b* in Example 2 and Example 13). Several motivic details and the strong moves to ii and v are closely related to the second section of the symphony.

Such links are carried, in a suitably contrasted way, into the recitatives. One

EXAMPLE 13

could mention the first recitative's melodic C-A in bars 69-70 and its early move to vi (bars 72-73, Example 6), or its extensive use of B-flat in bars 84-90, the harmonic context of which leans now towards IV rather than v. Such links can be found throughout the three recitative sections, and no less than those in the triple-time sections are central to the piece's continuity of thought; but it is the balancing of these similarities against much more overt contrasts with the surrounding material, which gives those sections their telling effect.

With the first recitative, it is not just the recitative character which stands out against the preceding vocal section. The pace at which material unfolds is much more expansive, and more opportunity is offered for locally expressive effect. Such contrasts are intensified for the next recitative. Immediately after the full close in C which end the symphony repetition, this expressive duet begins on E major as V of vi, an intensification of the minor mode inclinations already heard in the first recitative. This is neatly complemented by the third recitative, the beginning of which overlaps into the end of the triple-time section. While the first harmony after the new signature is E major, it is as a close in iii, and the recitative proper gets under way with a move back to C, an apt reversal of the move at 'Dicite virgini', considering that the piece is approaching its conclusion.

The way in which Purcell overlaps the first restatement of 'Laudate Ceciliam' into the preceding section is a particularly telling example of his sensitivity to structural balance. The principle common to the periodic phrase structures of all triple-time sections is set out in the first (see Example 14).

EXAMPLE 14

	4	+	4	+	3	+	7	+	4	+	4
bb.	43-46		47-50		51-53		54-60		61-64		65-68
	I-I		I-I		V of I-V		V-vi		I		I-I
	'Laudate Ceciliam'				'In voce et organo'		'Laudate Ceciliam'			'In voce et organo'	

N.B. All closes except the final ones stress the third of the relevant harmony.

This section operates a circuit based on departure from and return to a four-bar norm. The operation is coincident with a complementary harmonic circuit. The movement away from the tonic in bars 51-53 coincides with new material setting 'in voce organo'. This phrase too could readily have been of four bars, ending on the downbeat of bar 54. Purcell's compression of the alto-line and the overlapping entry in the bass effect a shortening of that phrase, and inject a tension neatly picked up by the irregularity of the next series of entries, which generates a seven-bar phrase ending on vi. The material which formerly was used to leave the tonic, and which was associated with phrase disruption, now is used to return to the tonic area, and twice appears with a tonic full close, each appearance concluding on the downbeat of the phrase's fourth bar. The crucial point here is that the two statements of this phrase (bars 61-64 & 65-68) are identical in content but different in function. The first (bars 61-64) effects the return from vi to I; the second effects closure of the section by reinforcing the return of harmonic and phrase stabilty.

The second triple-time section (Example 12) exploits the balance principles involved in the first, and combines these with the previously mentioned melodic and harmonic links so that the first statement of 'Laudate Ceciliam' (bars 108-111) stands as the balancing harmonic statement which otherwise would be required to close the section. The entry of 'Laudate Ceciliam' is made plausible by the similarities between bb. 43-46 and bb. 104-107, and by the latters' strong move from IV to I. The harmonic stability posited by this move is neatly effected by the return of the opening vocal material.

Comparable methods are used to make the final statement of 'Laudate Ceciliam' especially effective. The phrase and harmonic structures of the preceding triple-time section (bars 192-205, Example 13), are much less stable than those of any other triple- time section. As this one is short, and dovetailed into the surrounding recitatives, it is dominated by these, and never suggests completion in the way which 'Quia preceptum' (example 12) did. The extended harmonic diversions of the 'Dicite virgini' recitative and the short triple-time section are followed by the more C-major oriented recitative 'Nobiscum Martyri'. But the piece requires a conclusion more straightforward than this recitative could possibly offer. The diatonic clarity and phrase stability of 'Laudate Ceciliam' amply fulfil this requirement.

One of the most remarkable features of this piece is its control of context. It is from this that detail acquires the focus necessary for it to have expressive substance. Moreover, it is not just that the setting convincingly expresses textual detail: the compositional process itself reflects a view implicit in the text, but rendered explicit textually and musically by the repetitions of 'Laudate Ceciliam'. And all this is in spite of the work's polyglot stylistic background.

Laudate Ceciliam was written during a crucial period in Purcell's compositional development. A number of earlier works took the imitation of Italian music as their starting point. Perhaps the earliest is the anthem *Let God Arise* (Z.23), which reworks passages of Monteverdi and Peri. Its short-breathed discontinuity and the evidence of a primary source place it certainly earlier than 1679, and probably well before that.[21] Then there are the two Latin motets mentioned above; but above all there are the trio sonatas.

It is not appropriate here to detail the strengths and weaknesses of the sonatas, but thirty years ago Michael Tilmouth noted that the most Italianate movements were not always the most successful.[22] The substance of the difficulties in such movements lies in Purcell's failure to discriminate when applying his superlative technique to a style fundamentally different from that in which the technique was nurtured. For example, once he latched onto an idea which offered possibilities for triple invertible counterpoint he found it hard to resist putting it through every possible combination. The result, combined with the strongly periodic phrase structures inherent in the Italian style, was often tediously predictable.

One might imagine that vocal setting was even more hazardous. But in *Laudate Ceciliam*, written maybe a year or more after the 1683 sonatas and probably most of those of 1697 also, he seems to have been able to take an imaginatively flexible approach to the repetition techniques of the adopted style. Whether in the superbly controlled phrase structure of 'Laudate Ceciliam' or in the contrapuntal elaboaration of 'nobiscum Martyri', this is the authentic voice of the Henry Purcell who just three years earlier was fully absorbed in the composition of fantasias.

Laudate Ceciliam is probably the first vocal work on a path which was to see an increasingly mature conflation of the Italian and English styles. This process was continued in the following year by choruses such as 'Welcome home' and 'With trumpets and shouts' from the ode *From those serene and rapturous joys* (Z.326.4 & 11), and continued right up to Purcell's death.

ACKNOWLEDGEMENTS

I am grateful to the following for help in the preparation of this article: to Professor Thomas Mitchell of Trinity College Dublin for advice on the Latin text and for the translation given in

Example 1; to Dr Richard Rastall of Leeds University and Dr Geoffrey Chew of Royal Hollaway and Bedford New College for advice on Purcell's notation; to Christopher Bornet of the Royal College of Music Library for information on MS 518; to the staff of the Manuscripts Room, British Library, for help with manuscripts contemporary with *Laudate Ceciliam.*

NOTES

1. There is no doubt that *Raise, raise the voice* (Z.334), which has sometimes been claimed for 1683, is later. The stylistic evidence for a date of around 1685-7 is particularly strong in the ground bass song 'Mark how heavily', the techniques of which are far more elaborate than in any equivalent song from 1683-4; they are, however, comparable with those from odes from 1684-7.

2. W.H. Husk, *An Account of the Musical Celebrations on St Cecilia's Day*, (London, 1857).

3. Franklin B. Zimmerman, *Henry Purcell, 1659-1695, His life and times*, second, revised edition (Philadelphia, 1983), 237. J.A. Westrup, *Purcell* (revised Nigel Fortune) (London, 1980), 220-1.

4. The dates of most pieces by Purcell mentioned in this article can be surmised from their positions in the autographs. Nigel Fortune and Franklin B. Zimmerman, 'Purcell's Autographs', *Henry Purcell, 1659-1695. Essays on His Music*, ed. Imogen Holst (London, 1959). Franklin B. Zimmerman, *Henry Purcell 1659-1695. An analytical catalogue of his music* (London, 1963).

5. *Welcome to all the pleasures* (Z.339) is not in this autograph. It seems likely that the autographs for this piece and for Purcell's major publication of 1683, the *Twelve Sonatas of Three Parts*, were sent to the publisher.

6. The path these composers and Purcell took in developing the English court ode can be traced by examining B.L. Add. MS 33287, which includes most of Humphrey's and Blow's odes, plus many by Purcell. See Ian Cheverton, 'Captain Henry Cooke (*c*.1616-72), the beginnings of a reappraisal', *Soundings*, 9 (1982) 74-86, and Rosamond McGuinness, *English Court Odes, 1660-1820* (Oxford, 1971).

7. E. Walker, *A History of Music in England* (revised J.A. Westrup) (Oxford, 1952).

8. See Odes 61 and 62 by Catullus as examples of classical precedents. I am grateful to Professor Thomas Mitchell of Trinity College, Dublin for assistance and advice on this and other matters concerning the text of *Laudate Ceciliam.*

9. See Preface & Commentary in *Musica Britannica, 50 – Blow: Anthems with Orchestra*, ed. Bruce Wood (London, 1984).

10. See Introduction to *Purcell Society Edition, Volume 13 – Sacred Music Part I*, ed. Peter Dennison (London, 1988).

11. Purcell's barring is irregular. I have here adopted Arkwright's practice in his generally sound Purcell Society Edition of 1899, i.e. barring is regular, editorial insertions being indicated by dotted lines. Bar numbers follow the regular pattern.

12. R. North, *Roger North on Music*, ed. John Wilson (London, 1959), 113-114.

13. *Roger North on Music*, 120-2, 300, 350.

14. According to British Library Catalogue.

15. *Roger North on Music* (as n. 12), 120-2.

16. Husk, *An Account* (as n. 2), Zimmerman, *Analytical Catalogue* (as n. 4), 150.

17. Richard Luckett, 'St Cecilia and Music', *Proceedings of the Royal Musical Association*, 99 (1972-3).

18. See Introduction to *Musica Britannica, 38 – Locke: Anthems and Motets*, ed. Peter Le Huray (London, 1976).

19. See Husk (as n. 4) and 'Cecilian Celebrations', *The New Grove Dictionary of Music and Musicians*, ed. Stanley Sadie (London, 1980), vol. 4, 46-7.

20. Don Franklin, 'Review of *Musica Britannica, 34 & 35*', *Journal of the American Musicological Society*, 28 (1975) 143-9. Also correspondence between Peter Dennison and Don Franklin, *Journal of the American Musicological Society*, 31 (1978), 541-3.

21. J.A. Westrup, *Purcell* (as n. 3), 215. Eric van Tassel, 'Purcell's *Give Sentence*', *The Musical Times*, 118 (1977), 381-3.

22. Michael Tilmouth, 'The Technique and Forms of Purcell's Sonatas', *Music and Letters*, 40 (1959), 109-21.

Vivaldi's Marginal Markings

CLUES TO SETS OF INSTRUMENTAL WORKS AND THEIR CHRONOLOGY

PAUL EVERETT

A problem which continues to limit our understanding of the music of Antonio Vivaldi (1678-1741) is the lack of a chronological perspective which might govern the study of stylistic factors and generally inform the appraisal and performance of his works. With the exception of the operas (whose dates are known from contemporary notices and other documentary evidence) and the relatively small number of instrumental pieces which were published during the composer's lifetime, most of Vivaldi's hundreds of works are shrouded in mystery because their sources are undated and may have seemed to be undatable. It has recently become clear, however, that a reasonably complete chronology of the music may successfully be based largely on certain kinds of evidence yielded by the numerous autograph and copied manuscripts which survive in Turin, Dresden and elsewhere. There is no shortage of relevant data, especially when the sources' *non-textual* characteristics – handwritings, styles of calligraphy, patterns of stave-ruling, types of paper, the collation of leaves, and so forth – are analysed in relation to the documents' texts. The problem lies, in fact, in the interpretation of evidence of such great diversity and the difficulty of relating one conclusion to another.

The present article concerns one small but important aspect of this complex investigation: the significance of certain kinds of annotations appearing in some of the manuscripts preserved in the Foà and Giordano collections in the Biblioteca Nazionale, Turin. Twenty-seven large volumes contain what is believed to have been Vivaldi's 'working stock': the manuscripts which he retained and supplemented throughout his life and which probably travelled with him on his journeys away from Venice. Discounting several scores of other composers' music which Vivaldi appears to have possessed, this remarkable collection comprises 446 manuscripts: 365 autographs, 57 partly autograph copies and 24 non-autograph copies.[1] Most of the autographs are composition drafts, replete with corrections, revisions and aborted sketches; others are copies which may represent second or subsequent versions of the works they contain. It hardly needs to be stated that, for the purposes of assembling a chronology, the importance of this extraordinarily rich corpus of music is immeasurable. The natural premise for the investigation of documents which relate so exclusively to the activities of the composer himself is that any non-textual or textual feature, no matter how small or seemingly insignificant, is potential evidence for relative dating.[2]

Many manuscripts – including several whose musical texts were entirely copied by scribes – exhibit inscriptions in Vivaldi's hand which must relate to the composer's initial use and later adaptation of the music. Some of the obvious examples – which normally have clear chronological implications – are remarks concerning the transposition of vocal parts, new instrumentations substituted for original ones, instructions to copyists, and, in the case of several concertos, markings connected with the conversion of a solo part to one for a different instrument. A few annotations are particularly fascinating because they are each of an unique kind. One is the famous autograph 'thematic catalogue': brief incipits of seven instrumental pieces noted on the otherwise blank folio 284[v] in Foà 30, the last page of the autograph score of RV 251 (ff. 275-284).[3] (There is a danger is misinterpreting such evidence, of course. Although it is possible that the seven compositions were in existence by the time Vivaldi created what appears to be the composition draft of RV 251, it is equally possible that, at a later time, he listed here works more recent than RV 251 simply because the blank page was to hand.) Another example is one of Vivaldi's rare doodles: a vertical stream of letters down the right-hand margin of f. 238[r] in Giordano 29, a page of the autograph score of RV 212a (ff. 233-235 and 238-244), which spell out the words 'don antonio uiualdi maestro di capela del sige prencipe'. There can be no doubt that this little piece of self-congratulatory vanity relates to the period, from 1718 to 1720, when Vivaldi was *maestro di cappella da camera* (maestro, that is, for secular music) in the service of Prince Philip of Hesse-Darmstadt, Governor of Mantua, or that the concerto RV 212a itself was composed during that time. It may be argued, of course, that the inscription could have been added at any time after (or even before) the music was notated. But evidence more concrete than the annotation allows us to attribute both this manuscript and companion sources to the Mantuan interlude, as we shall see.

The meanings of other kinds of inscription, and the extent to which they are indicative of contemporaneity or chronological ordering, are not so easy to determine when the markings themselves are either rare or, because they are very brief and thus not explicit, subject to diverse interpretations. To begin to understand them, one must of course note their characteristics and positions on the page, and try to judge when and by whom they were written. From these details it is possible to conclude that certain markings may belong together in a series, and that each series must have its own significance based on the set of works it circumscribes. The notion that such markings are labels of one kind or another, and that they were therefore imposed as identifications of constituent documents in sets, is most certainly valid, not only because several series of marks are indeed discernible but also because the practice of grouping works in sets was an exercise Vivaldi must often have undertaken.

It was common for a composer of the time to prepare small-scale works in sets – or at least to assemble sets from a repertory of existing pieces – in order to form collections for publication, for presentation to a patron, for sale to a customer, or to fulfil commissions. In Vivaldi's case, his intermittent service at the Ospedale della Pietà in Venice, and his duties both in Mantua and as the *maestro di musica in Italia* of the Bohemian count Wenzel von Morzin (to whom the op. VIII collection of 1725 was dedicated), would have required him to furnish quotas of instrumental works, cantatas and, for the Pietà, motets and other sacred vocal pieces too. Twelve collections of sonatas and concertos were published between 1705 (op. I) and 1729 (op. XII), and the composer himself almost certainly organized as a set the six cello sonatas which are preserved both in a copyist's manuscript and a print of 1740, even though it remains possible that he did not authorize their publication in Paris by C.-N. Le Clerc.[4] We know from the testimony of Edward Holdsworth, who met Vivaldi on 13 February 1733, that the composer had decided not to publish any more sets because the sale of manuscript copies – at what Holdsworth judged to be a high price – was more lucrative.[5] Indeed, Vivaldi must regularly have fulfilled commissions from private customers, especially foreign visitors to Venice, by supplying sets comprising as many works as they wished to purchase.[6] This perhaps explains the existence in Paris of the manuscript of cello sonatas, while other surviving manuscript collections were compiled for different reasons:

(1) Twelve concertos (RV 360, 189, 202, 286, 391, 526, 183, 322, 203, 271, 277 & 520), entitled *La cetra*,[7] dedicated to the Austrian emperor Charles VI. Autograph parts (lacking the solo violin part), with non-autograph title-pages dated 1728. Vienna, Österreichische National-bibliothek, Cod. 15996.

(2) Twelve violin sonatas (RV 3, 12, 757, 755, 759, 758, 6, 22, 17a, 760, 756 & 754) notated by Scribe *4* with a few corrections and a title-page in Vivaldi's hand, believed to have been presented to Cardinal Pietro Ottoboni of Rome in the mid-1720s.[8] Manchester, Central Library, MS 624.1 Vw81.

(3) Twelve concertos without soloist (RV 157, 133, 119, 136, 114, 154, 160, 127, 164, 121, 150 & 159); partbooks compiled by Scribe *4*, perhaps intended for Jacques-Vincent Languet, comte de Gergy.[9] Paris, Biblio-thèque Nationale, Ac. e.[4] 346.

(4) RV 558, 552, 540 & 149; copies of the instrumental works performed

at the Pietà on 21 March, 1740, before Frederick Christian, Prince-Elector of Saxony. Two scores (RV 558 & 552) are in the hand of a copyist; the others are autograph. Dresden, Sächsische Landesbibliothek, Mus. 2389-O-4.

These sets raise three further points. The first is the obvious observation that, for Vivaldi, a set typically comprised works of a single genre, and that this is therefore a criterion by which the sense of each series of Turin markings may be judged. Secondly, it appears that Vivaldi regularly assigned the task of preparing a set to a copyist, a factor which alone might account for many of the marginal annotations on Turin autographs if we suppose that the scores needed to be specially labelled as exemplars to be copied. 'Scribe 4', responsible for the sets of Manchester sonatas and Paris concertos and many other Vivaldi sources, was Vivaldi's most regular and reliable assistant to whom such tasks might frequently have fallen; I have elsewhere proposed that he is likely to be none other than the composer's father, Giovanni Battista Vivaldi (1655-1736).[10] Thirdly, the connection between Vivaldi and musicians of the Dresden court, fostered initially at the time of the visit to Venice in 1716-17 of Johann Georg Pisendel and three of his colleagues, should not be overlooked. The autograph references to Pisendel, *Sassonia* and *l'Orchestra di Dresda* in certain Turin manuscripts are well known; perhaps some of the more obscure annotations also relate to Vivaldi's provision of works for the repertory of the *Hofkapelle*.

The compositions represented in the Vienna, Manchester, Dresden and Paris manuscript sets would originally have existed separately as individual autograph drafts, and it is not at all surprising that the Turin collection includes no example of two or more sonatas, concertos or cantatas written out and bound as one unit. Nevertheless, some of Vivaldi's annotations leave us in no doubt that certain manuscripts belong together.

Let us take the simplest example first. It has correctly been assumed that the autograph scores of RV 68, 70, 71 and 77 – the only trio sonatas for violins preserved in the Turin collection – are a set of four works or parts of a larger collection. The numerous signs of a close relationship both between the manuscripts and between the compositions (which, for Vivaldi, are in an unusual style) can hardly be coincidental: (1) similarly worded superscriptions at the head of each manuscript (RV 71, for instance: *2.ª Suonata à 2 Viol.ⁱ dà Camera da suonarsi anco senza basso Del Viualdi*); (2) RV 70, 71 and 68 are consecutively numbered *P[ri]ma, 2.ª* [seconda] and *3.ª* [terza]; (3) the manuscripts are bound contiguously within Giordano 28, in an order which reflects the works' numbering (ff. 56-61, 62-66, 67-72 and 73-78: RV 70, 71, 68 and 77, respectively); (4) all show a late style of autograph calligraphy; (5) Vivaldi terminated each work with the word *Fine* – a characteristic of his late manuscripts, especially those of the 1730s; (6) musical features common to the sonatas include a three-movement structure and an optional bass.[11] These factors – especially the uniformity of Vivaldi's handwriting and his similar superscriptions – naturally lead us to suspect that the four manuscripts are contemporaneous. But such a conclusion is not necessarily correct; it needs ideally to be corroborated by firm evidence which is independent of the texts themselves and the manner in which they were written. If the manuscripts which form an apparent set were compiled at precisely the same time, their materials might be expected to reflect the fact. Such evidence, of the strongest kind, does indeed exist in this case; one batch of music-paper is common to the four manuscripts, and a second occurs in RV 68, 70 and 77.

The concept of a 'batch of music-paper' requires explanation. Vivaldi and other musicians active in Venice purchased paper of standard sizes and formats from local dealers who were supplied by paper-manufacturers in the region. The preferred unit was a sheet of *foglio reale* dimensions (typically with the generic three-crescents watermark), folded twice in oblong quarto format but not yet cut into two bifolios, which was already ruled with staves – normally ten across an oblong page. The materials Vivaldi and his copyists used may therefore be analysed by classifying, in a very precise way, each paper-type and each stave-ruling (or 'rastrography'). Over 70 paper-types appear in the Turin collection; Vivaldi used some more frequently than others, but, because any type may have remained in production for many years, the incidence of papers serves only as a general guide to the documents' chronology and fails to demonstrate the contemporaneity of two or more sources. In contrast, a rastrography is most useful as a 'date-substitute' because it is related to a very limited period: the time in which the rastrum continued to draw precisely similar rulings. Almost 400 distinct rastrographies are exhibited by the Turin manuscripts; most occur in very few sources, and it seems reasonable to believe – unless the manuscripts in question show evidence to the contrary – that two or more documents or portions of documents which possess the same rastrography are approximately contemporaneous, having been compiled from the same batch of music-paper.[12]

The most common markings to be found in the margins of the manuscripts are simply numbers. With few exceptions, they appear to be autograph – it is often impossible to be certain from the appearance of only one or two digits – and many are underlined in the way the composer normally styled the gathering-signatures of his opera manuscripts. Most appear against either concertos with solo parts for stringed instruments or concertos without soloist, and most are located near the upper left-hand corner of the first page. In contrast, numbers appearing near the lower left-hand corner neatly define a set of six works for solo bassoon, strings and continuo (a concerto-type represented in Turin by no fewer than 39 examples):

TABLE 1

Bassoon concertos

Mark	Work	Key	Location
1	RV 490	F major	Foà 32, ff. 403-10
2	RV 494	G major	Foà 32, ff. 394-402
3	RV 503	B flat major	Foà 32, ff. 386-93
4	RV 489	F major	Foà 32, ff. 333-40
5	RV 504	B flat major	Foà 32, ff. 376-85
6	RV 498	A minor	Giordano 31, ff. 18-25

Unlike the trio sonatas, these autograph scores employ distinct music-papers (although quires of a single batch were used for RV 490 and 504); all were certainly compiled late in Vivaldi's career, but probably at quite different times. It is a case of the composer assembling a set by selecting existing works, and he must have done this and imposed the numerical sequence at some point after he had completed the last of the manuscripts to be written. That date was probably around 1737. The batch of music-paper used for both RV 490 and 504 was also employed for an autograph solo violin part for the concerto RV 367 (Giordano 34, ff. 103-5 and 110). Belonging with this part is a non-autograph second violin part (ff. 108-9) for the same concerto, whose music-paper appears also in the autograph score (Foà 38, ff. 110-84) of the opera *Catone in Utica*, RV 705, produced in Verona in the spring of 1737.

A set of at least seven concertos for solo cello, strings and continuo is similarly suggested by numerical markings, although its full sequence cannot be defined. The scores of RV 406 and 412 are marked '5' and '7', respectively, each in the upper left-hand corner of the first page. Numbers less than ten appear in the same position on several other manuscripts, however, and we need to be certain that these particular markings relate to each other. Again, the analysis of the manuscripts' materials reveals connections of apparent contemporaneity between these and other sources which cannot be purely coincidental. One variety of music-paper, belonging to the very early 1730s or perhaps the late 1720s, was used for both RV 406 and 412: paper-type *B5* with *10/190.2(2)* rastrography.[13] This batch was also employed for other manuscripts, including those of three further cello concertos, RV 399, 403 and 414, which might therefore be considered to be possible works in the set despite the fact that their sources lack numerical markings. Although the autograph score of RV 414 is located separately (Foà 29, ff. 101-111), the remaining four manuscripts are bound contiguously in two pairs, separated only by the score of a sixth cello concerto, RV 424:

TABLE 2

Cello concertos

Markings	Work	Location
Originale	RV 399	Foà 29, ff. 134-141; autograph.
5 Originale	RV 406	Foà 29, ff. 142-149; copy in hand *16*, completed by Vivaldi.
	RV 424	Foà 29, ff. 150-157; autograph.
7	RV 412	Foà 29, ff. 158-165; copy in a hand unknown from other Vivaldi manuscripts.
	RV 403	Foà 29, ff. 166-173; copy in hand *16*, with autograph annotations.

The word 'originale', common to the sources of RV 399 and 406, is found only rarely in manuscripts of Vivaldi's music. It is exhibited elsewhere in certain opera scores and as part of the composer's superscription, *Originale del Viualdi*, on the first pages of the two trios for violin, lute and continuo, RV 82 and 85 (Foà 40, ff. 6-9 and 2-5), dedicated to Count Johann Joseph von Wrtby,[14] and seems to be a marking used to label a score as a definitive exemplar to be copied. At the time when the set of cello concertos was being compiled, it is possible that a copy was made from the autograph score of RV 399, that Scribe *16* transcribed the word 'originale' from an autograph exemplar, and that the copy-scores of RV 412 and 403 were also derived from autographs each labelled in this way.

We notice, not for the first time, that the order in which manuscripts are bound in the Foà and Giordano volumes reflects some of the links of apparent contemporaneity between sources of similar kinds. Because the sorting of works by genre and instrumentation was undoubtedly the principal process by which the volumes were defined prior to being bound, it is not at all surprising to find that most cello concertos are located in Foà 29 and most bassoon concertos in Foà 32. But the scores of RV 399, 406, 424, 412 and 403 within Foà 29 and those of RV 504, 503, 494 and 490 within Foà 32 cannot have been bound contiguously by chance. Unlike in the case of the trio-sonata scores, RV 68, 70, 71 and 77, which could easily have been gathered together because their similar superscriptions were noticed, there is no simple explanation for the fact that companion manuscripts like these are frequently located consecutively unless we suppose that the order of binding preserves, in a fragmented and rearranged manner, the state in which the documents are likely to have been stored by Vivaldi himself. Although the date and place of binding, and the circumstances of how the manuscripts came into the possession of Jacopo Soranzo between 1741 and 1745, remain unknown, this factor increases the probability that the volumes were bound fairly soon after the composer's death.

The remaining numerical markings, listed in Table 3, are not easily explained. Some undoubtedly belong with others, but, because the style in which they were written and their positions on the page vary, it is impossible to define, with any certainty, sets of works comparable with those of bassoon and cello concertos. The facts that certain markings ('2', '4', '6', '9' and '10') were duplicated and that three scores (RV 94, 156 and 544) possess two numbers indicate, at any rate, the existence of two or more series of marks dating, probably, from distinct times. It is possible, however, that Vivaldi added many of these markings not as labels for works in sets but as references in some kind of inventory. The numbers run from '2' to '67', but the isolated case of RV 548 suggests that the sequence was extended to '205' and possibly beyond. Are we to suppose that over 170 further manuscripts of instrumental works – those which exhibited numbers missing from the sequence – must once have existed? It is possible that some markings, noted in the upper left-hand corner of the page, were removed from extant manuscripts when the upper edges of the leaves were trimmed at the time of binding, but it is hard to believe that this could have happened in so many cases: it is clear, from the measurements of watermarks bisected by the upper edges of the oblong leaves, that the strips of paper cut away were typically very narrow.

Several negative conclusions may at least be drawn about the elusive significance of the sequence. If the numbers relate to the making of an inventory, they do not appear to have been imposed logically by a musical criterion. The works were not ordered by key, for instance; it seems coincidental, to judge by the whole sequence, that RV 156 and 104 (both in G minor) were numbered consecutively, and that RV 94, 564 and 248 were labelled '31', '32' and '33', respectively, in their natural progression from D major to D minor. Nor were the manuscripts sorted by concerto-type; randomly represented in the sequence are six chamber concertos (without a *ripieno* band), nine concertos without soloist, ten with solo violin, two with solo viola d'amore, and six scored for two or more solo instruments. Neither the existence of the numbers nor the sequence which they form seems to have any direct connection with the dates when the marked manuscripts are likely to have been compiled: at various times from the late 1710s to the late 1720s (discounting the seemingly later score of RV 93, datable to *c*.1730-31). To judge by the documents' non-textual characteristics, there is no correlation between low and high numbers and relatively early and late works, and thus the sequence seems unlikely to be a running tally of the works supplied to a single customer over a long period. (The delivery to the Pietà of two concertos per month from 1723 to *c*. 1729 is a case which springs to mind; Vivaldi presumably kept some kind of account, but it is hard to believe that his method depended on unqualified numbers.) While it is possible that most of the markings were applied at one particular time, the notion that the composer made an inventory, with arbitrary figures, of all the concerto manuscripts he possessed at that date is ruled out by the fact that he did not label numerous surviving scores of comparable works which are demonstratively earlier than, or approximately contemporary with, these documents.

TABLE 3

Other numbered concertos

All sources are autograph scores (except RV 544 and 229 which are partly autograph), and, unless noted otherwise, each marking appears in the upper left-hand corner of the first page. Entries prefixed with an asterisk refer to manuscripts which exhibit other markings; see Table 4.

RV 397	Foà 29, ff. 293-300	A minor	2
RV 544 *Il Proteo*	Giord. 28, ff. 2-9	F major	2
RV 93	Giord. 35, ff. 297-302	D major	2 [upper right corner]
*RV 387	Giord. 30, ff. 129-138	B minor	3
RV 94	Giord. 31, ff. 412-419	D major	4 [with] 31
RV 575	Giord. 28, ff. 134-150	G major	4
RV 261	Giord. 29, ff. 225-232	E flat major	5
RV 136	Giord. 30, 63-66	F major	6 [upper right corner]
RV 140	Foà 30, 101-105	F major	6 [upper right corner]
RV 166	Giord. 30, 168-171	B flat major	6 [f. 171ᵛ]
*RV 250	Foà 30, ff. 61-68	E flat major	7
*RV 156	Giord. 29, ff. 29-35 *bis*	G minor	8 [with] 66
RV 164	Giord. 30, ff. 35-40	B flat major	9 [altered to] 9x
*RV 225	Foà 31, 200-209	D major	9 [lower right corner]
RV 247	Giord. 29, ff. 73-81	D minor	10 [also upper right corner]
RV 271 *L'amoroso*	Giord. 29, ff. 82-89	E major	10
RV 157	Giord. 30, ff. 248-255	G minor	13 [altered to] 13x
RV 395	Foà 29, ff. 301-310	D minor	16 [f. 301ʳ and f. 310ʳ]
RV 547	Giord. 28, ff. 171-179	B flat major	18 [possibly '78'?]
*RV 127	Giord. 30, ff. 108-111	D minor	20
*RV 119	Giord. 30, ff. 112-117	C minor	26 [altered to] 26x
*RV 234 *L'inquietudine*	Giord. 34, ff. 79-87	D major	28
RV 94	Giord. 31, ff. 412-419	D major	31 [with] 4
RV 564	Giord. 28, ff. 151-170	D major	32 [f. 151ʳ and f. 170ʳ]
RV 248	Giord. 30, ff. 47-56	D minor	33 [f. 47ʳ and f. 51ʳ]
RV 107	Giord. 31, ff. 314-323	G minor	34
RV 233	Giord. 29, ff. 283-294	D major	45
*RV 128	Foà 30, ff. 232-239	D minor	47
RV 103	Giord. 31, ff. 228-234	G minor	55 [upper right corner]
RV 229	Giord, ff. 12-21	D major	56
RV 546	Giord. 28, ff. 180-189	A major	60
RV 87	Giord. 31, ff. 404-411	C major	64
RV 544 *Il Proteo*	Giord. 28, ff. 2-9	F major	N[?] 64 [f. 9ᵛ]
*RV 156	Giord. 29, ff. 29-35 *bis*	G minor	66 [with] 8
RV 104 *La notte*	Giord. 31, ff. 243-249	G minor	67
RV 547	Giord. 28, ff. 171-179	B flat major	78 [probably '18'?]
RV 548	Giord. 34, ff. 133-140	B flat major	205

RV 93: a source belonging with the autograph score of the sonata RV 85 (Foà 40, ff. 2-5). Both sources carry dedications to Count Wrtby, and RV 85 exhibits the number '5' in the upper right-hand corner of the first page.

RV 94: the marking '4' is faded; '31' was perhaps added later.

RV 156: the marking '8' appears both to the left and to the right of the highest stave; the number '66' is closer to the upper left-hand corner.

RV 261: '5' also appears near the upper right-hand corner of the first page.

RV 387: also marked '3' before the inscription *Con:^{to}* (centre, top of first page).

RV 544: the score's complete title is *Il Proteò ò sia Il Mondo al rouerscio*.

There is little doubt, however, that some of the markings relate to the assembling of sets of works. It is perhaps no coincidence that *L'amoroso*, RV 271, is labelled '10'; the concerto is preserved elsewhere as the tenth work in the autograph manuscript collection, *La cetra*, dated 1728. This raises the possibility that further scores, those which served as the exemplars for the Vienna set, may have been similarly marked; although the three remaining concordant scores in Turin – of RV 183, 286 and 391 – lack numbers, there is a chance that Vivaldi once possessed separate copies of these works which did exhibit appropriate marks. (It is interesting to note also that the other score marked '10', RV 247, is bound contiguously with *L'amoroso*. Could it be that Vivaldi at first intended RV 247 to be included in *La cetra* and later changed his mind?) Concordant sources for ten out of the twelve concertos in the Paris set are preserved in Turin; of these, five exhibit numerical markings. Except in the case of RV 164, which is labelled '9' in Turin and appears as the ninth work in Paris, these is no relationship between the Turin scores' markings and the order in which the works occur in the set: RV 157 ('13', Paris No. 1), RV 119 ('26', Paris No. 3), RV 136 ('6', Paris No. 4) and RV 127 ('20', Paris No. 8). What does appear to be connected with the compilation of the Paris set is the alteration of three of these markings (those on the scores of RV 119, 157 and 164) with a small subscript 'x', in a shade of ink distinct from that of the figures. The explanation, above, for the lack of markings on three Turin concordances of works in the Vienna set is equally applicable to the five unmarked Turin concordances of Paris works, but this somewhat unconvincing theory could so easily be wrong, of course. Nevertheless, the twin arguments that Vivaldi must have possessed exemplars for all the works which were copied in sets and that these scores were not necessarily the documents which have come down to us, together support the notion that a significant number of manuscripts, exhibiting the missing numbers in the sequence, once existed.

FIGURE 1

a:

b:

c:

d:

e:

Whereas most of the numerical markings signify that Vivaldi occasionally grouped together manuscripts of widely differing dates, non-textual factors show that annotations of other kinds typically appear on sources which more naturally belong together, having originally been compiled as companion documents. The autograph scores of RV 533 and 427, bound contiguously in Giordano 31 (ff. 206-12 and 213-19, respectively), each exhibit a special sign, deleted with two cross-strokes, in the upper left-hand corner of the first page: see Figure 1a. Their identical materials appear to date from the late 1720s; the same batch of music-paper was used also for some revisions made to the score of *Orlando*, RV 728 (Giordano 39 *bis*, ff. 2-153), an opera produced in the autumn of 1727. It seems, moreover, that the works were initially conceived as identically scored concertos; the superscription at the head of RV 427 was originally the same as that for RV 533 – *Con.^{to} p(er) 2 Flauti Trauersieri* [space] *Del Viualdi* – before Vivaldi amended it to read '... p(er) il Flauto Trauersiere ...'. In a similar fashion, the scores of RV 336 (autograph, Giordano 30, ff. 286-95) and 182 (partly autograph, Giordano 30, ff. 296-307) constitute a pair of contiguously-bound solo violin concertos, marked 'Primo' and '2do', respectively. While none of their various music-papers is common to both sources, Vivaldi simultaneously employed paper from batches represented separately in RV 182 and RV 336 when compiling a third concerto manuscript: RV 582 (Giordano 34, ff. 22-43). Although the relationship between the materials of RV 336 and 182 is thus an indirect one, there is every reason to suppose that these companion scores were written out at about the same time: a date most probably within the early 1720s.[15]

Larger groups of companion manuscripts are distinguished by other special signs and letters, seemingly in Vivaldi's hand: see Table 4. Several sources carry two labels, having presumably been marked for copying on separate occasions; RV 128 and 234 each possess three, taking into account their numerical markings. Were these perhaps some of Vivaldi's favourite works – those which he was most inclined to offer to his customers and patrons? The markings are evidence, perhaps, of Vivaldi's desire to distribute his concertos widely; they may also reflect a concentration on composition in this genre during the late 1710s and early 1720s – the period to which most of these sources appear to belong.

TABLE 4

Concerto manuscripts marked with letters and special signs

All sources are autograph scores of concertos for solo violin unless otherwise noted. Entries prefixed with an asterisk refer to manuscripts which also exhibit numerical markings; see Table 3.

'D', 'D.', 'D. B.' or '. D. B.', beyond the right-hand end of the first stave

D[?]	RV 199, *Il sospetto*	C minor	Giord. 34, ff. 141-150
D.B.	RV 218	D major	Giord. 29, ff. 295-303
D.	*RV 234, *L'inquietudine*	D major	Giord. 34, ff. 79-87
D.	RV 252	E flat major	*I-Af*; Mss. N. 318/4
D.B.	RV 343	A major	Giord. 28, ff. 96-103
D.B.	RV 379	B flat major	Giord. 30, ff. 147-157

'M.', 'M[?]' or 'M. B.', beyond the right-hand end of the first stave

M.	RV 207	D major	Giord. 30, ff. 158-167
M[?]	*RV 250	E flat major	Foà 30, ff. 61-68
M.	RV 306	G major	Giord. 30, ff. 256-263
M.B.	RV 362, *La caccia*	B flat major	Giord. 29, ff. 245-253

'P.' beyond the right-hand end of the first stave

	RV 118	C minor, without soloist	Giord. 30, ff. 57-62
	*RV 119	C minor, without soloist	Giord. 30, ff. 112-117
	*RV 127	D minor, without soloist	Giord. 30, ff. 108-111
	*RV 128	D minor, without soloist	Foà 30, ff. 232-239
P.[?]	RV 252	E flat major	*I-Af*; Mss. N. 318/4

'/o/' (Figure 1b) in the upper left-hand corner of the first page

	RV 138	F major, without soloist	Giord. 29, ff. 120-125
	RV 199, *Il sospetto*	C minor	Giord. 34, ff. 141-150
	*RV 234, *L'inquietudine*	D major	Giord. 34, ff. 79-87
	RV 246	D minor	Giord. 29, ff. 63-72
	RV 270, *Il riposo*	E major	Giord. 34, ff. 88-95
	RV 553	B flat major, 4 solo violins	Foà 29, ff. 47-68

Figure 1c near the upper right-hand corner of the first page, beyond the end of the first stave

	*RV 128	D minor, without soloist	Foà 30, ff. 232-239
	*RV 156	G minor, without soloist	Giord. 29, ff. 29-35 *bis*
	*RV 225	D major	Foà 31, ff. 200-209
	RV 343	A major	Giord. 28, ff. 96-103
	RV 379	B flat major	Giord. 30, ff. 147-157

'#' (Figure 1d) beyond the end of the first stave

| | RV 436 | G major, solo flute | Giord. 31, ff. 396-403 |

Figure 1e in the upper right-hand corner of the first page

| | *RV 387 | B minor | Giord. 30, ff. 129-138 |

RV 252: an autograph score preserved in the library of the Convento di San Francesco, Assisi (*I-Af*). The 'P.[?]' marking is below the 'D.', to the right of the second stave.

RV 306: a partly autograph score, copied by Scribe *4* and Vivaldi in collaboration.

RV 362: the title, 'La Caccia', is a later annotation than the original superscription (simply 'Con:^{lo}') and appears to have been added in the same ink as the marking 'M.B.'.

It is difficult to know what to make of the letters. We should beware of equating 'D.' with 'D.B.' or 'M.' with 'M.B.', of course, but it is curious, if the letters are simply initials which stand for the names of persons to whom the works were destined, that 'B' should be the only suffix in evidence. An alternative theory is that 'D', 'M' and 'P' might denote destinations (Dresda? Mantova? Parigi?) or patrons (Morzin? Prencipe?), while the 'B' has a quite distinct function – of differentiating these manuscripts from other copies of the same works Vivaldi might have possessed, for instance. It seems a weak hypothesis, to be sure, but three observations may be made in support of it. First, two of the scores marked 'P.' are concordances of works in the Paris set of concertos: RV 119 (Paris No. 3) and 127 (No. 8). Discounting the marking for RV 252 which was drawn in a different manner, the remaining labels in this category also appear on concertos without soloist. It therefore seems possible, assuming that the set was destined for Paris in the first place, that these markings may relate to the process by which Vivaldi selected, and in some cases later rejected, the works which were to form this collection. Second, the 'P' marked on the score of RV 252 might conceivably stand for 'Padova'; the Franciscan convent in Assisi, where this source is preserved, is known to have exchanged manuscripts with its sister house in Padua. Third, at least three of the four sources marked 'M' were available to Vivaldi while he was in the service of the Governor of Mantua. Although the manuscript of RV 207 cannot yet be dated with any certainty, that of RV 306 was probably copied during the mid-1710s but before the Mantuan interlude.[16] The scores of RV 250 and 362 separately employ batches of music-paper which, on the evidence of cantata manuscripts, are closely associated with Vivaldi's activities in Mantua.[17] One of these varieties, paper-type *B6* with *10/184.7(1)* rastrography, was used also for the autograph draft score of RV 212a mentioned earlier, on which Vivaldi referred to his appointment.

The incidence of some of the markings corresponds very closely with the incidence of varieties of music-paper; the scores of RV 156, 343 and 379 exhibiting the triple cross-hatched sign, for instance, comprise quires of a single batch. It therefore seems probable, in such cases, that Vivaldi decided that certain concertos should form a set very soon after he had completed the texts of the manuscripts. It is even possible that the grouping of works labelled '*/o/*'

(Figure 1b) was determined *before* the scores were written out, and that Vivaldi created the manuscripts in quick succession with this idea in mind. For five out of these six scores, he used a single batch of music-paper (*B14, 10/190.8(1)*) – a variety found also in the autograph score of *La verità in cimento*, RV 739 (Foà 33, ff. 142-316), dating from 1720. The sixth source, of RV 553, is probably contemporary with the others; its rastrography appears to be a variant of another exhibited by the opera manuscript. This set is characterized by the presence of *Il sospetto, L'inquietudine* and *Il riposo*, and one wonders if other concertos with fanciful titles, belonging with these three, once existed. As is shown in the high incidence of titled concertos – including companion sources of *L'inquietudine* and *Il riposo* – among the manuscripts Vivaldi is believed to have given to Cardinal Pietro Ottoboni,[18] the composer well understood the value of 'packaging' sets of his works.[19]

NOTES

1. These statistics depend on how one defines a 'manuscript', and are based on the present writer's analysis of the whole collection. Scores of operas, even those which are accretions of two or more versions, are counted singly; other composite documents – particularly the collection of arias in Foà 28 – are reckoned as separate items distinguished by the disposition of texts in relation to the collation of leaves within the structure of the volume. Portions of originally whole sources are counted separately if they are no longer bound together. The most recent catalogue of the Turin collection is Isabella Fragalà Data & Annarita Colturato, *Raccolta Mauro Foà, Raccolta Renzo Giordano*, Associazione Piemontese per la Ricerca delle Fonti Musicali (Torre D'Orfeo, Rome, 1987), with an introduction by Alberto Basso which includes important information on the history of the manuscripts. Far more useful for details of the contents of the Vivaldi items are Peter Ryom, *Les manuscrits de Vivaldi* (Antonio Vivaldi Archives, Copenhagen, 1977), and the same writer's *Répertoire des oeuvres d'Antonio Vivaldi; les compositions instrumentales* (Engstrøm and Sødring, Copenhagen, 1986).

2. Some characteristics are far more indicative than others of the dates when manuscripts were compiled, of course. Reasonably secure conclusions can be attained only by a hierarchical use of the evidence, whereby the interpretation of the most apposite features (Vivaldi's calligraphy, relevant notational features and textual clues) is governed by the implications of data most capable of being analysed objectively (principally paper-types and stave-rulings). See Paul Everett, 'Towards a Vivaldi Chronology', *Nuovi studi vivaldiani; edizione e cronologia critica delle opere*, ed. Antonio Fanna & Giovanni Morelli, 2 vols. (Olschki, Florence, 1988), 729-57.

3. See Jean-Pierre Demoulin, 'Indice thématique "pro memoria" autographe', *Vivaldiana* (Centre International de Documentation Antonio Vivaldi, Brussels, 1969); and Ryom, *Les manuscrits* (as n. 1), 449-51. 'RV' work-references follow Peter Ryom, *Verzeichnis der Werke Antonio Vivaldis (RV); kleine Ausgabe* (VEB Deutscher Verlag für Musik, Leipzig, 1974) and Ryom, *Répertoire* (as n. 1).

4. RV 47, 41, 43, 45, 40 & 46. The manuscript preserved in the Bibliothéque Nationale, Paris, shelf-marked Vm^7 6310, is undoubtedly of Venetian provenance and was notated –

probably to Vivaldi's order – by a professional Venetian copyist whom I have labelled 'Scribe 9'. See Paul Everett, 'Vivaldi's Italian Copyists', *Informazioni e studi vivaldiani, Bollettino dell'Istituto Italiano Antonio Vivaldi*, 11 (1990), forthcoming. Now that the scribe is known to have been active in Venice during the 1710s and 1720s and to have copied at least one other Vivaldi manuscript (two movements of the Turin copy of RV 455), there is reason to doubt Ryom's view (*Répertoire*, as n.1, p. 8) that the manuscript is probably a copy of the print. The reverse relationship – that the manuscript, or a copy of it, was used as the printer's exemplar – is more likely.

5. A letter dated Venice, 13 February 1733, to Charles Jennens in England, reproduced in facsimile in Michael Talbot, *Vivaldi* (Dent, London, 1978) between pp. 100 and 101.

6. One documented case, of a 'packet' of music which Vivaldi provided for the merchant Joseph Smith for delivery to William Capel, Third Earl of Essex, is mentioned in Michael Talbot, 'Charles Jennens and Antonio Vivaldi', *Vivaldi veneziano europeo*, ed. Francesco Degrada (Olschki, Florence, 1980), 72.

7. Not to be confused with the printed collection of the same name: op. IX (1727), also dedicated to the Emperor. One work (RV 391) is common to both sets, however.

8. The set is discussed in Michael Talbot, 'Vivaldi's "Manchester" Sonatas', *Proceedings of the Royal Musical Association*, 104 (1977-78), 20-29, and in the Critical Notes to the edition (by Everett and Talbot) of each sonata, published in 1982-83 by the Istituto Italiano Antonio Vivaldi and Ricordi, Milan.

9. See Michael Talbot, 'Vivaldi and a French Ambassador', *Informazioni e studi vivaldiani, Bollettino dell'Istituto Italiano Antonio Vivaldi*, 2 (1981), 38.

10. Everett, 'Vivaldi's Italian Copyists' (as n. 4), where a full catalogue of his contributions may be found.

11. Talbot observes that in their version without bass these works are stylistically akin to Leclair's op. III (1730) and Telemann's *Sonates sans basse* (1727). *Vivaldi* (as n. 5), 128.

12. Many qualifications must, of course, be applied to the argument; it would be foolish to believe, for instance, that Vivaldi always exhausted a batch of music-paper within a short time. A properly complete discussion of this central and most important aspect of the investigation is given in Everett, 'Towards a Vivaldi Chronology' (as n. 2), where the system adopted for the classification of paper-types and rastrographies is described. This article also contains some of the first results of the study; further data gathered by the present writer is interpreted in Michael Talbot, 'Vivaldi and Rome: Observations and Hypotheses', *Journal of the Royal Musical Association*, 113 (1988), 28-46. The analysis of non-textual data as the means of discerning the relationships between textually-discrete manuscripts in whole repertories is elsewhere demonstrated in Paul Everett, *The Manchester Concerto Partbooks*, 2 vols. (Garland, New York, 1990), in press; Everett, 'A Roman Concerto Repertory: Ottoboni's "what not"?', *Proceedings of the Royal Musical Association*, 110 (1983-84), 62-78; Everett, 'Vivaldi Concerto Manuscripts in Manchester: II', *Informazioni e studi vivaldiani, Bollettino dell'Istituto Italiano Antonio Vivaldi*, 6 (1985), 3-56; and Everett, 'The Application and Usefulness of "Rastrology", with particular reference to Early Eighteenth-Century Italian Manuscripts', *Musica e filologia*, ed. Marco Di Pasquale (Edizioni della Società Letteraria, Verona, 1983), 135-58.

13. 'B5' is one variety of three-crescents paper; '10/190.2(2)' is a label for a particular ruling comprising ten staves across the oblong page spanning 190.2 mm. from the uppermost to the lowest lines. Each rastrography is actually classified by recording a cross-section of all the lines drawn, and a number within parentheses ('2', in this case) serves to distinguish one ruling from another which coincidentally possesses the same span measurement.

14. Two of 14 Turin sources of putative Bohemian provenance probably dating from Vivaldi's

visit to Bohemia in *c.* 1730-31. See Everett, 'Towards a Vivaldi Chronology' (as n. 2), 739.

15. It is beyond the scope of the present article to present the complex evidence for such a conclusion. This approximate dating is based on the non-textual characteristics of over fifty manuscripts besides the scores of RV 182, 336 and 582.

16. A conclusion based on the calligraphy of Scribe *4* which this manuscript exhibits. See Everett, 'Vivaldi's Italian Copyists' (as n. 4).

17. See Everett, 'Towards a Vivaldi Chronology' (as n. 2), 752-6. The eleven cantata manuscripts which I have attributed to the Mantuan period themselves exhibit several series of markings (not related to those peculiar to concertos), and the presence of such annotations clearly distinguishes Vivaldi's early cantatas from those which belong to distinctly later periods.

18. Paul Everett, 'Vivaldi Concerto Manuscripts in Manchester: I', *Informazioni e studi vivaldiani, Bollettino dell'Istituto Italiano Antonio Vivaldi*, 5 (1984), 31-2.

19. I am grateful to the Faculty of Arts and the President of University College, Cork, for granting both financial assistance and leave of absence which have supported and enabled the research on which this article is based. Special thanks are due also to the staff of the Biblioteca Nazionale, Turin.

Fauré's First Successful Sonata Movement

PATRICK DEVINE

BACKGROUND

Gabriel Fauré celebrated his thirtieth birthday on 12 May 1875, probably at his home at 7 Rue de Parme in Paris. He had graduated from the École Niedermeyer in the capital in 1865, and the intervening ten years had witnessed service as church organist in no less than five positions, in Rennes (1866-70), then in Paris at Notre-Dame-de-Clignancourt (March-August 1870), Saint-Honoré-d'Eylau (March 1871), Saint Sulpice (October 1871-January 1874) and at the Madeleine (from January 1874). His career as a professional musician had been dramatically interrupted for five months when he fought in the Franco-Prussian War as an infantry soldier of the Imperial Guard between August 1870 and January 1871. In the summer of 1871 he made his way to Cours-sous-Lausanne in Switzerland, where he taught composition at the relocated École Niedermeyer for four months.

From 1861 Fauré had experienced a deepening friendship with Camille Saint-Saëns (1835-1921), whose influence on the younger composer was to remain until his own death. When they first met at the École Niedermeyer Saint-Saëns, then twenty-five, had been appointed teacher of piano, while Fauré was a fifteen-year-old student. Out of the formal academic atmosphere was to develop a lasting relationship which had a positive bearing on Fauré's career and on his music.

Saint-Saëns' teaching curriculum at the piano embraced the leading contemporary and near-contemporary Romantics: Schumann, Liszt and Wagner – names absent from the official syllabus of the school; Mendelssohn and Chopin might be added to the list. Although Fauré's teachers for composition had been the conservative Abraham Niedermeyer (1802-61), founder of the school, and his successor Gustave Lefèvre, author of the *Traité d'harmonie* (1889), it is probable that Saint-Saëns, whose works had already earned him considerable kudos in France and who was then poised on the brink of international success, also gave advice freely to the more enthusiastic pupils.

By the time Fauré left the school he had already compiled an impressive folio of compositions which included about seven songs, four choral works, three piano pieces and a three-voiced fugue. Between 1865 and 1875 the range of works remained largely similar, with songs, isolated movements for piano solo and duet, and choral motets constituting the bulk of creative achievements to date. However, these works include the composer's earliest attempt at symphonic form, and specifically sonata design, in the *Suite d'orchestre*, also known as the Symphony in F op. 20 of 1869-73. The first movement, an *Allegro symphonique* is, according to Robert Orledge, cast in 'conventional sonata form',[1] but its themes are 'not ideally suited to symphonic development.'[2] Versions of the movement were prepared for orchestra and for two pianos, and the music was published in 1895 in a transcription for piano duet by Léon Boëllmann as op. 68. The presence of three alternative forms indicates to some extent the composer's unhappiness about a definitive conception.

It was Saint-Saëns who partnered Fauré in the two-piano première of the *Suite d'orchestre* on 16 May 1874, and Saint-Saëns introduced Fauré to many influential musical families and patrons as well as to other composers on the former pupil's return to Paris from Rennes. However, the older master was also to further the cause of several French composers of the younger generation when on 25 February 1871[3] with Romain Bussine (1830-99), a professor of singing at the Paris Conservatoire, he founded the Société National de Musique, with its motto 'Ars Gallica': the promotion and performance of French music. Fauré participated in the society's activities from its inception, becoming secretary after the death of Alexis de Castillon (1838-73) in November 1874. In the period 1872-77 some ten songs and one choral work of his, as well as the above-mentioned *Suite d'orchestre*, received their first performances at the society's concerts.[4]

Fauré was introduced by Saint-Saëns to the Viardot family c1872. Pauline Viardot (1821-1910), a Spanish contralto, had by then attained the height of her fame. Her two daughters Claudie and Marianne became the dedicatees of several compositions,[5] and Fauré soon fell for Marianne. His love was not returned, and after a short engagement in 1877 she changed her mind and subsequently married another composer, Victor Duvernoy (1842-1907). Paul Viardot, the girls' brother and a violinist, was remembered by Fauré for the dedication of the First Violin Sonata in A op. 13.

The Clerc household in Paris represented another venue for soirées frequented by the musical establishment. Fauré was made to feel equally welcome at the Clercs' summer houses in Normandy, where he wrote much of the A major Violin Sonata in the summer of 1875. He was considerably facilitated in his work by the presence of another guest, the Belgian violinist Hubert Léonard, who performed and advised on the latest section to emerge on paper. The sonata was completed in the following year and, thanks to the Clercs' benefaction, published in 1877 by Breitkopf und Härtel. Fauré accompanied the violinist

EXAMPLE 1
(a) First subject; (b) Subsidiary theme (transition); (c) Second subject; (d) Codetta

Marie Tayau in the first performance of the work on 27 January 1877 at a concert of the Société Nationale de Musique.[6]

STRUCTURE

The sonata contains four movements the first of which is an Allegro molto in A of 409 bars. A sonata form design comprises exposition (bars 1-99), development (bars 100-267) and recapitulation with coda (bars 268-409).[7] Each of the four principal themes is conceived in units of four bars. Here the melodic line tends to form a single energetic sweep rather than a series of minute cells arranged organically. This unity is enhanced by the appearance of the full phrase in either instrument or in both, but not divided between them. Nevertheless, recurrent rhythmic patterns represent a basic ingredient (Example 1).

The initial phrase of each theme continues upwards in sequence, either by step (bars /6-9 and /28-31) or by a third (bars 61-4). Alternatively the theme is extended by a varied repetition (bars 69-72 and 90-3). The four-bar phrases eventually give way to shorter two-bar patterns which likewise avail of sequence (bars 12-13 and 76-7) or varied repetition (bars 39-40, 43-4 and 47-8). From this method of construction each theme generates a broad paragraph which is characterised by a forward drive. Towards the end of the paragraph the lyrical content of the music becomes less distinct; this is replaced either by a type of passage work (bars 20-2, 51-6 and 94-9), or at one point by a series of chord-progressions which usher in the next theme (bars 79-85).

The closing bars of the first paragraph introduce a rhythmic procedure which becomes characteristic of the composer. Here, a series of quavers is built from units of five, producing an irregular pattern of accents (Example 2):

EXAMPLE 2

The perfect cadence, traditionally the primary boundary line, functions here as an internal indicator only, serving to announce the subsidiary theme in each of the two subject groups (bars 22-3 and 85-6).

The first noticeable change in the central part of the movement concerns the treatment and distribution of the thematic material. Now the violin and piano share rather than combine. The contrasting elements which form the first subject and which receive little more than an introductory statement in the exposition are now discussed in turn, and along familiar contrapuntal lines. Phrases built from the first five notes are immediately echoed and imitated in canon, first by the piano and later by the violin (bars /106-136). The addition of a second device, augmentation, facilitates the first local climax (bars /138-153).

For the remainder of the development section both instruments participate fully and on equal terms. The constant presence of an ensemble sound after the previous temporary lull restores the momentum of the exposition. A repetitive two-bar unit from the first subject group, melodically static, focusses the attention on the alternative harmonisations. This procedure reveals Fauré's economy of material, with a four-note figure used in both ascending and descending forms (Example 3):

EXAMPLE 3

In a final development of the two-bar unit the composer reverts to sequence (bars 184-9) and varied repetition. Here, the first note is progressively shortened (Example 4).

The earliest reference to material from the second subject group disguises an insignificant link (Example 5).

This is followed by an unequivocal working of the second subject itself, now placed over successive dominant pedal points (bars 210-23).

EXAMPLE 4

EXAMPLE 5

A mainly quiet interlude recalls the only homophonic moment in the exposition. Once again the unrelieved repetition of a rhythmic pattern draws attention to the harmonic and textural interest (bars 226-51). Some further application of sequence (bars 250-60) and varied repetition (bars 261-4) brings the development section to a close. Here, for the second time in the movement, Fauré effects a link from passage work which comprises units of three crotchets reiterated in a rising sequence. These units undermine the prevailing metre in the manner of a hemiola (Example 6; see Example 2):

EXAMPLE 6

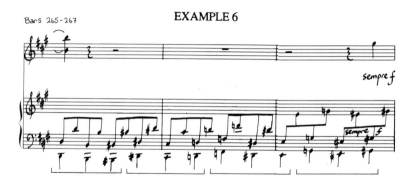

As Robert Orledge has stated, the recapitulation is 'literal but differently scored'.[8] The first subject, now played by the violinist as well as the pianist, begins on the leading note rather than on the tonic. This curious flexibility operates throughout the movement, although the less symmetrical opening is the more frequent and strategically important (see for instance bars 241-2 in Example 12 and bars 380-1 in Example 13).

The necessary tonal adjustment takes place during the reprise of the subsidiary melody (compare bars 34-6 and 300-6), now one bar shorter than the original. Both second subject themes return in their transposed versions, but otherwise unchanged.

The substantial coda sustains the forward drive of the music. Based on two unpromising ideas from earlier moments (compare bar 364 with 95 and bars 365-7 with 198ff.), it rises sequentially over a tonic pedal to achieve a fine climax on the opening three notes of the first subject (see bars 380-1 in Example 14). Even the last allusion to this theme reveals further development, when the first eight bars of the original are now condensed to six (bars / 385-90). The familiar repetition of patterns which suggest hemiola leads to the final statements of the tonic chord (Example 7):

EXAMPLE 7

TONALITY AND HARMONY

In terms of key the principal events of the movement conform to the traditional procedures of sonata form, with tonic (A) and dominant (E) serving as tonal contexts for the exposition of first and second subject groups respectively. Both groups are duly presented in the home key during the recapitulation. Here, the conventional modification with music transposed up a fourth or down a fifth is reflected faithfully, despite the fluid modulations (Example 8):

EXAMPLE 8

		D	c#	B	b	A	A/c#
EXPOSITION	Keys:	D	c#	B	b	A	A/c#
EXPOSITION	Bars:	34-36	37-40	41-42	43-44	45-48	49-56
RECAPITULATION	Keys:	G	f#	E	e	D	D/f#
RECAPITULATION	Bars:	303-305	306-310	311-312	313-314	315-318	319-326

Both first subject themes include early excursions to the supertonic minor key, a favourite trait of Schumann's (bars 6-11 and 28-9).

The second subject hovers uncertainly between the dominant E and distant relative G, with as many as three brief visits to each region alternately before the dominant prevails (bars 57-77).

Fauré's music frequently eludes description in terms of a specific tonality, and the passage which immediately precedes the entry of the second subject represents an early instance (Example 9):

EXAMPLE 9

Is this music in A or C-sharp minor? Arguments are easily found to support both. The raised fourth (D-sharp) and flat seventh (G natural) degrees are readily incorporated into the major key. If G natural is interpreted as F-double sharp, its enharmonic equivalent, the progression in bars 53-7 may be indicated as follows:

c-sharp: augmented sixth – IIIb.

Here, the mediant substitutes for the dominant chord. Similarly the submediant often occurs where one would expect the tonic: Example 3(b) provides an excellent instance; F-sharp is subsequently confirmed as a tonality (bar 170).

Enharmonic progression comes naturally to the composer, and a hypothetical instance has already been suggested above. The chord in bars 74-5 appears in two forms, as a dominant seventh (in the piano part) and as an augmented sixth (in the violin). In the development section the same music is presented in F-sharp and G-flat respectively (bars 170-85).

If the harmonic language of this movement is not remarkable for its originality, it demonstrates amply Fauré's familiarity with contemporary developments. In particular, the freedom in the resolution of sevenths is already integrated in the composer's vocabulary, as is shown in the following progressions (Example 10; see also bars 80-1 in Example 11):

EXAMPLE 10

The juxtaposition of the standard and flat seventh degrees of the scale features in the approach to the codetta (Example 11):

EXAMPLE 11

The augmented triad and subdominant seventh[9] appear in several guises, and combine at the beginning of the second subject (see bars 57-9 in Example 1(c)).

A distinctive progression which involves two root position major chords, the second a tone below the first, points to modal rather than purely diatonic origins.

Modal inflections in the composer's musical language stem from the training received at the École Niedermeyer which included among its subjects the accompaniment of Gregorian chant (see bars 25-6 in Example 1(b) and bars 86-7 in Example 1(d)).

Another example occurs during the quietest passage of the development (see bars 245-6 in Example 12). This is preceded by a progression which not alone reverses the orthodox order of chords but also removes them from their traditional context (bars 241-2 in Example 12):

EXAMPLE 12

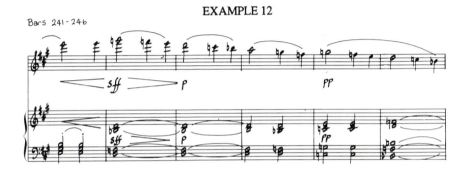

Where formerly this progression had exclusive connotations with the tonality of A major/minor, it now enjoys a new unfettered existence in the modulation from E to F.

Apart from featuring a further instance of the distinctive progression mentioned above, the climax of the movement highlights an appoggiatura, a form of dissonance employed here for the maximum expressiveness and associated with both the first subject and codetta theme (Example 13; see also Example 1(d)):

EXAMPLE 13

RHYTHM AND TEXTURE

As stated above, the momentum which characterises this movement from beginning to end is sustained to some extent by the concept of large paragraphs which are propelled by extended themes. However, the principal agent is a thread of continuous quaver motion, whether in the piano part (for the exposition, recapitulation and coda) or played by the violin (on two occasions during the central development). Phrases without quaver movement are surprisingly few: these generally resort to an uncomplicated homophonic layout (bars 226-51; see also Example 11).

In the piano part arpeggio figuration constitutes the main form of accompaniment. Alternative procedures include a type of written-out tremolando (bars 102-37) and the sequence of parallel split octaves (see Example 6). The latter transfers idiomatically to the stringed instrument (bars 90-3), which also proceeds in repeated-note pairs (see Example 5(b)). Rhythmically the writing is never more complex than two-against-three, confined to a mere two bars in the entire movement (bars 362-3).

The use of irregular patterns to hint at hemiola has already been described, and earlier comments about augmentation may also be freely applied in this context (Example 14):

EXAMPLE 14

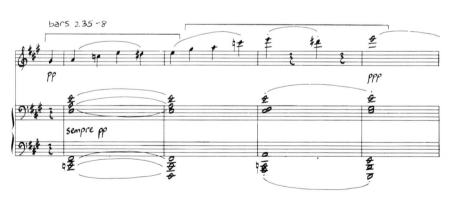

Fauré's predilection for short-long rhythmic patterns, the mainstay of the second movement in the A major Violin Sonata, is given expression in two discreet appearances during the development section of the first (see Example 3(b) and Example 5(b)).

The largest textural span created by both instruments, that of five octaves and a major sixth, coincides with the climactic point of the coda (see bar 381 in Example 13). However, the writing is consistently expansive in layout throughout the movement, the momentary exception being a single bar in which the violin part functions as a bassline (bar 285).

In the exposition the piano and violin parts proceed independently for the enunciation of all four principal themes. The lines draw closer together when, in the course of the development section, two isolated phrases show them in parallel sixths (bars 118-20 and 134-6). Eventually the violin and piano right-hand parts merge completely for an assertive interpretation of the second subject in octaves (bars 218-25). This marks the zenith of its development, in contrast with the first subject whose climax is reserved for the coda.

An enviable facility in counterpoint enables the composer to explore the imitative properties of three of the four main themes. Beginning in the exposition with the second subject (bars 31-48), Fauré turns to the first subject to launch the central development (bars 106-18). Material from the codetta is treated in a similar type of interplay between the instruments at the start of the coda (bars 364-71).

THE SAINT-SAËNS CONNECTION

As stated above, Fauré had known Saint-Saëns closely for fourteen years by 1875, initially as teacher and mentor, then as someone who visited him in Rennes in 1866 and who dedicated to him the *Trois rapsodies sur des cantiques bretons* for organ op. 7, written in the same year. Saint-Saëns proved an invaluable contact when Fauré began to participate in the frequent soirées and musical events at the homes of influential patrons. From 1871 the composers' paths crossed regularly, whether at Société Nationale de Musique meetings or at the Madeleine, where Fauré became Saint-Saëns' deputy in 1874.

Saint-Saëns had shown a genuine interest in his students' compositions at the École Niedermeyer, and it is probable that this involvement had continued during Fauré's ascent to the summit of his professional career. Certainly Saint-Saëns' glowing critique of the First Violin Sonata in the *Journal de Musique* on 7 April 1877 indicated a complete sympathy to, and support for, the direction which Fauré's creative development was taking. The older composer's corpus of chamber music up to 1875 included two representative works, the Piano Quintet in A minor op. 14 of 1855, published in 1865, and the Piano Quartet in B-flat op. 41, written and published in 1875.[10] It is not known how familiar Fauré was with these works, nor how they might have helped to determine his approach to the very first chamber work of some twenty-three in all, including the ten major compositions in this category.

The extent of Saint-Saëns' influence on Fauré may be gauged by a comparison of the opening movements of his Piano Quintet[11] and Piano Quartet with the first movement of the A major Violin Sonata. Results show that elements held in common by all three movements are considerably outweighed by fundamental differences in proportion, in the nature of the thematic material, in the treatment of tonality, and in the concept of rhythmic movement.

Aspects shared by the three movements include a first thematic group which is longer than the second, the omission in the central development of any reference to the codetta material from the exposition, and a faithful reprise of the second subject in the recapitulation in terms of its length.

The dimensions of sonata form in Fauré's movement reveal a shorter exposition than those found in the Saint-Saëns works. By contrast his themes are more extended, usually beginning with a four-bar phrase. They are more homogenous in effect, and less repetitive in content. While Saint-Saëns divides the first subject between the piano and strings, Fauré introduces his material on either instrument or on both simultaneously. The second subject is tonally less stable than its counterparts. The closing idea or codetta possesses a greater significance for the younger composer.

Thematic development as such is allocated by Fauré to the central part of the movement, so that this section is a good deal more substantial than the equivalent passages in both Saint-Saëns works. Nevertheless, Fauré's concentration on the second subject here is relatively slight in comparison with that of Saint-Saëns. One of the major differences concerns the range of keys employed at this point in the movement. Modulation is more frequent and varied in the Violin Sonata than in either movement by the older composer.

The coda is conceived by Fauré as a tautly organised conclusion to the movement, and his example is less diffuse than those of Saint-Saëns. Rippling arpeggio patterns in the piano accompaniment, a form of rhythm and texture which Fauré may have inherited from his former teacher, permeate the Violin Sonata movement in a manner which would have seemed excessive to the latter.

The characteristic procedures outlined here in relation to Fauré are not confined to op. 13; they also apply to the first movements of his next two largescale chamber works, the First Piano Quartet in C minor op. 15 of 1879 and Second Piano Quartet in G minor op. 45 of 1885-6.

It is generally agreed that Saint-Saëns' musical language is more conservative and less individual than that of Fauré. For this reason it may come as no small surprise to observe some of the latter's more telling progressions and other features foreshadowed in the chamber music of the former, albeit in far less striking contexts. These include the presence of the augmented triad (e.g. op. 14 I, bar 76), raised fourth above the root (e.g. op. 41 I, bars 36 and 53), standard and flat seventh degrees of the scale in close proximity (e.g. op. 14 I, bars 36-7), submediant chord in a prominent position (e.g. op. 41 I, bar 79), and progression III(major)b-V7 (e.g. op. 14 I, bar 30). The anticipation of Fauré extends even to actual melodic ideas (compare Saint-Saëns op. 14 I, bars 102-3, violin and cello parts, with Fauré op. 13 I, bars 198-200), while parallel fifths infiltrate the texture in all three movements (e.g. Saint-Saëns op. 14 I, bar 230; op. 41 I, bar 38; Fauré op. 13 I, bars 37-8).

CONCLUSION

As a structure sonata form assumed a special significance for Fauré, as he was to avail of this design in two out of every three movements in the ten largescale chamber compositions.[12] The confidence and sureness which emerged from the opening bars of the First Violin Sonata were to establish a facility and a mastery in the creation of the later chamber works which only rarely encountered difficulties of a fundamental nature.

NOTES

1. Robert Orledge, *Gabriel Fauré* (London, 1979), 71.
2. Orledge (as n. 1), 72.
3. This date is given by Jean-Michel Nectoux, 'Fauré, Gabriel (Urbain)', *The New Grove Dictionary of Music and Musicians*, (London, 1980), vi, 418; see also Martin Cooper, *French Music* (London, 1974), 9. February is mentioned by Laurence Davies, *César Franck and His Circle* (London, 1970), 136. The date 17 November 1871, offered in Robert Orledge (as n. 1), 9 is a surprising alternative.
4. For details relating to the date and venue for the first performances of individual compositions see Robert Orledge (as n. 1), 275-81.
5. Fauré dedicated *Puisqu'ici-bas toute âme* op. 10 no. 1 and *Tarantelle* op. 10 no. 2 to both sisters, and *Au bord de l'eau* op. 8 no. 1 to Claudie; Robert Orledge (as n. 1), 280-1.
6. Norman Suckling, *Fauré* (London, 1946), 15 mentions a performance of the sonata at the Trocadéro in 1878, with the violinist Jean Pierre Maurin (1822-94) and composer at the piano.
7. According to David Tubergen the recapitulation begins at bar 289; see his study *A Stylistic Analysis of Selected Violin and Piano Sonatas of Fauré, Saint-Saëns and Franck* (diss., New York University, 1985), 49.
8. Robert Orledge (as n. 1), 62.
9. These chords are listed as typical tools of the composer's harmonic apparatus in analytical studies such as those of Richard Crouch, *The Nocturnes and Barcarolles for Solo Piano of Gabriel Fauré* (diss., Catholic University of America, 1980), 23 and Charles Navien, *The Harmonic Language of 'L'Horizon chimérique' by Gabriel Fauré* (diss., University of Connecticut, 1982), 8.
10. The Piano Trio in F op. 18, composed in 1863 and published in 1867, is considered unrepresentative, principally because of the monothematic nature of its first movement and opening in the form of a fugal exposition.
11. I am indebted to Hugh Taylor, former Music Librarian of Trinity College, Dublin, who lent me a personal copy of the Saint-Saëns Piano Quintet in A minor op. 14.
12. Margaret Barshell, *Gabriel Fauré: a Biographical Study and a Historical Style Analysis of His Nine Major Chamber Works for Piano and Strings* (diss., Ball State University, 1982), 122. The same feature applies to the tenth chamber work, the String Quartet in E minor op. 121.

Atonality, Modality, Symmetry and Tonal Hierarchy in Bartók's Improvisation op. 20, no. 8

MICHAEL RUSS

Bartók composed his eight *Improvisations on Hungarian Peasant Songs* op. 20 in 1920.[1] In each a diatonic melody is given an intense chromatic setting. The final Improvisation, the longest and most complex, takes the form of a thematic presentation (bars 1-12) and three variations (bars 28-39, 53-61, 69-82) separated by interludes.

Example 1a gives the opening theme and its accompaniment; beneath it are various analytical interpretations of the passage derived from recent work by Antokoletz (Example 1(b)), Lendvai (Example 1(c)) and Wilson (Example 1(d)).[2] In this essay I will explore the divergent approaches these analysts take to this piece and investigate why each appears to ignore the work of the others.[3] The main body of this exploration is primarily analytical, the conclusion theoretical.

While it cannot be disputed that the tune is in the Dorian mode on B, I refrain from calling this note a 'tonic' because there is disagreement between our three analysts as to whether this piece is tonal or not. As can be seen, Wilson (Example 1(d)) takes an atonal view, classifying the pentachordal harmonies with Forte's pitch-class set nomenclatures, revealing sets like 4-Z29 and 5-32 both of which occur frequently in the music of Schoenberg and Webern.[4] Further evidence of 'atonality' is provided by the complementation between melody and harmony. In contrast, Lendvai views these same chords as 'alpha' harmonies (Example 1(c)) retaining the three functions of traditional tonality (I IV and V) while Antokoletz takes the view that this piece is moving towards a new system of tonality (as formulated by George Perle),[5] the principal symptoms of which here are Bartók's use of symmetry and the interpenetration of modal and octatonic scales.

I will begin a more detailed examination of Example 1 with the Antokoletz strand.[6] He explains the chordal succession as a rotation through the three forms of the octatonic scale returning to the original one at the end.[7] A sense of tonality claims Antokoletz, arises out of the special relationship between what he calls the 'basic' collection (that at either end of the melody) and the B-Dorian scale. This scale is a segment of the cycle of fifths bounded by the tritone D/G-sharp with the tonic symmetrically located at the centre, a quality unique to this mode (Figure 1(a)). The left-hand tetrachord which occupies the first five bars shares this 'defining' tritone and is referable to the basic octatonic collection C, D, E-flat, F, G-flat, A-flat, A, B. Another of its tones, A, then occurs in bar 6 allowing the tetrachord D, E-flat, A-flat, A to be formed among the left-hand pitches. This, one form of a special tetrachord which Antokoletz calls 'Z' (or, in pitch-class set nomenclature, 4-9), has the special quality that it is symmetrical about four axes[8] and therefore has only six possible forms.[9] As these may be arranged in three pairs synonymous with the three forms of the octatonic scale, it follows that only one form of the tetrachord is necessary to define an underlying octatonic collection. In the present context, 4-9: [D, E-flat, A-flat, A] not only defines the basic collection, but also has a close relationship with the B Dorian scale in that its extra tritone is formed by adding a further fifth at one end of the B Dorian segment (Figure 1(b)).

B Dorian cycle of fifths:

axis:

(a) D A E B F# C# G#

(b) D A E B F# C# G# D#

defines Antokoletz's basic collection:

C, D, E, F, F#, A, A, B

(c) G D A E B F# C# G#

defines collection 2:

C#, D, E, F, F, G#, A#, B

FIGURE 1:

Once the melody has been stated, F double-sharp (=G) becomes prominent (bars 13-17, left hand and bar 17 right hand), moving the segment of the cycle of fifths to the left and defining a new octatonic collection (figure 1c) which then becomes influential in the first interlude. This kind of shift is a neat theoretical extension of the idea that modulation to a nearly related key area is achieved by a one-step clockwise or anti-clockwise shift round the cycle of fifths, but, like the rest of Antokoletz's approach to this passage, it raises the fundamental issue of whether scales and segments of the cycle of fifths are axiomatic to tonality or are a reflection of other, more fundamental, kinds of harmonic process. For example, when analysing tonal music we generally assert that new keys are established through a conclusive harmonic progression rather than through a change of scale. We should also note that Antokoletz's approach pays little attention to chordal ordering and layout.

Lendvai recognises the importance of rotating octatonic collections here, but calls them by a different name and regards them less as scales than eight note chords he names 'alpha' which, rather than appearing complete, are almost always represented by their tetrachordal and pentachordal subsets. Unlike Antokoletz, Lendvai gives considerable attention to chordal layout, indeed these chords have a specific ordering in that they place two diminished sevenths one above the other (reflecting another quality of the octatonic scale: it contains two diminished sevenths). Example 1(c)[10] shows the close correspondence between the pentachords in bars 1-16 and the source forms of alpha.

Lendvai asserts that alphas take on functional characteristics with respect to any tonal centre, hence my I IV V I figuring in Example 1c. These functional designations are an outgrowth of Lendvai's well-known axis theory, which itself derives from Riemann's ideas on chordal function and substitution (i.e. VI for I, II for IV, VII for V etc.). Lendvai assigns each of the twelve chromatic tones to one of the three functional groups (axes) within which tones may substitute for their partners (Figure 2). The axis concept, according to Lendvai, enabled Bartók to meet his desired intention to use all twelve tones while remaining tonal.

(a)

	C			G			F	
E-flat	I	A	B-flat	V	E	A-flat	IV	D
	F#			C#			B	

(b)

A F# E-flat C	} roots	E C# B-flat G	} roots	D B A-flat F	} roots
B-flat G E C#	} fifths	F D B A-flat	} fifths	E-flat C A F#	} fifths
Tonic 'alpha'		Dominant 'alpha'		Subdominant 'alpha'	

Functional designations are given for a piece in C or one of its three substitute tones
(E-flat, F#, A).

FIGURE 2

Lendvai's axes are synonymous with the diminished sevenths making up the alpha chords; each alpha consists of two layers: its functional axis (i.e. I for a tonic alpha) and, beneath it the axis containing the fifth of each note in that above it. Lendvai derives this two-layered approach from the way the root of a conventional triad is defined by its fifth, but in Lendvai's alpha chords, fifths are placed below roots because in ancient folk music 'the perfect fifth represents the most vigorous dissonance' and prefers the 'pentatonic six-four system, the plagal way of thinking'.[11] The present folksong has a pentatonic framework (B, F-sharp, E, D, B) and a reiterated fourth at the end. Whether the various 'alpha' derivatives actually function is open to question; Lendvai himself confesses at one point that the 'tonality of bars 1-12 is determined by the B root of the folksong' rather than by the 'harmonies accompanying it'.[12] Their functional capacity is curtailed by a number of factors. Firstly, any alpha chord may be represented by a very large number of subsets all of which are supposed to retain its function. Secondly, whereas the idea that the fifth above defines a tonic not only has the precedent of three hundred years of common-practice tonality but also of the harmonic series, the notion that the fourth below has the same capacity has much less justification. Thirdly, the major, minor and diminished attributes that help make functional distinctions between diatonic triads in music in major and minor keys are entirely absent here; indeed many of the alpha subsets contain major-minor tetrachords (e.g. bar 8 which contains G major- minor).

Lendvai's axis theory makes a cunning attempt to extend conventional, hierarchical, fifth-based tonality by integrating symmetrical modes of organisation which must at the same time exert a destructive force against it. How far tonality can survive such an onslaught must surely be open to question. Lendvai frequently reminds us that 'tonality goes hand in hand with asymmetry, atonality with symmetry'[13] yet, paradoxically, he still asserts that 'alpha has strong tonal even functional character'.[14] Lendvai's interest in alpha chords also stems from his belief that the chords which accompany folk songs should be rich in Fibonacci intervals, i.e. those of 2, 3, 5 and 8 semitones, intervals which also characterise the pentatonic scale; the importance of these intervals should be self-evident in Example 1.

As I indicated above Wilson considers this passage to be atonal, for him B is only a priority of localised importance in a context primarily controlled by atonal means. Wilson is forced to this conclusion by his strict Schenkerian view of tonality; since this piece cannot be explained in terms of a closed system of prolongations emanating from an *Ursatz*, the deepest level projection of the tonic triad, the piece cannot be tonal. Wilson does not attempt to find functional or octatonic qualities in the harmony, he does not even include 8-28 (the set name for the octatonic scale) among his sets even though it is the superset of a great many of his atonal harmonies. Wilson's use of pitch-class set analysis implies that he regards the specific qualities of individual chords as less important than the way they relate through the classic atonal measures of total interval content, invariance, inclusion and complementation. He also attempts

EXAMPLE 1

to uncover whether any residue of prolongation remains in this atonal context, whether there are any aspects of its construction which are prolongational 'in some sense of that term'.[15] Recognising that atonal (unlike tonal) harmony provides little or no basis for distinguishing between structural and ornamental tones, he nonetheless attempts to make this distinction within melodic statements purely on grounds of contextual emphasis. He then looks to the set structure to see if it supports his findings. In the present piece he notes that within the pentatonic framework remarked upon earlier, the descent F-sharp, E, D, B receives the support of a whole-tone bass line C, B-flat, G-sharp, F-sharp and a series of pentachords all linked by a common subset, 4-17 (the major-minor tetrachord) in a variety of transpositions (Example 1d). Although these three elements create a structure which is, for Wilson, loosely prolongational, the extent to which this deeper structure is goal-directed and always implied

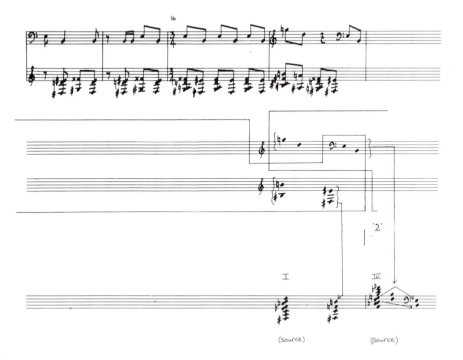

when temporarily replaced by surface diminutions (both important attributes of a prolongational structure) is surely open to question. It is arguable that in such a context we hear associations between elements rather than true prolongations.[16]

Wilson also observes that each of the chordal sets in this passage contains a form of 3-5 (some are shown in Example 1(d). This trichord contains both the 'primary tonal interval, the fourth or fifth, and the primary atonal interval, the stable tritone',[17] it also contains the semitone, probably the most potent interval of melodic voice leading in both tonality and atonality. In making this statement Wilson recognises that 3-5 encapsulates the tension that exists not only between tonal and atonal elements in this piece, and in much of Bartók's music of this period, but also between the intervals that divide the octave symmetrically and the fourth and fifth which do not. Unfortunately he chooses to focus on atonal prolongation rather than further exploring this tension and looking for larger scale projections of 3-5.

Although he recognises that 3-5 may be prominent at deeper levels of structure he does not demonstrate the importance of this to the present passage. For example, the set is outlined by the melodic 'tonic' (B) and the first and last notes of the bass descent (C and F-sharp). (C, F-sharp and B = 3-5:[0, 6, 11]). 3-5 is the set class of all four trichordal subsets of 4-9 (Antokoletz's 'Z'). Interestingly, if E-sharp (the alternative axis tone of the melody and a tone prominent in the left hand in bars 12-17 is added to 3-5:[0, 6, 11] then 4-9:[0, 5, 6, 11] results, this tetrachord partners 4-9:[2, 3, 8, 9] in the opening octatonic collection.

A way of viewing these larger-scale projections of 3-5 and 4-9 not explored by any of of our three analysts, is to see them as part of an expansion of the legitimate goals of voice-leading motions, particularly in the bass, to include the tritone as well as the fourth and fifth. While the motions to these goals might not be strongly directed harmonically and only become comprehensible once the whole passage is perceived, the loss in harmonically-directed dynamism that accompanies them is compensated for by the tension generated between them.

Having aired some of the issues that arise from the setting of the theme, we can now look briefly at the remainder of the piece.

In the first variation Bartók strengthens the melody's pentatonic framework by increasing the durations of its elements but this is matched by the introduction of chromatic interjections in its second half. The latter enable Bartók to create a whole-tone line rising from D to G-sharp within the melody itself rather than in the bass (Example 2).[18] Wilson, while observing the importance of this line, gives scant regard to the accompanying chords apart from observing that 4-13 is significant at the beginning of this passage. Since the chordal structure does not appear to mimic either the whole-tone or

EXAMPLE 2

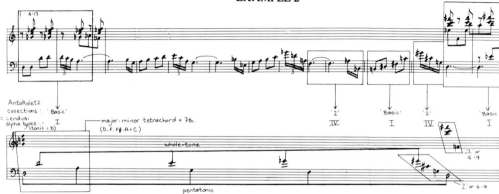

pentatonic element in the melody, Wilson resorts to an explanation of the harmony in terms of free association. Antokoletz draws attention to the fact that this variation begins with a return to the basic octatonic collection found at the beginning of the piece; as the variation progresses we lose touch with this collection only to have it restored at the beginning of the next interlude (see bars 38-40).[19] While Lendvai doesn't discuss this passage in either of his English texts, it is obvious that what Antokoletz somewhat limply calls a return to the basic collection, Lendvai might well regard as a return to the tonic; in other words this melody is framed by tonic alpha chords in the 'key' of D and this centre is supported by at least one feature of a tonal system; the idea that we depart from, and return to, chords of common origin. It should also be realised that the tonic alpha collection with regard to D is synonymous with that for B at the beginning of the piece since both tones originate in the same subdominant axis (given that the tonic axis for the whole piece is C, E-flat, F-sharp, A).

4-9's ability to define octatonic/alpha collections has already been observed. Two of these tetrachords occur in bar 38, one (C-sharp, D, G, G-sharp) in linear form in the bass, the other (B, C, F, F-sharp) embedded in the chord which follows; these two tetrachords define a subdominant-tonic octatonic/alpha succession with regard to the local tonic D, supporting the characteristic fourth-to-tonic ending of the melody.

In this variation voice-leading motions traversing both fourths and fifths and stable tritones are again in evidence. The melody moves from D to A at the beginning of the variation (via the tetrachord D, C, B, A, common to both the Dorian scale and to the basic octatonic collection) and the diatonic elements in the melody then concern themselves with filling in the fifth from A down to D; at the same time the upward moving whole-tone line ascends to G-sharp. The three crucial pitches D, G-sharp, A create 3-5: [2, 8, 9].

In the next, canonic, variation two slightly modified statements of the theme are in canon at the tritone; one is E Dorian the other B-flat Dorian becoming Aeolian. This variation presents the clearest example in the piece of fifth-based diatony combining with structural use of the stable tritone to produce octatonic collections and their characteristic subsets, 4-9 and 3-5; indeed the variation opens with a form of 4-9 and a complete octatonic collection (see Example 3). More 4-9s appear as the variation progresses, and two combine to form the striking eight note chord in bars 65-68 (the pairing is non-octatonic producing 8-9, the complement of 4-9 rather than 8-28).

Antokoletz views this variation as a 'focal point in the development of diatonic and octatonic interactions'.[20] He places particular importance on the shift to B-flat Aeolian that comes with the G-flat in bar 58 since this, by extending the Dorian cycle of fifths segment and thus adding another tritone, creates a new form of 4-9 which is then able to indicate a change in underlying

EXAMPLE 3

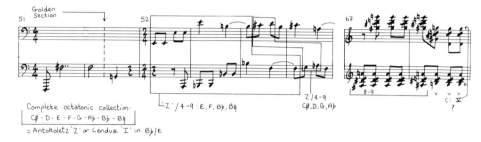

octatonic collection (a similar extension was described with regard to bars 14–17). Antokoletz clearly overstates the significance of the octatonic collections here, they are a surface symptom of the deeper process (the combination of diatonic collections at the stable tritone) rather than part of the process itself.

The prominence of 4-9 here prepares us for its important role in the final variation where a slightly reworked form of the melody, now in the bass and unquestionably C-centred, is entirely accompanied by right-hand 4-9 (Z) chords (example 4). The basis on which Bartók chooses from the six available versions of Z at any point is unclear. Lendvai, while citing this passage as an example of the '1-5 model' deriving from the 'scale equivalent of chord alpha' (i.e. the octatonic scale)[21] gives no reasons for the choice of particular chords, nor does Wilson, although he does hear some loose imitations of the melody in the upper line of the chords. If we consider the set-structure of this final variation further we will find that 4-9 is a subset of only two pentachords, 5-7 and 5-19, so the high degree of tetrachordal consistency is almost matched by the complete harmonies here in terms of their intervallic, rather than pitch, similarity. One distinction between the chords is that 5-7 is a classic atonal set whereas 5-19 is

EXAMPLE 4

an octatonic subset. Antokoletz, predictably, draws only on the octatonic and modal qualities, ignoring any atonal relationships. After pairing statements of 4-9 to generate complete octatonic collections, Antokoletz is left with a recalcitrant tetrachord (bar 69, last beat, C, F, F-sharp, B) whose partner fails to appear anywhere in the variation. Antokoletz explains this as the result of what he calls the 'bimodal' nature of the melody; the A-flat in bar 4 (Example 4) marks a shift from the Dorian to the Aeolian mode (a similar shift was noticed in the canonic variation). Combining the two modes produces an eight-note segment of the cycle of fifths bounded by the two tritones necessary to construct the missing form of 4-9. Antokoletz's approach is very much one of studying the relationships between various types of symmetrical collections rather than looking at the attributes of specific chords and the details of their ordering. He does not, for example, deal with why some pentachords are octatonic and others not; his quest for a unitary symmetrical 'tonality' results in his overlooking such difficulties.

Having briefly considered each setting of the tune we can now take an overview of the piece. Example 5 brings together all the modal tonics and the highly significant pedals for which the deepest register of the bass part is almost exclusively reserved. Taking C as the overall tonic and grouping the tones according to Lendvai's axes a clear I, IV, V, I pattern emerges. The crucial turning point in the piece comes in bars 51 and 52 where we shift from the subdominant to dominant axes. At the precise point of change the music becomes monophonic (see Example 3) as if Bartók is drawing attention to this crucial change at the precise Golden Section of the piece. Furthermore, the symmetrical divider of the octave, F-sharp, plays a pivotal role in the shift from the lower fifth of C (F) to the upper fifth (G) an event recalled in the final bars of the piece where Bartók places C symmetrically between F and G and then follows this with a strong G-flat (Example 5). Simply because the points of

EXAMPLE 5

tonal focus create a I IV V I pattern when axis substitution is allowed does not guarantee that this piece is 'in C' or that C is the inevitable and goal-directed (rather than simply logical) outcome of tonal practices operating from the beginning of the piece. Nevertheless, the principal tonal centres are all from the C major scale except for B-flat and F-sharp (the nearest chromatic tones to the C cycle of fifths) and the three tonal centres in the first part of the piece do spell out the C- defining diminished triad B-D-F.

In contrast to common-practice tonal pieces, tonal centres in this Improvisation result more from contextual emphasis than from harmonic process and any harmonic support they receive is highly ambiguous. Even so, each tonal centre is associated with its appropriate I IV or V octatonic/alpha collection with respect to the overall C tonality (these are defined in Figure 2b), all that is except for C in the final variation where the weight of contextual emphasis on this tone is so great that extra harmonic support almost becomes superfluous. The important question here is the extent to which the octatonic collections supporting subdominant and dominant axis tones are actually heard to ascribe functions to these centres and create a harmonic preparation for the final variation. The question is one which does not have a clear answer and to some extent the answer will vary with each listener's reaction to the piece. All the analyst can do is to show, as I have done that the system of tonal axes and the rotation of octatonic/alpha collections does retain some characteristics of the tonal system.

Of course, functional thinking is only one approach to tonality, even more widespread now is the Schenkerian theory, at the heart of which is structure and prolongation. While to assert that the principal harmonies in this piece are in any way capable of prolonging the tonic is probably fanciful and it is clear that there is no descending diatonic *Urlinie*, the progression of the deepest bass register does bear a passing resemblance to the obligatory bass register of an *Ursatz*.

Despite the rather negative tone of this discussion, there is evidence that Bartók felt the final variation on C to be the inevitable outcome of what precedes it. This is clearly evident in bars 65-67 where Bartók builds towards the C in bar 69 with a *crescendo molto* and a high inverted pedal G. The crucial point comes in bar 68 where Bartók destroys the symmetry of the octachordal harmony (8-9) by raising its lowest note, A-sharp, to B, the leading tone of C: a clear case of remnants of tonal hierarchy taking precedence over symmetrical and set-structural considerations.

Both Antokoletz and Wilson, from different standpoints, reach the conclusion that processes which control short spans in Bartók's music often do not operate at deeper structural levels. They would consequently interpret the sequence of tonal centres in this piece as being a structure independent of the short-term prolongations or localised interactions of diatonic and octatonic scales. The strength of Lendvai's approach is that it identifies a system of relationships (or at least provides a model of possible relationships) capable of operating both on the surface and at deeper levels of structure which integrates the principal intervals of tonality and atonality/symmetry into a tonal system embracing all twelve tones. If we dislike the functional aspects of Lendvai's work it remains possible to take an overview of the piece based simply on recognising that fifths and tritones are both stable in this piece and that voice-leading motions spanning both intervals are possible over large and small spans. The multiple occurrences of 3-5 and 4-9 at the surface and over larger spans and the fact that the piece ends by spelling-out 3-5 F, C, G-flat at the end of a melody accompanied by multiple forms of 4-9 is surely in itself a convincing argument for the more widespread significance of these sets. However, I am not arguing for the recognition of 4-9 and 3-5 as prolonged dissonant sonorities in this piece, I am simply identifying them as large-scale motives which can take the form of harmonies and be unfolded over large spans as the result of allowing both the fifth and tritone to be the legitimate goals of linear motions.

CONCLUSION

Bartók's *Improvisation* raises important issues which face us when examining highly chromatic music which, while having little or nothing in the way of triadic harmony, remains tonal in some sense of the term. It is to the nature of this tonality that I wish to turn first in this conclusion.

Not so long ago it was common to consign a large number of works by Debussy, Stravinsky and Bartók to a kind of rag-bag labelled 'extended tonality' even though the harmonic language in their pieces might go far beyond (and be fundamentally different in nature to) the techniques described by Schoenberg when he coined the term in his *Structural Functions of Harmony*.[22] Now analysts are becoming much stricter in their definitions of 'tonality' and disallowing extended tonality. Wilson is a good example; because this piece does not fit his strict Schenkerian definition of tonality he is forced to consider it atonal and therefore requires what for a Yale-trained scholar is the appropriate alternative analytical method: Forte's theory of pitch-class sets. A similar strategy is used by another scholar of the same pedigree, James Baker, in his recent book on Scriabin (another problematic 'transitional' composer): 'If one is to discover the extent to which a structure is determined by tonal procedures, one must first begin as a strict constructionist examining every possibility for interpreting the structure in conventional [i.e. strictly Schenkerian] terms'[23] even if (as in several of Baker's analyses), this means implying rather than actually finding an *Ursatz*. If such an examination produces a negative result then we must construe that the piece is not tonal since Baker, like his teacher Forte, holds that 'tonality and atonality are distinct structural attributes of music and they can be best revealed by Schenkerian and set-complex analysis respectively'.[24] Both Wilson and Baker, because they are 'strict constructionists' reject the freer definition of tonality as simply structure and prolongation, a definition which, having grown out of the work of Salzer, gave rise to the idea that dissonant prolongations could give rise to a new tonal system in the work of Travis and Morgan.[25]

Even though Wilson reaches the conclusion that the piece is atonal this does not prevent him from looking for atonal equivalents to prolongation; those he finds are in general much weaker and clearly less goal-directed than their tonal counterparts. Two important features of tonal prolongation are, firstly, that at all points deeper-level controlling structural tones and harmonies are always implied if not actually present and, secondly, that prolongations are always part of a closed hierarchical system in which each level of structure is controlled by the same set of rules. Wilson's atonal prolongations seem to lack both these characteristics, indeed he freely admits in the context of his analysis of the second Improvisation that while he can identify some prolongations and a 'transpositional plan' for statements of the melody these 'two structures exist independently of each other, though they converge at their end-points' and they 'interlock but do not control one another'. It may well be that prolongation is not the best term for these kinds of structure, 'association' might be better.[26]

The Schenkerian definition of tonality is not the only one, another rests on scales and functions. Toorn in his recent book on Stravinsky's *Rite of Spring* concludes that the piece is 'unquestionably non-tonal' since it does not possess 'a hierarchical system of pitch relations based referentially on the major-scale ordering of the diatonic set and encompassing an intricate, yet fairly distinct, set of harmonic and contrapuntal procedures commonly referred to as tonal functionality'.[27] So when Toorn discusses the interpenetration of diatonic and octatonic sets in Stravinsky's piece he is describing what is for him a non-tonal system of pitch relations. Yet, as we have seen, for Antokoletz a diatonic/octatonic interpenetration is at the heart of a new principle of tonality in Bartók, albeit one with a greater emphasis on axial symmetry than is the case in Stravinsky.

Antokoletz, unlike Wilson begins his work from a historical rather than a theoretical perspective. Instead of beginning with a statement on the nature of tonality he takes a historical perspective identifying passages from nineteenth-century works where symmetrical and octatonic formations occur in contexts which are otherwise unquestionably tonal (principally in music from nineteenth-century Russia). While he admits that the 'symmetrical formations contributed to the dissolution of traditional tonal functions' he also claims that 'they contributed to the establishment of a new means of progression'. These new means of progression become much more sophisticated in the music of

Bartók and 'the specific means by which Bartók employed symmetries on all levels of his music led to a new sense of pitch-class priority'.[28]'Pitch-class priority' and 'means of progression' seem to add up to Antokoletz's rather minimal definition of a tonal system. One is left with the feeling that he is describing various manifestations of a system without defining its essential nature.

Antokoletz's may well consider that Perle's *Twelve-Tone Tonality* contains the theoretical justification for his work and that he does not need to go over this ground again. While exploring Perle is beyond the scope of this essay, it is appropriate to make a few broad points. For Perle common-practice tonality is a set of normative relationships to which 'every simultaneity and every progression is referable'.[29] Conversely, in atonal music, where this system is removed, each piece becomes reflexive and has to create its own unique set of internal relationships. Realising the severe limitations this places upon atonal music Perle looks for a new kind of tonality in which all twelve notes can be used freely while retaining a common set of relationships from work to work. After examining a large number of early twentieth-century compositions in which symmetry plays some role (although the extent to which its role is decisive must be open to question) Perle reaches the conclusion that systematically exploiting symmetry in a system of inversionally related interval cycles provides the only other possible basis for a new referential system. The complete system is only exploited in works by Perle and his circle, but elements of it occur in pieces by early twentieth-century composers not least in the music of Bartók examined by Antokoletz; herein lies the weakness of the theory: early twentieth-century European masterpieces are all interpreted as working towards a system of pitch organisation that manifests itself only in a few obscure American compositions.

Perle's new system is antithetical to the common-practice tonal system in that it regards inversional equivalence as axiomatic; traditional tonal relationships are clearly non-invertible (a major triad when inverted becomes a minor triad: the two things have quite different meanings within the tonal system). Antokoletz finds elements of both old and new systems in Bartók's music: in order to reconcile them he has to place them on different structural levels. For me, Bartók's music thrives on the tension between symmetry and traditional tonal hierarchy at all levels of structure, this symmetry does not arise out of any new tonal system but out of the extension and redefinition of relationships within the old. Nevertheless, one must guard here against the danger that 'tonality' rather than being a particular system, is simply a name for the composer's choice from a multitude of pre-compositional possibilities.

One reason why Lendvai receives scant attention from American writers is that he does not belong to any theoretical ghetto. His work is often intuitive and often seems to take place in a theoretical vacuum. For Lendvai theory and

analysis seem to be uncomfortably sandwiched between hypothetical ex-
planations of Bartók's manner of composition and discussions of the emotional
effects of his music. Lendvai, much more than Antokoletz, haphazardly resorts
to nineteenth-century precedents to explain harmonic processes in Bartók rather
than to theory. The key word in Lendvai's definition of tonality is 'function',
but he sets aside the degree to which the very functions he seeks to identify are
undermined by their symmetrical extension through the axis system and the
vast number of alpha substitutes. In his most recent text he simply and baldly
states that: 'The functional system of Bartók and Kodály merges elements of
three separate (seemingly opposite) approaches to tonal organisation:

1) the functional thinking of Western classical music; 2) the distance principles [=symmetry] and atonal trends of twelve-tone music, and 3) the pentatonic thinking of Eastern folk music.' He goes on to say that 'Bartók's tonal
system grew out of classical harmony, it represents an organic development –
and in a certain sense the completion – of European functional thinking.'[30]

While such claims need more careful theoretical justification than they
receive in Lendvai's books, his freedom from Schenkerian and other dogmas
is refreshing. His intuitive enquiries often seem to bring him closer to the spirit
of Bartók than other more methodologically-conscious writers.

In my own view the way forward in Bartók analysis is not to be found solely
through prolongation and pitch-class sets, neither is it to be found through
'twelve-tone tonality' and the interaction of diatonic and octatonic sets; it seems
unlikely too, that the three functions can be meaningfully preserved in such
complex chromatic music. All of these approaches have a place but we must
look to broader concepts as well, in particular we must give more attention to
the way elements are associated with each other and the nature of the motions
(not prolongations) that occur between them. We must also look to the extension
and widening of the concept of tonality not its outright replacement with either
symmetrical systems or atonality.

In the last resort all of these enquiries emanate from the belief that despite
all the surface disruptions and all the complexities, we hear Bartók's music as
highly connected and highly organic, we believe Bartók to be a musician's
musician, a master craftsman. But, conceptualising what we hear in this
complex music is a difficult matter and what we say about it possibly says as
much about our own prejudices and education as about Bartók.

NOTES

1.   The reader is advised to have a score to hand while reading this essay.
2.   E. Antokokletz, *The Music of Béla Bartók*, (Los Angeles and London, 1984). E. Lendvai,
     Béla Bartók: An Analysis of his Music, (London, 1971). E. Lendvai, *The Workshop of
     Bartók and Kodaly*, (Budapest, 1983). P. Wilson, *Atonality and Structure in Works of Béla*

Bartók's Middle Period, Ph.D. dissertation, Yale University, 1982). P. Wilson, 'Concepts of Prolongation and Bartók's Op. 20', *Music Theory Spectrum*, 6 (1984), 79-89.

3. Of the three analysts only Wilson, in his doctoral thesis, makes anything approaching a comprehensive study of pitch relations in this piece. Antokoletz and Wilson, while not analysing the complete improvisation, make substantial references to it in support of their larger arguments.

4. See A. Forte, *The Structure of Atonal Music* (Yale, 1973). Using the idea of the pitch-class set, Forte developed a method of classifying all the possible horizontal and vertical pitch combinations. All tones are regarded as one of twelve pitch classes, so C-natural, B-sharp, D-double flat, in whatever register, are all forms of pitch-class 0. C-sharp/D-flat=pitch-class 1, D-natural/C-double sharp/E-double flat=2 and so on. Pitch classes combine to form pitch-class sets of which there are 208 possibilities (excluding sets of only one pitch-class or the unwieldy 11 pitch-class set). Sets are unordered groupings without internal hierarchies and are subject to both transposition and inversion, they are consequently deployed in different ways in compositions. They are classified such that the left hand 'cardinal' number represents the number of (different) pitch classes in the set, and the right hand number its position on Forte's list (pages 177-188) which is ordered according to the interval content of sets. Sets with the designation 'Z' have the special quality that while being made up of different groups of pitch classes they have the same interval vector (a count of the intervals possible between every pair of pitch-classes in the set) as some other set of the same size.

5. G. Perle, *Twelve-Tone Tonality* (Los Angeles and London, 1977).

6. Perle (as n. 5), 216-217.

7. An octatonic scale (Messiaen's second mode of limited transposition) is an eight-note scale of alternating whole-tones and semitones. Being symmetrical it has only three distinct forms in rather the same way that the whole-tone scale exists in only two.

8. A group of pitches is symmetrical if it can be disposed in a balanced manner about an axis which may, or may not, be a member of the group. Furthermore, axes never occur singly but always in tritone related pair. For example, the set 4-9:[D, E-flat, A-flat, A] can be symmetrically disposed about the axis B/C or F/G- flat (this special set is also symmetrical about two axes lying within the set itself: D/E-flat and A-flat/ A).

9. Non-symmetrical sets have 24 possible (unordered) forms (twelve transpositions, plus twelve transpositions of the inversion). Tetrachord Z or 4-9 replicates itself if transposed by the tritone or if inverted and then transposed by a semitone or fifth.

10. Based on Lendvai, 1983 (as n. 2), 359.

11. Lendvai (as n. 2), 369.

12. Lendvai (as n. 2), 709.

13. Lendvai (as n. 2), 293.

14. Lendvai (as n. 2), 357.

15. Wilson, 1982 (as n. 2), 79.

16. See J. Straus, 'The Problem of Prolongation in Post-Tonal Music', *Journal of Music Theory*, 31, no. 1, 1987, 1-21.

17. The important set 4-9 (=Z) contains three trichordal subsets each of which is a form of 3-5.

18. Derived from Wilson, 1984 (as n. 2), 119.

19. Antokoletz (as n. 2), 218.

20. Antokoletz (as n. 2),, 218.

21. Lendvai, 1983 (as n. 2), 371.

22. A. Schoenberg, *Structural Functions of Harmony* (London, 1969).

23. J.M. Baker, *The Music of Alexander Scriabin* (New, Haven and London, 1986), x.
24. A. Pople, Review of Baker, *Music Analysis*, 7, no. 1, 215.
25. R.P. Morgan, 'Dissonant Prolongation: Theoretical and Compositional Precedents', *Journal of Music Theory*, 20, no. 1 (1976), 49-91. R. Travis, 'Towards a New Concept of Tonality?', *Journal of Music Theory*, 3, no. 3, 220-84. R. Travis, 'Directed Motion in Schoenberg and Webern', *Perspectives of New Music*, 4, no. 2, 85-9.
26. See Straus (as n. 16).
27. P. van den Toorn, *Stravinsky and the Rite of Spring* (Oxford, 1987), 211.
28. Antokoletz (as n. 2), 4.
29. Perle (as n. 5), 162.
30. Lendvai, 1983 (as n. 2), 269-270.

Musicology, Positivism and the Case for an Encyclopaedia of Music in Ireland: Some Brief Considerations

HARRY WHITE

However generously we define musicological thought, there is no longer much dispute as to its origins in German positivism. Joseph Kerman's brilliant and incisive survey of the discipline of musicology repeatedly and justifiably draws attention to the influence of positivist ideology on the development of quite separate strands of musical inquiry.[1] Whether musicology is taken to comprehend cultural history, textual criticism and interpretation, scientific analysis or ethnological research, it is not hard to discover the impact of systematic, information-based modes of thought in each of these pursuits. The monumental achievement of late-nineteenth and early twentieth-century German musical research heroically attests to the extreme pertinence of positivist assumptions about the nature and primary importance of (musical) knowledge.

The further acceleration of this research since 1945, particularly in terms of Anglo-American scholarship, also testifies to the immense reliability of a method of musical inquiry which has produced a pantheon of rigorous critical editions, a well-wrought (if polarised) system of structural theory and analysis, and a systematic integration of anthropology with the social meaning and function of music. If Joseph Kerman rightly complains that this reliance on positivism has also produced work which is long on 'hard' information and conspicuously short on interpretation (and critical thought), the development of scholarly writing on music has nevertheless afforded historians of culture a vast resource of painstakingly acquired material and factual commentary. Whether or not we care to think further about such material, edited in abundance and placed in detailed, historical context, the sources now lie to hand. Kerman urgently advocates and occasionally discerns such further thought, which he discriminately describes as criticism. With special regard to European art music – a vast corpus of texts extending over several centuries – the positivist accumulation of information now demands a second phase of critical interpretation and assimilation.[2] And within the European tradition the prominent position of the music itself finds a correlative in the ready acknowledgement of music in the history of European ideas. To write *about* music follows, it would appear inevitably, from the pervasive role which music plays in certain forms of human behaviour.

If we attempt to apply these concepts in an Irish context, the gap between the achievement of musicological thought elsewhere and the extent of music in Ireland may appear dauntingly wide. Music has effectively failed to make its debut in the general history of Irish ideas. It lies remote, it would seem, from what Seamus Deane has called the Anglo-Irish intellect. If it appears dimly on the horizon of the cultural debate which in recent years has re-animated Irish intellectual thought, it never attains to a central focus. If it seems self-evident to suggest that music has been central in Irish life (as a manifestation of political dissent or distinction, for example, as a form of recreation, as an expression of religious conviction, as a means of livelihood, as a means of metropolitan celebration, and so on), our command of the facts about music in Ireland is nevertheless sketchy and insecure. Music does not form much (if any) part of the vigorous discourse which preoccupies thinkers in their assessment of the condition of being Irish and of Ireland.

It is not part of my purpose here to probe in detail the reasons for this failure, although I have tried to do so in a limited context elsewhere.[3] To be sure, the comparatively restricted state of music education in Ireland provides some explanation, if we admit political and economic well-being as preconditions for an *immanent* musical consciousness in any given society. How to develop an historiography adequate to the tenuous and vulnerable role of music in the gradual erosion of a popular Gaelic culture, for example, given the complex relations of that culture to the emergence of modern Ireland? And yet there have been essays in and surveys of Irish musical history within the century-and-a-half which encompasses the massive growth of systematic (and comparative) musicology in Britain, Europe and the United States. To complain of wholesale neglect would be to falsify the issue. Anyone at all interested in the subject of Irish music can reasonably point to the collection and preservation of native music materials in this country dating back at least two centuries, and to a virtually unbroken tradition of antiquarian and folkloristic studies during the same period. Joseph Walker's *Historical Memoirs of the Irish Bards*, published under the auspices of the Royal Irish Academy in 1786 and Donal O'Sullivan's full-length study of Turlough Carolan published in London in 1958 both belong to this distinguished tradition. Why then does music remain on the periphery of Irish cultural and intellectual discourse? A more profitable consideration from the vantage of these reflections might be: How to achieve a comprehensive notion of music in Ireland? Do the monuments of German positivism hold out a useful example of what might be achieved here? If music is at the edge of the Irish intellectual consciousness, how to move it to the centre? Certain precedents argue the case for one solution to these questions above all others. That solution lies in the making of an encyclopaedia of music in Ireland.

II

The *Encyclopedia of Music in Canada* (hereafter, *EMC*) was published in 1983 by the University of Toronto Press. Its editors succinctly described EMC as being 'about music in Canada and Canada's musical relations with the rest of the world'. Having identified a critical deficiency in the poor representation of Canadian music in various works of reference, the editors of *EMC* pursued the notion of a comprehensive research project far beyond the received idea of a national 'guide':

> The idea of devoting a dictionary to the music of one country has been realized before, but the editors are not aware of any previous attempt to describe a nation's musical culture in all its breadth and depth: the historical and the current aspects of popular, folk, religious, concert and other forms of music, and the educational, critical, administrative and commercial manifestations.... The step from narrative survey under broad headings to encyclopedic coverage under specific headings seemed pre-ordained [From the Introduction to *EMC*].

This step proved decisive. The accumulation and refinement of some four thousand subject headings led to a harvest of information easily recovered and assimilated by means of a structural format somewhat reminiscent of *The New Grove Dictionary of Music and Musicians* (1980). The result was (and is) not merely a dictionary of compelling magnitude, but a subsequently indispensable reservoir of information about music in Canada. (The use of computer technology means that a second edition of the encyclopaedia is a realistic prospect for the early 1990s.)

The scope and structure of *EMC* provide models for the form and content of an encyclopaedia of music in Ireland. The Canadian volume is prefaced, indeed, with a detailed explanation of research methods and subject headings which accommodate categories of information that range from local music history through to Canada's musical profile at international level.

To describe such categories here, or to nominate similar categories in the context of an Irish encyclopaedia is clearly beyond the speculative thrust of the present discussion. I have in fact recently surveyed some of these categories, together with the past and present state of specialised music research in Ireland. This research suggests and substantiates the possibility explored here.[4] In the present context, it is preferable to observe that a significant showing has been made in diverse Irish musical topics to facilitate a fair grasp of the size of the field in question. Individual research projects, for example, on opera in eighteenth-century Dublin, on the history of Anglo-Irish music in general from 1780-1830, on music in early Irish monastic liturgies, and on traditional music in Ireland testify to the wealth of material which lies to hand in these and many other related areas. Source studies, archival investigations and specialised works of reference exclusively concerned with music in Ireland precisely underwrite the detailed inquiries proposed in this paper. Certain source materials also lend support: the long run of the periodical *Counterpoint*, published from 1969 until 1981 by the Music Association of Ireland comprises a valuable foundation for a survey of music events in this country during that period. The considerably polemicised details of Roman Catholic church music in the late nineteenth century are available in the journal of the Irish Cecilian Society, *Lyra Ecclesiastica* (1888 onwards). The very history of Irish musical periodicals is also worthy of appraisal, and an encylopaedic article on this subject would clarify the role and content of music journalism as a (sometimes tendentious) commentary on music in Ireland. All of the above are assuredly random examples drawn from a corpus of documentary, archival and scholarly material which silently argues the need and possibility of a comprehensive scrutiny. With the methodology and realization of such works as *EMC* as guide (*The New Grove Dictionary of Music in the United States*, 1985, is another precedent), the gap between the identification and the fulfilment of this need could be considerably narrowed.

If, then, we are prepared to allow that the subject of music in Ireland is of sufficient magnitude to justify a co-ordinated research enterprise of the scope of *EMC*, it is not difficult to prefer encyclopaedic format over the claims of a narrative survey. The latter was in fact employed for *Music in Ireland*, a compendium of essays edited by Aloys Fleischmann in 1952 and published by Cork University Press. No-one who has consulted *Music in Ireland* could doubt the timeliness and usefulness of these essays individually or of the publication as a whole. Every aspect of music in Ireland covered by this book would find a place in the encyclopaedia mooted here. Nevertheless, in the (almost) four decades which have elapsed since the appearance of *Music in Ireland* two notable developments have occurred which argue against a second narrative survey, however enlarged or updated. The first of these developments is a radical advance in music information techniques which led to *The New Grove* and other works of reference. The second is the advent of musicology at large in Ireland. With these developments in mind, it is not surprising that Aloys Fleischmann, among others, also supports the idea of a musical encyclopaedia of Ireland, and has done so for several years.

III

Joseph Kerman warns clearly enough of the dangers of positivism: 'It will be a sad day for musicology', he observes, 'if dictionary fetishism becomes established along with edition fetishism.' A spate of dictionaries and reference works *has* been one apparent result of the outstanding success of *The New Grove*. Would the preparation of an Irish encyclopaedia distract scholars from other, more (individually) challenging musicological pursuits?

The polarisation of musical thought in the United States, and to an extent also in Britain and Europe, forces the issue of musical perception as musicologists and analysts debate or reject the role of criticism and interpretation in the study of music. As the nature of musical perception becomes more sharply defined and differentiated, the stringent demands of ever more specialised (and self-conscious) modes of musical thought alert scholars to the inherent dangers of such demands. When Leo Treitler writes of the 'deplorable rift that now exists in this country [i.e., The United States] between music history and theory', he adverts to a crisis of thought which sooner or later must be resolved, particularly in terms of its implications for music education.[5]

Such a crisis does not weaken the case for an encyclopaedia of music in Ireland. The regeneration of musicology and its neighbouring disciplines in North America derives from a position of scholarly achievement which validates this kind of re- evaluation and public scrutiny. The *a-priori* condition of this scrutiny in fact, is that which gave rise to the crisis in the first place. The great abundance of edited material, of factual detail, and of historical and cultural placement which characterises our understanding of European music from 1500 until 1900, for example, *radically* modifies the statement that a 'deplorable rift' exists between ways of musical perception. To press this point home, we should say that those who complain of the positivist programme and its inability to develop a sustained mode of critical inquiry congruent with the humanities in general, do so in the luxurious wake of musicology in the twentieth century. Joseph Kerman's own contributions to historical musicology amply demonstrate that he too consents to the fundamental order of things. 'Hard' information is a precondition for conceptual thought. Kerman's objections and advocations virtually take this for granted, and they do not therefore apply in an Irish context. How best to perceive music? How properly to address the role of music in society? How to develop a mode of musical criticism answerable to the musical text *and* its context? Such questions become redundant in the absence of basic information. That they can and should be asked in the retrieval of this information is scarcely at issue. But the information comes first. If a dictionary (or encyclopaedic dictionary) is 'a static rather than a dynamic thing, an immovable object rather than an irresistible force' (Kerman), it also stimulates research and promotes understanding. If a work of reference 'cannot be an end in itself' (Kerman's judgement on *The New Grove*), it can prove itself as an indispensable beginning. And as the editors of EMC point out, its preparation can mobilize and develop resources of scholarship hitherto untried.

Despite a plethora of musical encyclopaedias and other works of reference produced in the great (neo-) positivist surge of scholarship which has characterised musicology since 1945, music in Ireland remains a sparsely researched and poorly represented subject.

The New Oxford Companion to Music (1983) for example, simply reprints the article on Ireland which appeared in the first (1938) edition of the *Companion*. *The Thames and Hudson Encyclopaedia of 20th-Century Music* (1986) overlooks Ireland completely, although the music of some thirty other countries is included within its terms of reference. Even *The New Grove* (1980) affords a less than comprehensive point of departure for studies of music in Ireland, notwithstanding important entries which it contains on a number of Irish subjects.

To turn from the dictionaries to the field itself and to various research projects within that field is a move which promises hope. It would be premature in this context to name names, but the responsibility for the work proposed here lies in the main with scholars who live and work in Ireland. The well-proven effectiveness of a small, full-time panel of editors, together with the patronage of a learned society and the commitment of an Irish publisher are elements which would determine the success of this kind of venture. To cohere these elements, to produce an encyclopaedia of music in Ireland, would be to centralize music as a vital issue in the history of Irish ideas. The idea of 'Ireland' has shown itself fertile in literary, philosophic and historical terms. It also could yield much in terms of music. An encyclopaedia would quantify those terms. It would also offer a much needed resource of detailed information on a vast topic of enduring interest.

NOTES

1. Joseph Kerman, *Musicology* (London, 1985).
2. 'What appalls me', Kerman remarks, 'is that musicologists as a corps spend so much more time in establishing texts than in thinking about the texts so established' (*Musicology*, 226).
3. See 'Carolan and the Dislocation of Music in Ireland' in *Eighteenth-Century Ireland*, 4 (1989), 55-64.
4. See 'Musicology in Ireland', *Acta Musicologica*, LX, Fasc. III (1988), 290-306.
5. Leo Treitler, 'Structural and Critical Analysis', *Musicology in the 1980s*, edited by D. Kern Holoman and Claude V. Palisca (New York, 1982), 77.

Index

In this index of names, places, musical works, sources and instruments, musical compositions are indexed under the relevant composers; instruments appear under the heading 'Instruments'.